National Security
Policy-Making

National Security Policy-Making

Analyses, Cases, and Proposals

Morton H. Halperin

Lexington Books
D.C. Heath and Company
Lexington, Massachusetts
Toronto   London

Library of Congress Cataloging in Publication Data

Halperin, Morton H
    National security policy-making.

    1. United States-National security. 2. United States—Military policy.
I. Title.
UA23.H357   355.03'3073   74-16941
ISBN 0-669-96578-2

Contents

Introduction vii

Part I *Analyses*

Chapter 1 **Why Bureaucrats Play Games** 3

Chapter 2 **War Termination as a Problem in Civil-Military Relations** 17

Part II *Cases*

Chapter 3 **United States Policy Toward the Offshore Islands**
coauthored with *Tang Tsou* 31

Chapter 4 **The Gaither Committee and the Policy Process** 47

  The Gaither Committee Report (Text) 71

Chapter 5 **The Decision to Deploy the ABM** 111

Part III *Proposals*

Chapter 6 **The President and the Military** 143

Chapter 7 **The Good, the Bad, and the Wasteful** 155

Chapter 8 **Secrecy and Covert Intelligence Collection and Operations**
coauthored with *Jeremy J. Stone* 165

Index 183

About the Author 193

Introduction

These essays, written and published over the course of a dozen years or so, reflect a common theme: proposals to alter American national security policy must be based on an understanding of how the system works. Recommendations to change policy often will have unintended and undesired consequences if made without an appreciation of how such proposals will, if adopted, actually affect what is done by the United States.

Similarly, proposals to alter structures or procedures are often put forward as efforts to "rationalize" the system without regard for how the system really works. They often miss the essential point that proposals for restructuring are not value free; they make it more or less likely that a particular outcome will result.

An interest in structure then is not different from a concern with substance. The two should go together. These essays should give the reader a better understanding of how the system works so that the proposals put forward will be more realistic—more likely to bring about the desired change.

I have resisted the temptation to rewrite the various essays with the benefit of more hindsight or to reflect changes in my own perspective. They are, with the exception of obvious typographical errors, reprinted as they originally appeared. Having left the essays untouched, it seemed useful to provide here some further reflection on them and, where useful, some comments on their origin.

Part I, "Analyses," includes two papers both written after I left the government in 1969, having served in the preceding three years in the Pentagon and on the National Security Council Staff. The opening essay, "Why Bureaucrats Play Games," was an effort to focus attention on the interests of career officials in large organizations including the military services, the CIA, and the State Department. Much of the discussion of decision-making within the American executive branch proceeds on the assumption that the officials involved are searching together for what is in the national interest based on a common set of assumptions. Those making the analysis fail to realize that many officials interpret the national interest through the prism of organizational interests. They come to believe that what is good for the army, for example, is good for the United States.

Even analysts who consider organizational interests tend to make two errors. First, they do not disaggregate far enough. For example, to talk about the interests of "the military" in the United States is to miss the differing interests of the services and the sub-groups within the services. Second, they assume that all organizations are interested in growing bigger and getting a larger budget. This view fails to take account of an organization's interest in remaining as it is—in preserving its "essence"—and interest in growth only if compatible with the interests and expertise of its dominant career group.

The essay seeks to describe in some detail the organizational interests of the major national security bureaucracies and to show how these influence the information and advice they put forward to the president and the way in which they implement presidential decisions. The chapter emphasizes the importance of the organization's definition of its essence and the struggles over roles and missions aimed at protecting the vital interests of the organization.

The second piece, "War Termination as a Problem in Civil-Military Relations," is unique in two respects. It was written at the request of Professor William Fox for a symposium on war termination, and the focus is comparative. Materials from other countries, particularly France, are used. Its emphasis, as in the first essay, is on the need to disaggregate the military. Civil-military relations in periods of war termination actually involve at least three groupings in the military: (1) the field commanders, anxious to win the war, (2) the individual services seeking to protect service organizational interests, and (3) a few senior military officers in the capital who come to adopt the perspectives of political leaders.

Part II of the book is a series of cases. The first, "U.S. Policy Toward the Offshore Islands," written with Professor Tang Tsou of the University of Chicago, is part of a long-unfinished manuscript on China and the Offshore Islands. It attempts to explain how the United States went to the brink of nuclear war twice to defend several small islands just off the coast of China. The article was published in 1966 just as I was leaving Harvard to go into the federal government. As such, it reflects my groping toward a bureaucratic politics approach—as it has come to be called—prior to my direct immersion in the system. The essay emphasizes the importance of arguments and shows how those opposed to abandoning the islands always had the upper hand in the debate. It reflects McNaughton's Law, named after the late John T. McNaughton, Assistant Secretary of Defense and my first boss in the government. McNaughton's Law states that to be persuasive in the government an argument must be reducible to a simple declarative sentence which, once stated, is obviously true. The most important style of argument discussed is the "prediction of dire consequences" which warns that the sky will fall if the action one is urging is not taken. It is difficult to underestimate the degree to which this ploy is used effectively to prevent detailed debate on the consequences of alternate courses of action.

The second case study, "The Gaither Committee and the Policy Process," is the oldest essay in the volume, having been written in 1960. It was the piece I was most tempted to rewrite, both because it adopts much more of a cold war perspective than I would now take and because new information is available. The most significant additional data is the Gaither Committee Report itself. This study, prepared as a top secret document for the National Security Council in 1957, was declassified in 1973. It is the only significant internal document dealing with the strategic arms competition which has been made public. Because of its relevance for the case study and its historic importance, the text of the Report is reprinted as an annex to that chapter.

As the reader can see, the summary of the Report given in the essay is accurate in all essential respects. This underlines the point made in the piece about the struggle to get the Report released. Those urging its publication needed authoritative confirmation of the data contained in the Report, not the information itself, which had already leaked.

Readers of contemporary statements by administration officials on the strategic balance will find the Report hauntingly familiar. The United States is said to be superior to the Soviet Union, but the Soviets are gaining rapidly and the future is uncertain. The Russians are reported to be deploying forces larger than necessary for defensive purposes. Concern is expressed about the future vulnerability of American forces in the face of Soviet capability to target the forces precisely with ICBMs.

We now know that the fears expressed in 1957 were greatly exaggerated but this may not be an accurate guide to the reliability of current fears. What the reader can know is that the text of the Report gives him a rare glimpse into the style of argument used in the executive branch.

The final case study, dealing with the Johnson Administration and "The Decision to Deploy the ABM," was written in the early 1970s while I was working on a more general book, since published as *Bureaucratic Politics and Foreign Policy*. In my view, new approaches to analysis in political science often suffer from excessive abstraction. The author presents in great detail a new way to understand what is going on and promises that he (and others) will later apply this new approach to specific cases or issues. All too often the expectation created remains unfulfilled for a long period. Since the value of an approach can, in the end, be judged by how well it explains particular phenomena, it seemed important to me to work simultaneously on one or more cases while developing an approach.

Although it was published first, the ABM case study was meant to be a follow-on to the bureaucratic politics book and to show how the paradigm presented there could be applied. The essay emphasizes the role of the President as he interacts with the career bureaucracies and his senior advisors—notably, in this case, the Secretary of Defense and leaders of the Congress. The study points to the different set of players and considerations which affect implementation as contrasted with those involved in the decision to deploy. It portrays a Secretary of Defense struggling against a deployment and a President seeking to develop a consensus which would keep all of his principal constituencies on board. It shows the military services protecting their interests as they define them.

The final section of the volume, "Proposals," contains three essays presenting specific policy proposals. The first piece, "The President and the Military," is directed at the President and his closest advisors and suggests how to get better military advice and to increase the likelihood of military acceptance of presidential decisions. It returns to a theme present in many of the essays of the need to see past the label "military" to the three services—four counting the marines—and to their sub-groups. The essay argues that the president should seek advice directly from each service chief rather than pressing for a unified view, which often is a misleading compromise.

The second essay in this section, "The Good, the Bad, and the Wasteful," deals with the size and shape of the defense budget and is addressed primarily to the Congress. It suggests that the proper size of the budget is, within very wide limits, essentially arbitrary and needs to be judged in relation to national needs in other areas. It warns that the services, with their own interests, cannot be counted on to protect programs which increase the utility of the forces (the good) or to eliminate programs which decrease American security (the bad), and urges Congress to focus on these good and bad programs.

The final essay in the volume is "Secrecy and Covert Intelligence Operations," written (with Jeremy J. Stone) in the spring of 1973. After analyzing the effect of these operations and the way decisions about them are made, it recommends the end of super secrecy for intelligence collection and an end to the covert operations of the CIA. This issue has gotten considerably more attention since 1974 as a result of Watergate and revelations about the CIA role in Chile.

These essays were not originally written to be published together, but, taken as a whole, they do provide an in-depth look at some key issues in national security policy-making. The reader seeking an overall framework into which they fit may wish to consult the volume on *Bureaucratic Politics and Foreign Policy* (Washington: Brookings, 1974) mentioned above. Essays by other authors reflecting a similar approach have been collected by Arnold Kanter and myself in a volume called *Readings in American Foreign Policy: A Bureaucratic Perspective* (Little, Brown, 1973).

I am particularly grateful to Professor Tang Tsou and Dr. Jeremy J. Stone for their graciousness in permitting me to include our joint essays in this volume. My debts in connection with the various essays are acknowledged in footnotes at the beginning of some of the essays, as is my appreciation to the publishers of the journals in which the essays originally appeared for permission to reprint these papers.

Part I: Analyses

1 Why Bureaucrats Play Games

Charles Hitch, in the fall of 1962, was hard at work preparing the U.S. military budget for fiscal year 1964. As Comptroller of the Department of Defense, it was Hitch's responsibility to review weapons programs and make recommendations to his boss, Secretary Robert McNamara. One seemingly vulnerable item in the budget was Skybolt, an air-to-surface missile under development by the Air Force. It was designed to carry a nuclear warhead and to be fired from strategic bombers at a target up to 1,000 miles away. In 1960 President Eisenhower, at a meeting with Prime Minister Macmillan, had promised to share Skybolt with Britain. Without it, or some substitute, the U.K. would no longer possess a workable nuclear force beyond the mid-1960s.[1]

But by 1962 Skybolt was in trouble. The first five test launches were abortive, development costs had doubled, and the missile's operational date was already pushed back from 1965 to 1967. The further advanced seaborne Polaris and land-based Minuteman missile programs made a new airborne system seem all the more unnecessary. So Hitch, drawing the obvious conclusion, proposed to McNamara that Skybolt be cancelled. Eventually it was, but only at the cost of street demonstrations in London and tumult in Parliament, strains in the NATO alliance, a summit conference between President Kennedy and Prime Minister Macmillan, an offended President de Gaulle, and a U.S. offer of Polaris submarines to Macmillan to compensate for Skybolt.

These unhappy consequences occurred despite the fact that dozens of officials, from the President down to Pentagon colonels and State Department desk officers, devoted countless man-hours, meetings, messages and memoranda to grappling with "the Skybolt problem." Each of the main bureaucracies engaged in foreign policy in Washington became involved, but every separate organization saw the issue from its own perspective. Having different interests and perceptions, different bureaucrats took a different stand on what should be done.

For *Hitch* it was primarily a budget matter, a question of cancelling a program which he thought to be both technically difficult and strategically unnecessary. If such a program were allowed to continue, the defense budget would grow too large.

The *Air Force* saw the proposal to cancel Skybolt as a threat to the future of its strategic manned bombers, putting one of its basic missions in jeopardy. It might also mean a reduction in the Air Force budget.

Reprinted, with permission, from *Foreign Policy*, No. 2 (Spring 1971). © 1971 by National Affairs, Inc.

For the *Secretary of Defense*, this issue concerned his ability to demonstrate that defense budget decisions would be made on the basis of cost effectiveness analysis rather than by catering to the organizational interests of the services. McNamara also recognized that because Skybolt had been promised to the British for their bombers, the cancellation of Skybolt would create issues in U.S.-U.K. relations. But this was for him a secondary matter.

For the *State Department*, the Skybolt issue was seen largely in terms of U.S.-European relations. For the *Bureau of European Affairs*, the cancellation of Skybolt was seen as an opportunity to get the British out of the strategic weapons business. However, these officials also sensed a danger. The President, more anxious to avoid a crisis and less concerned about the British deterrent, might offer the British a substitute system, perhaps Polaris, which would extend the life of the British independent deterrent rather than shortening it, and would jeopardize Britain's prospects for gaining entry into the Common Market.

Secretary of State Rusk seemed not to have shared the desire of the Europeanists to get the British to phase out their nuclear deterrent and primarily saw cancellation of Skybolt as a threat to close U.S.-British relations.

The *President* appears to have shared Rusk's concern, but also was concerned about his relations with his Secretary of Defense and the Air Force and with controlling the defense budget.

Each participant saw a different face of the issue based on his own interests, and sensed dangers, opportunities, or both. For Hitch, for example, it was cancellation of Skybolt that was important, and the sale of Polaris to the British was a matter of indifference. For the Europeanists in the State Department, the money in the defense budget was a matter of indifference; getting the British out of the nuclear business was the important issue for them.

Skybolt was by no means unique. In seeking to understand why the U.S. government adopts a particular policy or takes a particular action, we can make no greater mistake than to assume that the participants in the process look at the issue in the same way and agree on what should be done. The reality is quite different.

The Way of the System

When American government officials consider a proposed change in American foreign policy they often see and emphasize quite different things and reach different conclusions. A proposal to withdraw American troops from Europe, for example, is to the Army a threat to its budget and size; to Budget Bureau examiners a way to save money; to the Treasury a balance-of-payments gain; to the State Department Bureau of European Affairs a threat to good relations with NATO; to the President's Congressional adviser an opportunity to remove a major irritant in the President's relations with Capitol Hill.

What determines what an official sees? What accounts for his stand? The examples provide some clues.

Participants in the national security policy process in the American government believe that they should and do take stands which advance the national security of the United States. Their problem is to determine what is in fact in the national security interest. Officials seek clues and guidelines from a variety of sources. Some hold to a set of beliefs about the world which provide strong clues, e.g., the Soviet Union is expansionist and must be stopped by American military power. Others look to authorities within the government or beyond it for guidance. Many bureaucrats define what is necessary for the nation's security by a set of more specific intermediate interests. For some these may be personal: "Since, in general, I know how to protect the nation's security interests, whatever increases my influence is in the national interest." For others, the intermediate interests relate to domestic political interests: "Since a sound economy is a prerequisite to national security I must oppose policies which threaten the economy"; or "Since only my party knows how to defend the security interests of the United States I must support policies which keep my party in power."

For many participants the intermediate objectives which provide strong clues for what is in the nation's security interest are the interests of the organization to which they belong. Career officials come naturally to believe that the health of their organization is vital to the nation's security. So also do individuals who are appointed by the President to senior posts in Washington foreign policy bureaucracies. This tendency varies depending on the individual, the strength of his prior conviction, his image of his role, and the nature of the organization he heads. On many issues a Secretary of the Air Force will be strongly guided by the organizational interests of his service. A Secretary of State on the other hand, is likely to be less influenced by the organizational interests of his Department and the Foreign Service, since these provide less clear-cut clues and in many cases conflicting guidelines to the nation's security interest. Some senior officials, moreover, will seek clues less from their organizations' interests than from the interests of the President as they define them.

Despite the different interests of the participants and the different faces of an issue which they see, officials still frequently agree about what should be done. This may occur when there is strong Presidential leadership or when there is a national security argument which most participants view as decisive. In many cases, however, officials reach consensus by designing an ambiguous policy which avoids substantial costs to the different interests of the participants, including the interests of the organizations involved. The compromise avoids making choices on priorities and leaves organizations free to continue operating as they have in the past and to control their own operations. Once a decision is made, the organizations themselves shape the way in which it is implemented.

Organizational interests, then, are for many participants a dominant factor in determining the face of the issue which they see and the stand which they take in pursuit of the nation's security interests. In large part they constitute U.S. foreign policy. Before there is any hope of mastering them, their mysteries—and their mystique—must be explored. What are these organizational interests? From what do they derive?

Organizational Interests

All organizations seek *influence*, many also have a *mission* to perform, either overseas or at home, and some organizations need to maintain expensive *capabilities* in order to perform their missions effectively.

Influence. Organizations with missions seek influence to promote the missions. Those that also have large operational capabilities—like the armed forces—seek influence on decisions in part to maintain the capability necessary to perform their mission. Some organizations such as the Office of International Security Affairs in the Office of the Secretary of Defense and the Policy Planning Staff in the State Department have neither large capabilities nor stable, organizationally defined missions. Hence their only organizational interest is in enhancing influence for its own sake and because individuals in such organizations share with those in other organizations the belief that they can best judge the nation's security interests.

Stands on issues are affected by the desire to maintain influence. This could lead to support for certain policies which will require greater reliance on the organization. It can also lead officials to avoid opposing a particular policy in the belief that to do so would reduce their influence on other issues.

Missions. Most organizations are charged with specific missions. Some of these can be accomplished entirely at home (such as maintaining good relations with the Congress); others require actions abroad (such as deterring a Soviet attack on the United States).

Bureaucrats will examine any policy proposal from the point of view of whether or not it will increase the effectiveness with which the mission of their particular organization will be carried out. For example, in examining a proposal for a new security commitment, the Budget Bureau and the Comptroller's Office in the Pentagon will ask themselves how it will affect their ability to keep down the defense budget, Treasury will ask how it will affect its ability to maintain the U.S. balance of payments in equilibrium, while the military will be concerned with its ability to meet existing commitments. State Department officials may be concerned with the impact of the security arrangement on political relations with that country and its neighbors.

Capabilities. The missions of some organizations in the national security field lead them to maintain substantial and expensive capabilities which may be employed abroad. The armed services, in particular, are responsible for creating very expensive military forces. Organizations with expensive capabilities will see the face of an issue which affects their ability to maintain what they view as the necessary capability.

Organizations with large capabilities will be particularly concerned about budget decisions and about the budgeting implications of policy decisions. Organizations with missions but low-cost capabilities will be primarily concerned with policy decisions and their implications for missions. This is an important difference between the armed services and the State Department.

Organizations with missions strive to maintain or to improve their (1) autonomy, (2) organizational morale, (3) organizational "essence," and (4) roles and missions. Organizations with high-cost capabilities are also concerned with maintaining or increasing their (5) budgets.

1. Autonomy

Members of an organization believe that they are in a better position than others to determine what capabilities they should have and how they can best fulfill their missions. They attach very high priority to controlling their own resources. They want to be in a position to spend the money allocated to them in the way that they choose, to station their manpower as they choose, and to implement policy in their own way. Organizations resist efforts by senior officials to get control of their activities by arguing that effective functioning of the organization requires freedom to determine its own procedures. The priority attached to autonomy is shown by the experiences of two recent Secretaries of Defense. Robert S. McNamara caused great consternation in the Pentagon in 1961 by instituting new decision procedures which reduced the autonomy of the services, despite the fact that he increased defense spending by six billion dollars and did not seek to alter the missions of the services. Secretary of Defense Melvin Laird, by contrast, improved Pentagon morale in 1969 by increasing service autonomy on budget matters while reducing the Defense budget by more than four billion dollars.

The quest for autonomy leads organizations to resist policies which will require them to yield their autonomy to senior officials or to work closely with another organization. The belief that autonomy is necessary in the performance of missions results in organizations informing senior officials that particular options are feasible only if full responsibility for carrying them out is delegated to the operating organization. During the 1958 Quemoy crisis, for example, the military repeatedly pressed for freedom to use nuclear weapons on their own authority. They informed the President that they could guarantee to defend this offshore island against a Chinese Communist attack only if granted this autonomy.[2]

2. Organizational Morale

An organization functions effectively only if its personnel are highly motivated. They must believe that what they are doing makes a difference and is in support of the national interest; that the organization's efforts are appreciated and that its role in the scheme of things is not diminishing and preferably is increasing; that the organization controls its own resources; and that there is room for advancement in the organization.

Because they have learned the vital importance of morale for the effective functioning of an organization, bureaucrats give close attention to the likely effects of any change of policy or patterns of action on the morale of the organization and will resist changes which they feel will have a severe effect on morale. Officials may resist changes which even they believe would improve their organization's effectiveness in carrying out its mission if they also believe that such actions would severely affect the morale of the organization. In particular, they will be concerned about the effects on the promotion patterns of the organization. Short-run accomplishments of goals, and even increases in budgets will be subordinated to the long-run health of the organization. Bureaucrats know that ignoring morale can have disastrous consequences.

For example, almost every observer of U.S. operations of Vietnam has concluded that extending the tour of duty of commissioned Army officers from one year to two or three years would substantially improve the U.S. military performance. Yet the Army has refused to make this change. This is not because the Army has differed with the assessment that there would be an improvement in effectiveness, but rather because (1) the Army has believed that there would be severe effects on morale if officers were sent to Vietnam either for an indefinite period or for a prolonged period, such as three years, and (2) particularly in the early stages of the war, Army leaders felt that there would be severe morale problems if only a small percentage of career Army officers had combat experience in Vietnam, since those officers would have an inside track on promotions. They believed it desirable not only for morale, but also to improve the effectiveness of the force over the long run, that an opportunity be provided for as many career officers as possible to have experience in Vietnam.

3. The Organization's "Essence"

Career officials generally have a clear notion of what the essence of their organization is and should be, both in terms of capabilities and of missions. In some organizations the same view of the essence will be shared by all of those in the same promotion and career structure; in other cases there will be differences of view. This can be seen in the following brief discussion of the organizational essence of some of the major U.S. national security organizations:

Air Force officers agree that the essence of their program is the development of a capability for combat flying, particularly involving the delivery of nuclear weapons. Officers whose orientation is toward the Strategic Air Command (SAC) emphasize the mission of strategic bombing; those in the Tactical Air Command (TAC) emphasize interdiction of enemy supply lines. Providing close combat support is not seen by most Air Force officers as part of the essence of their mission, nor is the development of a capability to transport Army troops and equipment.

Army officers seek to develop a capability to engage in ground combat operations employing traditional Army divisions deployed according to traditional Army doctrine. Some Army officers emphasize tank operations; others stress air mobility. Air defense, advisory missions for foreign governments, and "elite" specialized forces such as the Green Berets are not seen as part of the essence of the Army.

Navy officers agree only on the general proposition that the Navy's business is to man combat naval ships and that their mission is to maintain control of the seas. In fact, the Navy is split into three traditional groups and a fourth whose weight may be growing. Navy flyers (brown shoe) emphasize carrier-based air; others (black shoe) stress the surface Navy; the submariners focus on attack submarines. The fourth group looks to missile-firing submarines and puts emphasis on the mission of strategic deterrence (advocated in the 1940s and '50s by the flyers). No influential group sees the transport of men and matériel as part of the Navy's essence, and most senior naval officers have tended to view the Polaris missile-firing submarines as a service to the nation, extraneous to the Navy's "essential" tasks.

Foreign Service officers see their essential functions as representation and negotiation and political reporting. Managing programs and embassies and even analyzing policy alternatives are not part of the essence of the State Department's function.

Career *CIA* officials appear to be split between those who emphasize analysis and those who view the agency's essence as its unique role of covert intelligence gathering and operations.

The stand of bureaucrats on a policy issue is influenced by its impact on the ability of their organization to pursue its essential programs and missions. They resist most strongly efforts to take away these functions or to share them with other organizations. They also resist proposals to reduce funds for these programs or missions. Autonomy is most precious as it affects the essence of the organization.

Conversely, bureaucrats feel less strongly about "marginal" functions, particularly those which require cooperation with other organizations or are viewed as support for them (e.g., naval and air transport for the Army). Left alone, they will devote fewer resources to such programs and missions, and ambitious career officials will ignore them. For example, during the 1950s neither the Navy nor the Air Force built air or sealift capability. The best Army officers, to take another example, seek to avoid advisory assignments in Vietnam, seeking instead to lead troops in combat and to serve on a combat staff.

If pressed by senior officials they will take on new programs or missions if they believe that they can earn support which can be used on more crucial issues and if persuaded that the new activities will not divert funds from the essence of the organization. They resist or seek to give up functions which they believe will use up more resources than they bring in or which will require the recruitment of new personnel with new skills and interests who may dilute or seek to change the organization's essence. For example, the Army after World War II urged the creation of a separate Air Force in the belief that if this was not done flyers would come to dominate the Army. Similarly, State has resisted efforts to assign to it the operational responsibility for aid, propaganda, and intelligence functions.

Organizations seek new functions only if they believe that their failure to get responsibility for them would jeopardize their sole responsibility in critical areas. Thus the Navy and Air Force insist on performing the troop transport role and the Air Force rejects Army efforts to perform the close air support role. If the Army transported its own troops by sea they might well build ships which enabled Army troops to come ashore firing—the Marine function. By performing this mission the Navy is able, for example, to insist that the proposed Fast Deployment Logistic (FDL) ships be carefully constructed so that they cannot be used for amphibious operations, denying an option which in some crises a President might wish to have. The Air Force, to cite another example, fought for the medium-range missile program after it failed to kill that program because it feared that the Army would use the missiles as a foot-in-the-door on the strategic deterrence mission.

4. Roles and Missions

Few sharp dividing lines exist between the responsibilities for programs and missions of various parts of the U.S. foreign affairs bureaucracy. Some missions may be performed simultaneously by two organizations. Both the Air Force Minuteman force and the Navy Polaris force contribute to deterrence of a Soviet nuclear attack on the United States. Both the State Department and the Central Intelligence Agency evaluate the likely reaction of foreign governments to particular courses of action.

A program which at one time is shared may later be assigned to a single organization or be phased out. For example, at one time the Air Force and the Army shared responsibility for the development of medium-range missiles (MRBMs); the function was later assigned to the Air Force and still later eliminated.

Some missions, once the exclusive province of one bureaucratic entity, may at a later date be transferred to another—either an already existing organization or a new organization. For example, intelligence functions once performed by the military and the State Department were transferred to the CIA in 1947.

Organizations are specially sensitive to this issue because of a number of disputes about roles and missions extending back to the early postwar period, but continuing to be important now in Vietnam. The three classic disputes which divided the services in the 1940s and continue to divide them now are: the struggle between the Navy and Air Force over naval aviation; that between the Army and Air Force over combat support; and that between the Army and Marines over Marine participation in ground combat operations. The Air Force has sought authority for all combat air operations. The Navy fights hard to protect its role in air operations over the sea and has sought parity with the Air Force in tactical and strategic bombing, which it attained in Vietnam. The Army seeks control over close combat support air operations. The Army-Marine rivalry involves the Army effort to limit the Marines to amphibious operations and the Marine desire to participate in all ground combat.

Two other disputes have pitted the CIA against older established organizations. The CIA would like to have control over all *covert operations*. The military would also like control of all such missions, or at least those which involve combat operations. The military apparently pointed to the Bay of Pigs fiasco as proof that they and not the CIA should manage combat operations. The CIA and the Air Force have fought from the start over who should control U-2 operations.

State and the CIA have never agreed where the Agency's responsibility for "intelligence" *evaluation* ends and State's responsibility for political reporting begins. Nor has there been agreement on the line between CIA's functions and the military intelligence functions of the armed services and their responsibility for evaluating allied and U.S. military forces and operations.

New technology produces other disputes over nuclear weapons and space operations. Sensing that most of the money for aviation would be allocated to nuclear delivery, naval aviators sought to have the Navy share the nuclear deterrence mission with the Air Force, leading to the once famous but now forgotten "revolt of the admirals." With the development of missiles the Navy gained a role in strategic deterrence, as the Army did for a brief period when it had a medium-range missile under development. In a somewhat similar manner, first the Army and Air Force fought for a major role in space, with the Navy showing some interest. The Air Force, after winning, saw much of its function transferred to NASA, although it continues to seek a role in space.

Disputes over roles and missions affect the stands taken by organizations and the information they report to senior officials. For example, according to a former Air Force intelligence officer, both the Air Force and Navy exaggerated the effectiveness of their bombing of North Vietnam. Both recognized that the postwar dispute over the Navy's bombing role would be affected by evaluation of their bombing operations in Vietnam. Each, believing (or fearing) that the other service would exaggerate, was forced to emphasize the positive in order to protect its position.[3]

In implementing missions which they know to be coveted by another organization, organizations may bend over backward to avoid the charge that they demonstrated by their behavior that the mission should be shifted. Townsend Hoopes, who was then Under Secretary of the Air Force, reports that he saw this process at work in the Air Force request for an additional 17 tactical fighter squadrons as part of a proposed increase in American forces in Vietnam in March 1968 following the Tet offensive:

It was a matter of some delicacy in Army-Air Force relations because it touched the boundary line between the assigned roles and missions of the two Services. If the Air Force did not provide close air support in a ratio satisfactory to the Army, that would strengthen the Army's argument for developing its own means of close support. Already, through the development of helicopter gunships of increasing power, speed, and sophistication, the Army had pressed against that boundary.[4]

In periods of crisis, bureaucrats calculate how alternative policies and patterns of action will affect future definitions of roles and missions. They do not put forward options which might lead to changes in roles and missions to their detriment. They may argue that such options are in fact infeasible. Bureaucrats may also feel obliged to distort information reported to senior officials in order to guard against the danger that it will in the future affect roles and missions. Disputes over roles and missions also affect their policy stands and the way policy decisions are implemented.

Bureaucrats have learned over time that changes in roles and missions frequently occur during crisis situations. Thus an organization concerned about its mission and desiring either to expand it or prevent others from expanding at its cost may be particularly alert to both challenges and opportunities during a crisis. Because this phenomenon is widely understood, organizations cannot trust other organizations not to take advantage of a crisis situation, and must be on guard. Frequently, after a crisis, an organization whose functions were expanded during the crisis will try to argue that it has now established a precedent and should continue to perform the new function.

During the Cuban missile crisis, for example, both the CIA and the military were concerned with how intelligence operations during the crisis would affect future definitions of roles and missions. A key episode is described by Graham Allison:

The ten-day delay between that decision [to direct a special flight over western Cuba] and the flight is another organizational story. At the October 4 meeting, the Defense Department took the opportunity to raise an issue important to its concerns. Given the increased danger that a U-2 would be downed, it would be better if the pilot were an officer in uniform rather than a CIA agent. Thus the Air Force should assume responsibility for U-2 flights over Cuba. To the contrary, the CIA argued that this was an intelligence operation and thus within the CIA's jurisdiction. Moreover, CIA U-2's had been modified in certain ways which gave them advantages over Air Force U-2's in averting Soviet SAM's. Five days passed while the State Department pressed for less risky alternatives such as drones and the Air Force (in Department of Defense guise) and CIA engaged in territorial disputes. On October 9 a flight plan over San Cristobal was approved by COMOR [the Committee on Overhead Reconnaisance], but to the CIA's dismay, Air Force pilots rather than CIA agents would take charge of the mission. At this point details become sketchy, but several members of the intelligence community have speculated that an Air Force pilot in an Air Force U-2 attempted a high altitude overflight on October 9 that "flamed out," i.e., lost power, and thus had to descend in order to restart its engine. A second round between Air Force and CIA followed, as a result of which Air Force pilots were trained to fly CIA U-2's. A successful overflight took place on October 14.[5]

5. Budgets

Bureaucrats examine any proposed change in policy or patterns of action for its effect on the budget of their organization. They prefer larger to smaller budgets and support policy changes which they believe will lead to larger budgets.

There is, however, a substantial asymmetry between the Department of Defense and the Department of State in regard to the impact of policy issues on budget issues. The State Department budget is relatively small, and very few of the foreign policy matters with which the State Department deals have any direct effect on its budget. For the military services, most policy issues are likely to have important budgetary implications. For example, the question of the United States military forces in Europe does not have any implications for the State Department budget, while it could have very important consequences for the budget of the United States Army and the Defense Department as a whole.

An organization will be concerned with whether a proposed change in policy which generates a new function will in fact lead to a budget increase, or whether the new function may be added to its responsibilities without there being any corresponding increase in its budget. The estimate of whether a new function will lead to an increased budget will depend in part upon the nature of the budget-making process. For example, during the 1950s the budgets for the military services were largely determined by allocating fixed percentages of an over-all budgetary ceiling established by the President. Thus, in general, new responsibilities had to be financed out of existing budgetary levels. By contrast, during the 1960s there was at least no explicit budgetary ceiling. The budget was determined by the Secretary of Defense on the basis of functional categories and responsibilities. Thus the services believed that new functions tended to mean increased budget levels.

The question of whether a new function will lead to new funds and hence should be desired, or to a reallocation of old funds, which perhaps needs to be resisted, will also depend in part on whether the new function is seen as closely related to existing functions or substantially new ones. For example, the Army was interested in acquiring responsibility for the deployment of MRBMs in the 1950s, in part because this would give the Army a strategic nuclear role. The Army hoped that this would justify its getting an increased share of the over-all defense budget, since the existing allocation was based on the Army having no strategic function. On the other hand, the Air Force recognized that MRBMs would simply be considered another strategic weapon and that it would be forced to finance their development and deployment out of existing budget funds. Thus, in terms of its budgetary interests, the Army sought the MRBM role, while the Air Force was reluctant to take it on. (Concern with protecting its "essence," however, meant that if there was to be an MRBM program the Air Force was determined to have it.)

Organizations are concerned not only about their absolute share of the budget, but also about their relative share of a relevant larger budget. This proposition applies particularly to each of the military services, although it may also apply to parts of the AID organization. In part, this objective seems to be based simply on the sense of competition between the services. It also apparently derives from the fear that once established levels change in an adverse direction, they may continue to change, leading to substantial reductions in the activities of a particular service, which could have substantial effects on morale.

This objective frequently leads the services to resist proposals which may lead to increases in their own budget if they fear that it may lead to a less than proportionate increase in their budget as compared to other parts of the defense establishment. It also leads the services to prefer the certainty of a particular share of the budget to an unknown situation in which budgets may increase but shares may change. For example, in 1957 the Gaither Committee appointed by President Eisenhower recommended substantial increases in the budgets of all three services, arguing the need for secure second-strike retaliatory forces and for larger limited-war capabilities. However, none of the services supported these proposals, in part because they were uncertain what the implications would be for shares of the budget and preferred a known process with known division of the budget to a new process which, while it might mean increased budgets for all, might involve changes in the shares of the budget.[6]

What Every President Should Know

Organizations have interests. Career officials in these organizations believe that protecting these interests is vital to the security of the United States. They therefore take stands on issues which advance these interests and maneuver to protect these interests against other organizations and senior officials, including the President.

This process affects policy decisions and action in a number of ways and limits the power of the President and his senior associates. Every President needs to know how bureaucratic interests interact, in order to be the master rather than the prisoner of his organizations, and also in order to mold the rational interests of the bureaucracies into the national interest as he sees it. The beginning of wisdom for any Chief Executive is to understand that organizational interests and maneuvers affect policy in at least four main areas.

1. *Information.* Organizations focusing on acquiring the information necessary to protect their interests tend to supply to others information designed to protect their organizational interests and to lead senior officials to do what the organizations believe needs to be done. This means that the selection of information is different from what the President would like to have and many think he is getting.

2. *Presentation of options.* Organizations construct a menu of options to meet any situation based on their notion of what the essence of their mission is. Options which involve cooperation between organizations and which would require an organization to alter its structure or perform extraneous missions are unlikely to be advanced.

3. *Freedom to choose options.* Organizations seek to prevent the President from choosing an option which runs contrary to their interests. They do so by asserting that the option is infeasible or by demanding full freedom for implementation if the option is chosen. They may leak the proposed option to the press or to Congressional allies.

4. *Implementation.* In implementing Presidential decisions organizations feel free to vary their behavior from that required by a faithful adherence to the letter and spirit of the President's action. When organization interests conflict with directed behavior, organizations may obey the letter rather than the spirit, they may delay, or they may simply disobey.

In seeking to mitigate the consequences of this behavior, senior officials and the President must begin by accepting the inevitability of organizational interests and maneuvers to support them. Neither appeals to patriotism nor changes in personnel will lead career officials and many of their bosses to lose their belief in the importance of the health of their organization and the need to protect it.

Awareness of organizational interests would lead senior officials to recognize that those with whom they deal see different faces of an issue and, because they have different interests, reach different stands. Abstract national security arguments usually do not change these stands. Being aware of maneuvers in support of organizational interests, senior officials learn to be skeptical of information which tends to support these interests and of analyses of options presented by organizations. They can then look to other sources for options or information. Beyond that they can seek organizational changes to mitigate the consequences of organizational interests for high priority objectives, and they can seek to design programs, missions, and policies to reduce their incompatibility with organizational interests.

Organizational changes can involve creating new organizations, altering the internal structure of an existing organization, or changing the rules of the game by which decisions are made. NASA is an instance of the first option, the Green Berets of the second, and the McNamara program budgeting system of the third. Such moves are time-consuming and their consequences frequently difficult to predict.

Designing policies to reduce organizational opposition requires a clear understanding of the relevant interests and an ability to fashion an option which accomplishes its purpose while minimizing organizational costs. For example, proposals to withdraw forces from overseas are likely to meet less opposition if they do not appear to threaten service interests in autonomy (e.g., by delegating to the services the choice of the mix of forces to be withdrawn) or force levels and budgets (e.g., by decoupling force level and budget decisions from force dispositions).

Presidents need vigorous organizations manned by highly motivated officials who believe in what they are doing. Such men cannot be expected to have the same interests as the President, to see the same face of an issue or to take the same stand. These facts limit a President's options and make it impossible for him to do some things he would like to do. If, however, the President and his senior associates are clear about their own priorities, select options with care, and understand that the name of the bureaucratic game is "organizational interests," they can lead rather than follow the bureaucracies. They may even be able to put them to constructive use.

Notes

1. A fuller account appears in Richard E. Neustadt, *Alliance Politics* (New York: Columbia University Press, 1970), Chapter 3. For another view, see Lord Harlech's "Suez *SNAFU*, Skybolt *SABU*," *Foreign Policy*, No. 2 (Spring 1971): 38-50.

2. Dwight D. Eisenhower, *Waging Peace* (New York: Doubleday, 1965), p. 299.

3. Morris J. Blackman, "The Stupidity of Intelligence" in Charles Peters, ed., *Inside the System* (New York: Praeger, 1970).

4. Townsend Hoopes, *The Limits of Intervention* (New York: David McKay, 1969), pp. 161-62.

5. Graham Allison, "Conceptual Models and the Cuban Missile Crisis," *American Political Science Review*, September 1969, p. 705.

6. Morton H. Halperin, "The Gaither Committee and the Policy Process," Chapter 4 of this collection.

2

War Termination as a Problem in Civil-Military Relations

A war ends when there is agreement within the decision-making structures of the two or more belligerent governments to stop fighting. This occurs when there is internal agreement that they should be prepared to terminate the fighting if acceptable conditions can be reached and there is an overlap between the acceptable conditions of the contending parties. Each government, in arriving at a determination at any time as to whether to be prepared to terminate a conflict, and if so, under what terms, needs to take account of the views of its senior military leaders. Governments vary as to the degree that they take military views into account in high policy decisions, in peacetime as well as in war, but for any government the degree of attention given to military views will be greater during a war. This chapter examines the way in which civil-military relations affect the policies of a government toward war termination. General propositions about the impact of relations between military and civilians on war termination are suggested with some specific examples drawn from recent military conflicts, particularly in the developed countries.

We consider first the military and civilian participants in the process of determining conditions for war termination, and the different interests that these groups are likely to have.

Military Interests

The military participants in the process can be divided into a number of different groups. The most useful grouping will depend on the particular government involved and on the kinds of decisions one is trying to examine. However, it is possible to identify three individuals or groups who are likely to be important within the military in shaping attitudes toward war termination conditions at any time in any major government.

The Field Command

The first is the field command. Typically, the field commander himself will have become an important political figure with a popular following at home by the end of a military conflict. Even where he does not, he and his principal subordinate commanders and his advisory staff will have come to play a key role

Reprinted, with permission, from *The Annals of the American Academy of Political and Social Science*, Vol. 392 (November 1970), pp. 86-95.

in any decision. They will be the men in the field whose advice will have to be sought about future prospects and whose judgment on tactical military issues will count heavily with military leaders in the capital, as well as with civilians. Thus, the field commander, either as an individual or in terms of a staff unit, will play a key role.

All the participants in the process, whether civilian or military, will believe that they should advocate what is in the over-all interest of their country rather than what is in the interest of the particular organization to which they are attached or in their personal or internal political interest. Nevertheless, each participant will also view what is in the national interest from his own perspective. He will be influenced by his place in the hierarchy and his mission as he sees it. Thus, a field commander will tend to look at the national interest from the perspective of the local military theater in which he is engaged. He will come to believe that the war being carried out in his theater is of vital importance to the future of his country and to any higher ideal, such as democracy, Christianity, or communism, to which he is attached. A local field commander will also come to believe that success in the form of military victory is possible. He will come to feel that his government owes him support, additional troops, and equipment if necessary, but basically he will tend to be optimistic over the chances of military success. The field commander will also be concerned about the morale of his troops. He will tend to equate the successful performance of his mission with the national interest and therefore to equate things necessary to improve the morale and combat effectiveness of his troops with the national interest.

U.S. Army General Douglas MacArthur, in his conduct of the Korean war, exhibited these characteristics in classic form. MacArthur came to believe that success for the United States in the Korean war, by which he meant the defeat of the Chinese Communist armies, at least in the field, was vital to the security of the United States. He came to believe that American interests required that all that was necessary be done to win the war. He had faith in his ability to win, provided that he was given the necessary support and the necessary freedom to conduct combat operations as he believed necessary.[1]

This same general belief was exhibited by French generals, both in Algeria and in Indo-China. For example, General Navarre, commander of French forces in Indo-China in 1954, greatly underestimated enemy strength and overestimated his own ability to win, as well as the importance of Indo-China to France, at least as compared to the views of those in Paris.[2] The French commanders in Algeria came to feel that success was possible and crucial for France.[3]

Viewpoints of the Services

Two other military perspectives are likely to exist on questions affecting war termination. Both of these groups are situated in the nation's capital, but they approach the problem with different perspectives. The first group is composed of senior military officers of the various services—the Army, the Navy, and the Air Force—who remain attached to service perspectives and service outlooks on particular issues which affect war termination. The second group is the central general staff, the principal military advisers to the senior civilian officials, who come to be imbued with a perspective which leads them to focus on operational issues as they relate to the broad national concerns of the political leaders.

Let us consider service perspectives first. Service perspectives seldom come into play explicitly in determining high political strategy. However, service views do affect the perspective with which senior commanders play their roles in the general staff, and do directly influence certain kinds of events which in turn affect decisions regarding war termination. Service perspectives are also important because of the way the politics of budget-making in defense issues interacts with the politics of decision-making in policy issues, including war termination. (This subject will be considered shortly.)

It has frequently been said that military officers always fight the last war—that is to say, their preparations and calculations are always based on assumptions which were true in the war most recently fought by the nation. This is certainly to some extent true, although it is not clear whether military views or civilian views are the more dominated by the immediate past. However, it is also the case that those with a service perspective are greatly concerned about the post-war period—and about the next war. That is, they are concerned with how the conduct of the war will affect the future definition of the roles and missions of each service as compared to the others, and perhaps to such civilian agencies as intelligence organizations.

For example, the French army in Algeria during the Algerian war seemed to be concerned with the impact of various outcomes on the future of the Foreign Legion. The French army, navy, and air force were also concerned about the implications of how the war ended, and the political role of the army in ending the war, for the future division of power between the services. In the United States during the Second World War, the services were concerned about future roles and missions, including the possible unification of the armed forces and the creation of a separate Air Force.[4] In the Vietnam war, the services have been concerned with the future Army and Air Force roles in tactical air, the future of such elite organizations as the Green Berets, and the future role of the Marine Corps in ground combat operations.[5]

In focusing on the concern about other services as to how the conduct of a war and its termination will affect future roles and missions, we have already touched on one of the key interests of the services, namely that of their roles and missions in relation to other military organizations, in some cases other civilian organizations as well. The historic divisions between Navy and ground forces have been totally blurred by the developments of contemporary military technology. Thus, there is in all major military establishments now a competition between the services for roles and missions which are in the margin between the services. This means that services will desire to protect the missions which they have and in some cases to expand them, and they are concerned about how behavior during a war and also the process of war termination affect future assignments of roles and missions.

Services are also, of course, concerned about their budgets, both their absolute budgets and their relative budgets compared to other services. Thus, they will begin planning during war time for the postwar situation, and attempt to develop a strategic doctrine which will justify their own budgets in the postwar period. This cannot help but influence their attitude toward war termination issues.

Perhaps the strongest organizational interest of the military services is in autonomy, the drive to be left alone so that the organization can grow and prosper and survive according to its own desires. This drive for autonomy affects the way the services look at operational issues, including those which affect war termination.[6]

General Staff

Civilian leaders will feel the need to have in the capital a group of senior military leaders and staff to advise them on the conduct of the war. They will not be willing to deal directly with the field commanders and thereby be forced to accept their proposals. These military leaders, who obviously will have to come from the military services, will see their role in terms of giving broad-gauged military advice to senior political leaders. To a greater or lesser degree, they will be able to remove the blinders on the interests of the services to which they belong and to provide a view of the national interest through the perspective of the worldwide political and military interests of their country. The approach of these leaders is likely to be characterized by loyalty to political leaders and sensitivity to their domestic political as well as foreign policy interests, and focus on the several theaters of military operations or potential military operations with which their country may be faced. These leaders will also see their mission as attempting to compromise between service interests and field commander interests on the one hand and those of the civilian leadership on the other.

It is when this group determines that an ending of the war is in the over-all interest of the country that possibilities for an active effort to seek termination of a war greatly increase. Thus, in the United States, when the Joint Chiefs of Staff decided that following the Chinese entry into the Korean war the over-all interests of the United States required acceptance of an armistice along the existing lines, the civilian officials of the Truman administration were in a strong position to move in that direction, despite the objections of the field commander. Similarly, in 1954, the French government was able to get its senior defense officials, after a trip to the field, to conclude that the war was hopeless and that an armistice should be sought right away.

Civilian Perspectives

With this overview of the interests and perspectives of various military groups, we turn to a brief consideration of civilian perspectives. It is, of course, much more difficult to say anything general which applies to civilian leaders across the board, since the structures of government vary enormously and the roles assigned to different individuals also vary greatly. Nevertheless, we can identify the perspective of the senior political leadership and the perspective of the Foreign Office or State Department.

The senior political leadership of a country, even, or perhaps one might say particularly, during a war, will view the national interest largely through domestic constraints. What is in the nation's interest will derive in large part from their perspective on what the nation will support and what it will be possible to do, given constraints posed by domestic politics. Political leaders will also be concerned with the impact which various kinds of war termination conditions will have on the postwar politics of their country. They will be concerned with whether war termination on one set of conditions would give rise to the charge of a stab in the back, of selling out to the enemy, leading to a period of right-wing attacks of the kind known as McCarthyism in the United States. On the other hand, if the war goes on too long and there is growing disaffection from the left, civilian leaders will be concerned with the kind of outbreaks which affected American policy in the mid-1960s in Vietnam. They will be concerned as to whether or not the growing opposition to the war on the left will undercut the ability to pursue successfully the conditions for war termination which had previously been established. They will also be concerned about the impact, for the long-run conduct of the foreign policy of their country, of the growing disaffection of the left-wing group.

Political leaders will also, of course, be concerned with the impact of war termination conditions on elections and in some countries on the future survival of the current constitutional system. They will also be concerned with their support on other issues. Particularly during a limited war, when politics will be going on as usual at home on domestic welfare issues, political leaders will be concerned with how the conditions they put forward for war termination and continuation of the war itself will affect their ability to get desired programs.

Certainly, for example, Harry Truman during the Korean war was concerned with the impact on the Fair Deal of continuation of the Korean war; he was anxious to end the war, at least in part, to avoid interference with what were considered to be critically important domestic programs. With the image etched firmly in people's minds concerning what happened in the United States after the Korean war, Lyndon Johnson sought, and Richard Nixon is seeking, to end the Vietnam war in a way which would avoid another period of McCarthyism at home. General Charles de Gaulle, in maneuvering to end the Algerian war, was certainly concerned in large part with maintaining French society and avoiding charges of a sellout from the right, which came close to producing a coup d'état against the general.

Foreign Office Perspectives

If political leaders are focused on the implications for postwar politics of war termination conditions, so will Foreign Office and State Department officials be focused on the implications of war termination for postwar diplomatic relations. Thus, they wish to see war termination conditions which strengthen the hand of their country in what they will envision as the postwar political competition.

Different Perspectives

These different perspectives will lead each of the participants, in the process of determining a position on specific war termination issues, to view proposals differently. When an issue affecting war termination arises, field commanders will see it in terms of obtaining a military victory in the field, services will be concerned with the implications for postwar missions and postwar budgets, political leaders with the postwar domestic situation at home, and Foreign Offices with postwar diplomacy. Thus, various proposals will appear as either threats or opportunities, according to one's perspective. However, the internal dialogue will be conducted in terms of the over-all national interest.

Having sketched out interests as they will affect decisions, we turn briefly to a look at some aspects of the process by which civilian leaders and military leaders interact in considering questions affecting war termination.

Budgets and Wars

Civilians and military leaders interact with each other in two totally different processes. One involves decisions about size of armies and the kinds of weapons they will have—what are called budget decisions. The second concerns decisions on the use of military forces, on decisions to go to war, and, of concern to us here, to seek peace. These two processes critically affect each other in a number of ways. We can only briefly review some of the effects of the process of bargaining about defense budgets on policy issues, including war termination.

In arguing in support of the acquisition of new weapons systems, the services frequently find themselves in a position in which the logic of the debate forces them to overstate the likely performance characteristics of the system, or at least to be extremely optimistic about how well the system will perform. In convincing political leaders that a system should be procured, they create in the minds of these political leaders an exaggerated view of the effectiveness of the system. For example, when in 1970 President Richard Nixon described a potential ABM system against China as "virtually infallible," he was clearly reflecting the sense of salesmanship of those in the military in favor of the ABM system.[7] One can only speculate about how this belief would affect President Nixon's attitude toward policy issues with China, including questions of the initiation of military operations or their termination.

The services themselves, having promised certain performance from their military equipment when they were arguing for its procurement, find it difficult to come back later and argue that the systems cannot perform in that way during a particular crisis or war situation. Thus, if asked to carry out a mission, they may feel obliged to agree to it, while having their own doubts about whether it can be successfully accomplished.

The requirements of the budget debates also lead to statements about enemy capabilities which may affect future decisions about war initiation and war termination.

Military services tend to have a healthy respect for their potential opponents and to want to have very substantial superiority before they are prepared to engage in war. On the other hand, in order to get particular weapons systems, they are sometimes driven to promising that with those systems they will have superiority or an effective capability for military combat. For example, the Japanese navy, prior to World War II, pressed for certain naval forces. When they were given these forces, Japanese admirals found it difficult to argue that the Japanese navy was not prepared for war with the United States, since they had justified those forces as necessary for engaging in combat with the United States. Thus, in a critical moment in the decision to go to war with the United States, the Japanese navy was not prepared to state its full doubts about its ability to win such a war. Similarly, at the end of the war it was not prepared to admit that it had been defeated, having promised that it would do substantially better if given the naval forces with which it was provided.[8]

Thus, the debates about the procurement of new systems, in terms of promises of technical performance and of relative capability vis-à-vis potential enemies, will affect the positions that services feel free to take during war time, as well as the perspectives of political leaders on what their military forces can accomplish.

It is also the case that future competition about defense budgets will affect decisions about policy issues during a war. We have already discussed this question in considering future roles and missions and future budgets in terms of service interest. Here the point to be made is that the argument that the services are willing to put forward will be influenced by their judgment of how these will affect postwar struggles over defense budgets.

Information

Civilian leaders, in considering whether to continue a war, or on what conditions to be prepared to terminate it, frequently look to military leaders for information on questions defined as "military." What is a military question is, in fact, a matter of convention. Questions concerning the morale and effectiveness of the country's own troops will always be considered a military question, as to some extent will be the judgments about how well the forces will fight in the future. However, many countries, including the United States, now have intelligence services to share responsibility for questions of enemy intentions, and even enemy capabilities and judgments about what strategies the enemy is likely to pursue. Nevertheless, even where civilian groups such as intelligence organizations are given a hand in the evaluation of these questions, military judgments on them will play an important role in evaluations by political leaders.

A key question in the judgments of officials of a country about whether or not to continue a war is the question of whose side is helped by time. Field commanders tend to have a bias in favor of time being on their side. They see themselves as building up momentum toward a military victory. There does not appear to be any systematic bias from the point of view of military officers at home on the question of whether time will help. French military leaders in Paris differed with the field commander in 1954 in advising the government that time was not on their side and that they should sue for peace as quickly as possible. On the other hand, U.S. military commanders in Washington tended to support the field commander's judgment that time was on their side in the Vietnam conflict, and that therefore negotiations should be delayed.

A second critical question closely related to the question of whom time will help is the question of whether or not military victory is possible. Here again, field commanders tend to believe that victory is possible, while this may or may not be challenged by military officers in the capital. General Matthew Ridgway, who assumed command of UN forces in Korea after General MacArthur's removal, appears to be an exception to this rule. Ridgway recognized that victory against the Chinese forces was not possible and supported efforts toward a negotiated settlement. In the case of the Suez crisis in 1956, the British military believed from the start that the operation was hopeless and that neither a military nor a political victory could be obtained.[9] Japanese military leaders were very pessimistic about the possibility of a military success for Japan from the beginning of the war with the United States, and this pessimism grew as the war continued. Nevertheless, as we will see below, they came to different policy judgments from those of their British colleagues.

A third problem of evaluation concerns the question of enemy intentions and strategy. Traditionally, field commanders have been looked to for evaluation of this question, although in many cases their sources of information are less good than that of the central staff or of civilian intelligence organizations. Thus, during the Korean war General MacArthur's view that the Chinese would not intervene was given great weight despite the fact that Washington-based intelligence organizations with more information felt that the probability of Chinese intervention was considerably higher.

The military's advice on short-run tactical military questions can also be important in affecting decisions about war termination. For example, during the Suez crisis of 1956 the British cabinet was advised by senior military officials that it would take several days, perhaps as much as a week, for the British-French invasion force to reach the end of the Suez Canal. Knowing that it could not wait so long, the British cabinet ordered a cease-fire. In fact, military officials in the field believed that the canal could be seized in a matter of a few hours, and advance units were already at the end of the canal. However, when asked to give an official estimate, each unit of the chain of military command hedged somewhat as the estimate moved up the lines. By the time it reached the cabinet it was so hedged as to lead to a decision opposite from the one that might very well have been made had the original estimate in the field reached the cabinet. This hedging can go either way. Confronted with an operation of high uncertainty, military officers are likely to overstate the threats as a hedge against failure. On the other hand, in reporting on operations, they are likely to overstate the results.

Maneuvering for Power

In the struggle to obtain the outcome which they desire, military officials not only have control over information, but can engage in specific kinds of maneuvers to make more likely the outcome which they seek. At the same time, civilian officials can engage in maneuvers designed to reduce the influence of the military. Only a few of these can be reviewed.

One maneuver of great potency in many societies, but of little if any value even as warning in a few countries such as the United States or Great Britain, is the threat of a coup d'état if the civilian leaders order a policy not acceptable to the military. The threat of a coup played a major role in Japan during the latter stages of the Second World War in deterring moves toward a negotiated settlement. In fact, there was an attempted coup after knowledge reached senior military officers that the Emperor was about to broadcast a message ordering the Japanese people to surrender. The coup plotters sought to destroy the recording and prevent the Emperor from addressing the nation. They failed only because a few critical senior military officers refused to join them, and once the Emperor's message was broadcast they were in a hopeless position. French generals revolted in 1958 in order to prevent the government from remaining in power, which they felt would negotiate an end to the war, and again sought to revolt against General de Gaulle.

A second maneuver which military leaders can use is to threaten to resign. Political leaders will hesitate to adopt policies which could lead to resignations by senior military leaders, followed by a public denunciation of those policies.

A third maneuver which can be used by a military commander is to publicly announce a policy or publicly announce a judgment which forecloses the civilian government from moving in a different direction. Thus, MacArthur foreclosed Truman's plan to issue a statement expressing an interest in negotiations by publicly demanding that the enemy surrender.[10]

The most potent maneuver which civilian leaders have in dealing with a military leader, particularly with the field commander, is to replace him. Thus, the French government replaced General Navarre by General Ely, and Truman ultimately replaced MacArthur by Ridgway.

In some cases maneuvers are implemented to prevent a change in policy. More often they are undertaken to bring about such a change. This is because nations at war tend to remain at war. That is, nations tend to continue to engage in all the activities that they are pursuing at any one time. Thus, if a nation is to make a move toward seeking to negotiate a settlement of a military conflict, or to respond favorably to a move from the other side, there must be a group within the bureaucracy strongly committed to seeking termination of the conflict. The motive of such moves will be, at the one extreme, the fear of imminent, overwhelming, and total defeat, such as faced Japan at the end of the Second World War, or, at the other, the attainment of virtually complete victory and something close to unconditional surrender by the other side. In many cases the decision to work hard for an early termination comes from the perception that domestic political considerations require such action, or that it is important for the long-run future of the country in terms of its foreign policy relations. As was indicated above, these motives are likely to be held either by high civilian policy officials or by those in the Foreign Office or State Department, and not by the military. There are some exceptions. The German general staff appears to have favored an early end to the military conflict during the Second World War, precisely because it was concerned about postwar relations.

Those who oppose an end to the conflict will argue that better terms can be obtained at a later date, or that one should not bargain but rather seek a total military victory. These views are likely to be held particularly by the field commander. Thus, the military officials in the capital frequently find themselves in the position of a compromise group whose concurrence in the decision to move for a termination of the conflict is frequently required by the civilian leadership.

Notes

1. Matthew B. Ridgway, *The Korean War* (Garden City: Doubleday, 1967); David Rees, *Korea: The Limited War* (London: Macmillan, 1964); John W. Spanier, *The Truman-MacArthur Controversy and the Korean War* (New York: W.W. Norton, 1965).

2. Philippe Devillers and Jean Lacouture, *End of a War* (New York: Praeger, 1969); Bernard Fall, *The Two Viet-Nams* (New York: Praeger, 1967); Melvin Gurtov, *The First Vietnam Crisis* (New York: Columbia University Press, 1967); Ellen J. Hammer, *The Struggle in Indochina* (Stanford, Calif.: Stanford University Press, 1954).

3. John Steward Ambler, *The French Army in Politics, 1945-1962* (Columbus: Ohio State University Press, 1966); Michael J. Clark, *Algeria in Turmoil* (New York: Praeger, 1959); Edgar S. Furniss, Jr., *De Gaulle and the French Army* (New York: Twentieth Century Fund, 1964); George Kelly, *Lost Soldiers* (Cambridge, Mass.: M.I.T. Press, 1965); Dorothy Pickles, *Algeria and France* (New York: Praeger, 1963).

4. Vincent Davis, *Postwar Defense Policy and the U.S. Navy, 1943-1946* (Chapel Hill: University of North Carolina Press, 1966); Perry McCoy Smith, *The Air Force Plans for Peace, 1943-1945* (Baltimore: Johns Hopkins Press, 1970).

5. Morton H. Halperin, *Bureaucratic Politics and Foreign Policy* (forthcoming).

6. Ibid.

7. Transcript, press conference, *The New York Times*, January 31, 1970, p. 14.

8. Robert Butow, *Japan's Decision to Surrender* (Stanford, Calif.: Stanford University Press, 1954); Herbert Feis, *Japan Subdued* (Princeton: Princeton University Press, 1961); Paul Kecskemeti, *Strategic Surrender* (Stanford: Stanford University Press, 1958).

9. Anthony Eden, *Full Circle* (Boston: Houghton Mifflin, 1960); Hugh Thomas, *Suez* (New York: Harper & Row, 1966).

10. Richard E. Neustadt, *Presidential Power* (New York: Science Editions, 1962), p. 13.

Part II: Cases

3

United States Policy Toward the Offshore Islands*

Few of the foreign policies of the United States in the postwar period have been as controversial or as difficult to explain as the American actions in defense of the Offshore Islands of Quemoy and Matsu. At least once in the 1950s the United States went to the brink of war to defend these small islands off the coast of China and was prepared, according to the later account of President Eisenhower, to use nuclear weapons. Throughout this period, and particularly during the 1958 crisis, the United States acted in the face of widespread domestic and foreign discontent and almost no support from outside the government.

Not only is the continued American commitment to the Offshore Islands difficult to explain, but so also are the arguments with which various administrations have sought, both publicly and privately, to justify their decisions. As discussed below, one of the justifications used rests on predictions of dire consequences. The most extreme instance of predicting "dire consequences" can be found in a planning document drafted, according to President Eisenhower, by himself and his Secretary of State, John Foster Dulles, on September 4, 1958, during one of the Offshore Islands crises. That memorandum describes the results of the possible fall of the Offshore Islands as follows:

The consequences in the Far East would be even more far-reaching and catastrophic than those which followed when the United States allowed [sic] the Chinese mainland to be taken over by the Chinese Communists, aided and abetted by the Soviet Union.[1]

An effort is made here to explain American policy toward the Offshore Islands, first in historical terms and then in relation to the constraints of decision-making in a bureaucracy. We consider the process by which the United States became increasingly committed to the defense of Taiwan and slightly later to the defense of the Offshore Islands without ever being in a position to force the Nationalists off the Islands. We also discuss the stratagems used by those who sought to tie the United States to a defense of Quemoy and Matsu.

The Evolution of U.S. Policy

Prior to the outbreak of the Korean War, the United States had announced that it would not interfere in a Chinese Communist attempt to seize Taiwan. No

Reprinted, with permission, from *Public Policy*, Volume XV, 1966.
*Coauthored with Tang Tsou.

mention was made of the Offshore Islands, but obviously if no American force was to be used to defend Taiwan, the United States would *a fortiori* not act to hold the Offshore Islands.

On June 27, 1950, following the outbreak of the Korean War, President Truman issued an order to the Seventh Fleet to begin to patrol the Taiwan Straits to prevent Communist attacks upon Taiwan or attacks from Taiwan against the Mainland. The American statement did not make any mention of the Nationalist-held Offshore Islands, and it is not clear whether in the hectic period at the opening of the war officials gave much attention to these Islands.[2]

In the operations of the Seventh Fleet in the Taiwan Straits and in the statements of American officials on the scene, it generally appeared that the Offshore Islands were in fact excluded from the U.S. defense perimeter.[3] Moreover, U.S. ships did not try to prevent operations from the Islands directed at the Mainland. Truman was not prepared to defend the Offshore Islands. Nevertheless, having moved to defend Taiwan in order to get bipartisan support for the Korean War, he was unwilling to provoke a partisan row by trying to force a withdrawal from the Offshore Islands. The ambiguity which was to characterize the American commitment to the defense of the Offshore Islands was evident even at this time. Since Truman's statement had not specifically excluded the Offshore Islands from the U.S. defense perimeter, the Chinese Communists could not be sure whether or not the Islands would be defended by the United States.

In February of 1951, under the terms of a bilateral Mutual Defense Assistance Agreement, the United States undertook to provide military assistance to Taiwan with the understanding that the Nationalist government would "use the material to maintain its internal security or its legitimate self-defense."[4] No mention was made of the Offshore Islands in the agreement. Following the signing of the agreement, the United States began to train and give equipment to the troops on Taiwan but with the understanding that they would not be sent to the Offshore Islands.[5] Thus the ambiguity continued.

There is no record of any high-level consideration by the American government of the Offshore Islands question until March of 1952 when John Foster Dulles, then a Special Assistant to the Secretary of State and soon to become Foreign Policy Advisor to Presidential candidate Dwight D. Eisenhower, in a discussion with a group of State Department officials proposed that the Nationalists be authorized to increase their strength on the Offshore Islands.[6] Perhaps triggered by Dulles' remarks, the State Department undertook a study of American policy toward Taiwan including the Offshore Islands. A draft of the study was completed and sent for comment to the American Embassy in Taipei in January of 1953 just before the new Administration took office. In reaction to the study (which has not been made public), the United States Ambassador to the Republic of China, Karl Lott Rankin, proposed that the responsibilities of the U.S. Military Assistance Group (MAAG) on Taiwan be extended to include training and equipment for the 75,000 Chinese Nationalists troops on Quemoy, Matsu, and the Tachen Islands.[7]

Soon after taking office President Eisenhower informed Congress that the Seventh Fleet would no longer be used to prevent the Chinese Nationalists from carrying out operations from Taiwan against the Mainland. He did not refer to the Offshore Islands, however.[8] Rankin made it clear to Chiang Kai-shek that this public statement constituted no change in American policy; the United States would still expect to be consulted before any decision was made by the Chinese Nationalists to attack the Mainland.[9]

While the Offshore Islands were not mentioned in the "unleashing" statement, the action by the United States implied that Quemoy, Matsu, and the Tachens were still put in a different category. The 1950 inhibition on Chinese Nationalist actions against the Mainland applied only to Taiwan and the Pescadores, and the formal release of the Nationalists related as well only to these islands. The United States in early 1953 was acting as if the Chinese Nationalist troops on the Offshore Islands were irregular forces whose actions were not subject to the same restrictions as the troops on Taiwan. But this distinction was very soon to erode.

By mid-1953 the American Joint Chiefs of Staff had come to the conclusion that because of the Communist buildup opposite the Offshore Islands the Nationalists would have to improve their defenses if they desired to hold the Offshore Islands. Chiang had been informally advised that the Joint Chiefs of Staff no longer had any objection to the rotating to the Islands of some of the regular American-equipped units from Taiwan. Despite these hints the Chinese Nationalists had taken no action before July when Ambassador Rankin, back from a trip to the United States, met with Chiang to discuss the Joint Chiefs' position and a U.S. MAAG report which proposed a buildup on the Tachens. Rankin urged Chiang to strengthen his forces on the Tachens as well as the other Offshore Islands. Rankin warned the Chinese Nationalist leader that under existing conditions the United States would not intervene quickly in the event of an attack. For precisely this reason he urged the Chinese Nationalists to build up their own forces. In agreeing to the increase in forces on the Offshore Islands, Chiang made three counter-requests to the United States. He asked that renewed consideration be given to a formal integration of the Offshore Islands into the Taiwan defense system and that the U.S. assume direct responsibility to come to their aid. While this move was being considered, he suggested an immediate public statement by the President indicating an interest in the Offshore Islands. Finally, he asked for some military craft for use in the Offshore Islands area.[10]

Rankin told Chiang that it might be some time before his requests could be acted upon. Nevertheless the United States had given advice to Chiang as to how to defend the Islands and had made a specific proposal for an increase in military forces, particularly on the Tachens, which was accepted by the Nationalists. The distinction between Taiwan and the Offshore Islands was eroding.

Soon after the Korean War was terminated by the Armistice Agreement of July 27, 1954 and a Mutual Defense Treaty was initialed by Dulles and Syngman Rhee, Chiang, in an interview, called for the conclusion of a mutual defense pact between the United States and Taiwan. The Nationalists would also have liked to see the conclusion of a Pacific pact similar to the North Atlantic pact.[11] In December of that year, the Nationalist government proposed a security treaty with the United States.[12]

During 1954 the efforts of the American government to organize a Southeast Asia Treaty Organization led the Chinese Nationalists to press harder for a bilateral Sino-American defense treaty. As Dulles explained to the Senate Committee holding hearings on the treaty, it was difficult to reject the Nationalist request.

Under these circumstances [of seeking other security pacts] China began to take on significance. It was suggested that the reason for this omission was that the United States desired to keep open the possibility of trading Taiwan (Formosa) and the Pescadores to Communist China as part of a general settlement in the area.

Such ignoble suggestions were damaging to the morale and prestige of the Republic of China and they reflected on the integrity and honor of the United States itself.

The appearance of discrimination against the Republic of China could not be continued without prejudice to moral and political standards that we need to maintain.[13]

At the same time that its desire to establish a ring of military alliances around China led it to accept the Nationalist proposal for a Sino-American treaty, the Administration's policy of "liberation" also precluded any notion of demanding a Chinese Nationalist withdrawal from the Offshore Islands as one of the conditions for American willingness to conclude a treaty. The Administration, already embarrassed by its failure to implement the policy of rolling back the Iron and Bamboo Curtains, was in no position to urge Chiang Kai-shek to withdraw from the Offshore Islands, which both symbolized his determination to return to the Mainland and served as the area from which most of his harassing of the Mainland was carried out.

Thus a major opportunity was lost to force a Chinese Nationalist retreat from the Offshore Islands. Not only did the U.S. not press for a withdrawal, but the Administration suggested a willingness to defend the Offshore Islands. The treaty committed the United States to defend only Taiwan and the Pescadores, but it noted that the provisions of the treaty would "be applicable to such other territories as may be determined by mutual agreement."[14]

Three months before the signing of the treaty, the Chinese Communists launched an artillery bombardment of Quemoy which was preceded by a large-scale propaganda campaign for the liberation of Taiwan. In early November, they shifted their military operations to the Tachens and Ichiangshan Island off the coast of Chekiang and used air and naval forces as well as their artillery. On January 18, 1955, the Communists launched an amphibious attack on Ichiangshan and secured the island for two hours of intensive firing. The Communist control of the sea and air around the Tachens made it impossible for the Nationalists to get supplies to the other Offshore Islands, which were also vulnerable to sea attack.[15]

Confronted with this threat before the ink was dry on the Mutual Defense Treaty, the Eisenhower Administration apparently felt that it had no choice but to participate in the defense of at least some of the Offshore Islands. The President, therefore, on January 24, 1955, dispatched a message to Congress which led five days later to Congressional approval of the Formosa Resolution. The Resolution authorized the President

to employ the Armed Forces of the United States as he deems necessary for the specific purpose of securing and protecting Formosa and the Pescadores against armed attack, this authority to include the securing and protection of such related positions and territories of that area now in friendly hands and the taking of such other measures as he judges to be required or appropriate in assuring the defense of Formosa and the Pescadores.[16]

A few days after the passage of this authorization the United States announced that it was, under the terms of the Resolution, assisting the Chinese Nationalists in the evacuation of the Tachen Islands which had come under heavy fire.

In urging this evacuation, the United States made a secret commitment to the Nationalists to defend Quemoy and Matsu.[17] Eisenhower quoted Dulles as saying at the meeting at which the decision was taken to submit the Formosa Resolution to the Congress:

I believe we must modify our policy: we should assist in the evacuation of the Tachens, but as we do so we should declare that we will assist in holding Quemoy and possibly the Matsus. . . .[18]

The statement issued by the American government at the time of the evacuation of the Tachens maintained that:

The U.S. Government has further advised the Chinese Government that with the object of securing and protecting Formosa, in consonance with the congressional resolution approved January 29, 1955, the U.S. Government will extend assistance to the Republic of China in defending such related positions and territories now in its hands as the United States deems to be essential to the defense of Formosa and the Pescadores.[19]

Moreover, Rankin implies by his description of the event that a promise was made. He writes: "The Chinese had hoped for the formal inclusion of Kinmen [Quemoy] and Matsu in this [U.S.] defense area, but they had to accept second best in the shape of informal assurances as to firm intentions."[20] A U.S. commitment to Quemoy and Matsu was further implied on February 22, 1955, when the United States informed the Taiwan government that it would not defend Nanchi Island, which is south of the Tachens but north of Matsu. The Chinese promptly evacuated Nanchi, apparently feeling that at least by implication the United States had committed itself to the defense of the remaining island chains of Quemoy and Matsu.[21] Publicly Secretary Dulles continued to emphasize that the American commitment was to defend only those positions necessary for the defense of Taiwan and the Pescadores.

Thus in a successful effort to get the Chinese Nationalists to evacuate the most exposed of the Offshore Islands, the Tachens, the United States at least in the eyes of the Chinese Nationalists committed itself to the defense of Quemoy and Matsu, and the Formosa Resolution authorized the President to defend those positions should he consider it necessary.

With the crisis passed and the treaty ratified, the United States made what was apparently its only effort in the postwar period to secure Chinese Nationalist evacuation of the Offshore Islands. Assistant Secretary of State Walter Robertson and Chairman of the Joint Chiefs of Staff Admiral Arthur W. Radford were sent to Taipei in April, 1955, to ask the Chinese Nationalists to consider evacuation of Quemoy and Matsu.[22] Radford and Robertson were the two firmest friends of the Chinese Nationalists in the American government. This suggests either that Chiang's best friends were sent to bring the news that he would have to evacuate the Islands or that they were sent to make a passing gesture in order to satisfy critics within the American government who thought that the United States should at least try to get the Nationalists off the Islands. The absence of any signs of bitter debate at the time of the Radford-Robertson visit to Taiwan suggests that if they did propose evacuation of the Islands, they did so in very mild terms. Perhaps they indicated that if the Chinese Nationalists decided they had to stay on the Islands, the United States would understand.

There the matter rested until mid-1958, except that the Nationalists substantially built up their forces on the Offshore Islands with the aid of U.S. military advisors stationed on Quemoy and Matsu. In August and September, 1959, heavy Communist artillery fire against Quemoy brought the United States, according to President Eisenhower, to the brink of nuclear war. Eisenhower reports in his memoirs that he was determined to defend Quemoy and that he had reached the decision to use nuclear weapons if Quemoy were attacked.[23] There were several reasons why the Administration decided not to issue a public statement unequivocally committing itself to defend Quemoy. It was believed that such a statement would stimulate more intensive attacks by critics of American policy. Moreover, the Administration feared that the Chinese Nationalists might use such commitment to draw the United States into a large war. Finally, the Administration was unwilling to defend some of the smaller islands in the Quemoy chain but did not want to invite an attack on them by drawing a clear U.S. defense perimeter.[24] By military actions and by their public statements, however, the Secretary of State and the President sought to convince the Chinese Communists that an attack on Quemoy was likely to bring in the United States. The most publicized of these was the Dulles statement issued after his Newport meeting with Eisenhower. Dulles speaking for the President declared that "the securing and protecting of Quemoy and Matsu have increasingly become related to the defense of Taiwan."[25]

The internal memorandum quoted at the outset of this paper stated that the loss of Quemoy would lead ultimately to the collapse of the entire American position in the Far East. If these were the expected results, it is no wonder that the Administration felt that the extensive Congressional and public opposition should carry little weight.

With the ending of the crisis, the Administration apparently made no move to secure evacuation of the Islands, although Dulles, on a visit to Taiwan, did succeed in getting the Chinese Nationalists to agree to rely primarily on peaceful means to liberate the Mainland and persuaded them to cut back slightly the forces on Quemoy.[26]

There was no further public debate or, apparently, private discussion within the Administration of the Offshore Islands until the issue arose during the 1960 Presidential election. At that time in the heat of a TV debate with his Republican opponent Richard Nixon, John F. Kennedy suggested the desirability of trying to persuade the Chinese Nationalists to withdraw from the Offshore Islands. Although in later debates he drew closer to the Eisenhower position, there is no doubt that Kennedy came into office determined to try to find a way out of the Offshore Islands situation.

For a time, numerous press reports predicted that the Kennedy Administration would soon unveil a new China policy. But in fact no changes of policy toward the Offshore Islands were made. When a new crisis in the Taiwan Straits arose in June, 1962, Kennedy was forced by circumstances to state that his position would be the same as that of Eisenhower in 1958. He declared that whatever his own views, the United States would not request the Nationalists to withdraw from the Islands under the threat of a gun.[27]

There the matter stands. President Johnson, confronted with a threat in Vietnam which he associates with the expansionist desires of the Communist Chinese, is unlikely to make any move to try to force the Nationalists off the Offshore Islands.

The Rationale

Thus far we have attempted to present historical explanations of why the United States has not tried to force the Nationalists off the Offshore Islands in peacetime and why it twice was prepared to resort to military action to defend the Islands. These explanations can be summarized as follows.

When the Truman Administration first made the decision to defend Taiwan in

1950, it did so to secure bipartisan support for its Korean policy. It was unwilling to jeopardize that support by provoking a fight with the Nationalists over the evacuation of the Offshore Islands. In 1954, when the United States made a treaty commitment to defend Taiwan, the Eisenhower Administration policy of "liberation" made it impossible to surrender additional territory to Communist control or to give up territory which would be useful in attacking the Mainland. In 1958 the view of the Administration as to the disastrous consequences of the fall of Taiwan, together with Dulles' commitment to not retreating under military pressure, made consideration of a withdrawal impossible. Finally, in 1962 before the new Administration could work out a revised China policy, Kennedy was forced to commit himself to the defense of the Islands in the face of renewed military threat.

While historical explanation on the surface accounts for the continuing American commitment to the defense of small islands less than 5 miles from the coast of China, we believe that American behavior can best be understood in light of the fact that the decisions were made by a large bureaucracy. In the remainder of the paper we attempt to say why those within the bureaucracy who opposed withdrawal prevailed. Their arguments, embodying stratagems which had much to do with their success, can be outlined in capsule form: (1) Dire consequences can be predicted. (2) We must not yield to pressure. (3) Now is not the time. (4) The costs are clear but gains uncertain. (5) How would we do it? (6) No one directly responsible is for this.

The Prediction of Dire Consequences

Often during the postwar period the United States has committed itself to the defense of territories whose intrinsic importance to the United States is small. The Offshore Islands represent an extreme case of this type of commitment. Some of the Islands were uninhabited, others had very small populations. If there was to be a justification for the United States defending the Offshore Islands, it had to be found in the consequences of their fall to Communist control. There were many officials who did believe that these consequences made the Islands worth defending.

The particular reasons which led individuals and bureaucratic agencies to support a defense of the Offshore Islands were complex and varied. Those officials who were sympathetic toward the Chinese Nationalist regime believed that the Islands should be held simply because the American pressure to force a withdrawal might provoke a crisis between the two governments which would lead to the collapse of the Chiang Kai-shek government.

Others feared a withdrawal from the Islands would pave the way for a two-China policy. Once off these Islands, the Chinese Nationalists would be 90 miles from Communist guns and would no longer have possession of any territory which was indisputably Chinese. The Chinese Nationalists have been determined to hold the Islands precisely because they see them as a protection against a two-China policy.

Neither the possibility of instability on Taiwan nor the need for a bulwark against a two-China policy are sufficiently serious consequences on which to argue for the use of American military forces, however. Such arguments would not appeal to the President or the public. Thus other warnings had to be advanced. Many officials have discovered that any prediction of the consequences to be expected from a proposed course of action which is not expressed in absolute terms is taken as indication that one does not oppose the policy. Rankin, for example, reports that his assertion that the loss of the Offshore Islands by the Chinese Nationalists would be "very serious but not necessarily disastrous" was taken as meaning that he had withdrawn his very strong opposition to American efforts to force a Nationalist withdrawal from the Islands.[28]

With intelligence estimates taken as policy proposals and with real motivations complex, diverse, and not necessarily persuasive, American officials supporting a defense of the Offshore Islands felt it necessary to resort to the strategy of predicting dire consequences. Thus the President was told by his advisors in 1958 that the American position in Japan, Korea, Taiwan, the Philippines, Thailand, and Vietnam would be seriously jeopardized and that currently neutralist nations, such as Indonesia, Malaya, Cambodia, Laos, and Burma would come under Communist control.[29]

These predictions of dire consequences appear to have served two purposes in the eyes of those making them. First, they convey unmistakably the implicit policy recommendation. If the memorandum drafted for the President and the Secretary of State had said that the danger of subversion in Taiwan would increase if Quemoy had fallen, that steps would have to be taken to assure the continuation of the American presence in the Philippines and elsewhere, and finally that the drift of some Southeast Asian countries toward accommodation with China might be accelerated, the estimate would have appeared more accurate and probably more in line with the actual estimates of the officials. However, their policy proposal would not have been as clear. The President would not have known if these officials were leaving the decision up to him or were implying that the U.S. should not defend the Islands. Predictions of dire consequences served the purpose of implying policy recommendations in what appears to be an accepted bureaucratic shorthand.

Moreover, predicting dire consequences has the advantage of hedging against the actual consequence of an American withdrawal from the Offshore Islands. If the Islands fell with consequences almost as dire as predicted, the officials could have pointed to their warning. On the other hand if the consequences were less severe, the bureaucracy could have taken credit for shoring up American positions after the President had decided not to go to war in defense of what the bureaucracy asserted to be a vital interest. Or perhaps no one would remember the predictions.

The value which officials saw in predicting dire consequences, and their apparent confidence that these predictions would not simply be ridiculed, led those in favor of defending the Islands to agree that they should make such predictions. But ritualistic language comes to be believed by those writing and reading the policy proposals. Thus 7 years after the event, Eisenhower apparently still claims to feel that it is true that the loss of the Offshore Islands would have had consequences greater than those which followed the fall of China.

The tendency to believe what one reads in formal papers is reinforced by the problem of drafting public speeches explaining American policy. Both in 1954 and in 1958 there were some people who opposed an American defense of the Offshore Islands. In explaining its position, the Administration tended to rely on predictions of dire consequences for reasons analogous to those which led government personnel to such predictions in internal memoranda. That is to say, any public evaluation of the consequences of the fall of the Islands which discussed costs and gains and trade-offs in some detail would appear to undercut the argument that the use of American military policy was necessary and would have suggested that the United States was about to change its position. Thus public exhortation as well as bureaucratic communication requires the prediction of dire consequences which come to be believed and, in turn, influence the actual policy calculations of officials.

We Must Not Yield to Pressure

A second device for coordinating policy views in a bureaucracy with diverse motivations is to seize on an absolute principle of behavior. This is a particularly useful device if some of those involved in the process, particularly high policymakers, actually believe in the principle.

Secretary of State Dean Rusk appears to follow John Foster Dulles in genuinely holding to the principle that it is dangerous and immoral to yield to pressure and permit force to be used to effect political change. For such men, the lesson of Munich is that yielding to military pressure only whets the appetite of an aggressor who then will press for greater conquests. Thus Rusk continues to believe as Dulles did that the United States must if necessary use force to prevent the successful application of force, particularly by Communist China or the Soviet Union. It has, therefore, been possible for the bureaucracy to appeal to the principle that the U.S. cannot yield to pressure when the Offshore Islands have come under the threat of military attack from Communist China.

The principle of not yielding to pressure has been violated by the United States on a number of occasions, even in the Taiwan Straits where the Tachens were evacuated in 1954 under pressure. Nevertheless, the belief in the absolute principle of not yielding to pressure has made the appeal to this principle a useful strategy for those in favor of defending the Offshore Islands.

Now Is Not the Time

Another way to manipulate a policy proposal is to applaud the contrary position but to assert that now is not the time to implement it. Thus those opposed to an American effort to force the Chinese Nationalists off the Offshore Islands could seemingly accept the ultimate value of such a withdrawal while suggesting that it would have to be done at some other time.

Arguing that "now is not the time" has the effect of forcing the advocate of the policy to declare that this is the optimum time rather than talking about the merits of the action. The argument can be used both during crises and in calmer periods. When used at both times, as it has been in relation to evacuation of the Offshore Islands, it is the equivalent of saying there is never an appropriate time.

Apparently during both the 1954 and 1958 crises, as well as at the time of the fear of a Chinese Communist attack in 1962, those who opposed a withdrawal from the Offshore Islands argued that clearly now was not the time to carry out such a policy. This is close to saying that the U.S. cannot retreat under fire but has the added element of saying that the costs of withdrawal will be greater now than they will be at another time.

During a calm period, it is possible to argue that one should not stir up trouble in the area when the other side is leaving well enough alone. If the Chinese Communists are apparently not planning to attack the Offshore Islands, why should the United States stir up trouble by seeking to force a Chinese Nationalist withdrawal? Thus, like the man who will always repair his roof tomorrow, the United States has apparently always come to the conclusion (with the possible exception of the Radford-Robertson visit in 1955) that now is not the time for pressing for an evacuation. The advocates of evacuation have never been able to make the case that any given occasion offered the optimum moment to pursue the policy.

The first two bureaucratic stratagems discussed thus far are applicable only in periods of crisis, while the third is applicable both to crisis and non-crisis periods. We turn now to additional stratagems used to block American pressure for a withdrawal from the Offshore Islands in non-crisis periods.

The Costs Are Clear but the Gains Uncertain

In a crisis period, a major cost of continuing to defend the Offshore Islands is the danger of a nuclear war with China; hence, those desiring to defend the Islands had to predict less obvious but more dire consequences of backing down.

At the same time, they were able to assert that standing firm is the way to forestall nuclear war. In quiet periods, those advocating that the United States seek to force the Chinese Nationalists to withdraw from the Offshore Islands confront a situation in which the immediate costs of withdrawal could be clear-cut while any gains are uncertain.

In a situation in which the costs are clear and the gains uncertain, the opponents of the policy will dwell on costs. In the case of withdrawal from the Offshore Islands, they are able to indicate that such a move might provoke a rift with the Chinese Nationalists. They can point out that the President, the Secretary of State, and other high officials will need to spend considerable time on the problem; first evaluating the alternatives and then implementing a policy of forced withdrawal. Opponents of withdrawal discuss the severe moral problems on Taiwan and increased threat of collapse of the regime which would follow a forced withdrawal. Moreover, they point out the United States would have to act to assure its other allies that this move did not presage the withdrawal of the United States from other exposed positions.

The strategy which those advocating a withdrawal would like to adopt would be to point to the extremely favorable consequences which would inevitably result from forcing a withdrawal. But these are difficult to specify. One can argue that withdrawal would make a crisis in the Taiwan Straits less likely. To this argument the answer is that there is no sign of such a crisis developing and the act of attempting a withdrawal might provoke a Chinese Communist attack. Another possible argument is that a withdrawal would make it possible for other governments to associate themselves with the defense of Taiwan. This in itself is not a major gain for the United States, and moreover it is difficult to say which countries would do so and what "associating themselves with the defense of Taiwan" would mean.

There *is* one major consequence which forcing the Chinese Nationalists off the Offshore Islands might have. However, many people in the bureaucracy do not believe that this consequence is a desirable one. A Chinese Nationalist withdrawal from the Offshore Islands would pave the way for the adoption of a two-China policy by the United States. It would be possible for the United States to assert that she recognized the Chinese Nationalist government as the government on Taiwan and recognized the authorities in Peking as the government on the Mainland. It is likely that a number of other states would be prepared to adopt a similar policy. The UN might even be persuaded to find a way to have both Taiwan and China as legal members of the organization even though under present circumstances neither Chinese government would accept such arrangements and actually sit in UN chambers.

The gains reaped from such a policy could be extremely great. And it is likely that only when the President makes it clear that he attaches a very high priority to a two-China policy that the arguments for forcing the Nationalists off the Offshore Islands will carry significant weight.

In the absence of a clear sign from the President that he supports a two-China policy, it is difficult for officials within the bureaucracy to rest a proposal on the assertion that it is good because it will make possible a two-China policy. The obvious answer of the opponents of the policy is therefore that they will consider pressing for a withdrawal from the Offshore Islands only when the American government formally decides that it is in favor of a two-China policy. In the absence of this, the argument that the costs of the proposed action are clear and the gains uncertain will carry more weight than the argument that while the costs are clear, the gains may be great.

How Do We Do It?

Another strategy which has been used by those opposing an evacuation of the Offshore Islands is to argue that the United States does not have the power to force a withdrawal. Officials can point out that Robertson and Radford were unsuccessful in 1955. How, they ask, do we do it? They can point out that the Islands are the sovereign territory of the government of the Republic of China and that the United States has neither the right nor the power to decide that an evacuation is necessary.

The answer of those advocating a withdrawal rests on the notion that Taiwan depends on the American security guarantee for its very survival. In such a situation, it is argued, the United States can force a withdrawal if it is prepared to go to the brink of a break. However, the success of such a policy depends on the President and the Secretary of State standing firm in the face of substantial Chinese Nationalist resistance to proposals to withdraw from the Offshore Islands. Thus those in the bureaucracy advocating withdrawal must concede that it is desirable only if the President and the Secretary of State feel very strongly about the issue and are prepared to devote substantial amounts of their own time and energy to the successful implementation of the policy. Given the absence of evidence that the President and the Secretary of State are prepared to devote substantial amounts of their own personal resources, there is no answer to the question: how do we do it?

No One Directly Responsible Is for This

In weighing arguments advanced for or against a policy within a bureaucracy, officials tend to give greater credence to the views of those who would be responsible for implementing a given policy or who would have to deal with the consequences of failure to act. When the proposal to evacuate the Offshore Islands has been made within the government, it has been possible for opponents to argue that no one directly responsible is for this. The Joint Chiefs, for example, are responsible for defending the Islands when they come under attack. Those who conduct American political relations with the Chinese Nationalists have a responsibility for the consequences which would flow from an American decision to withdraw from the Offshore Islands.

It appears to be the case that nobody with responsibility of this sort has pressed for an evacuation of the Offshore Islands. Under the Eisenhower Administration, the Far East Bureau of the State Department had a strongly pro-Chinese Nationalist view and presented the case against withdrawal. The military appear to have counted on the right to use nuclear weapons if necessary to defend Quemoy and in this sense saw the Islands as defensible. Under Kennedy and Johnson, the Far East Bureau has been preoccupied with the Indochinese peninsula and is probably not eager to accept the additional responsibilities which would come from an attempt to secure an evacuation of the Offshore Islands.

Those who advocate the policy of forcing a withdrawal have apparently been in policy-advising roles of various kinds, and hence their views have carried less weight. Moreover, no part of the bureaucracy has seen itself gaining so much from an evacuation that it is prepared to press continually for the implementation of such a policy.

The bureaucratic strategies discussed here have been employed to maintain the status quo in American policy. They constitute a sobering example in the realm of foreign policy of the general proposition that to make a bureaucracy change its position is much more difficult than allowing it to continue a given policy: the bureaucracy prefers the known dangers of an existing course to the uncertain costs and gains of change. If the bureaucracy is unlikely to initiate the proposal to force an evacuation of the Offshore Islands, American policy will move in this direction only if a President or a Secretary of State sees a potentially significant gain from seeking a withdrawal. It has been suggested that only a firm commitment to a two-China policy would lead top officials to envision substantial benefits following from evacuation of the Offshore Islands. Thus any future withdrawal of the American commitment to defend Quemoy and Matsu is likely to stem from and therefore imply a fundamental alteration of American policy toward the acceptance of the existence in the world community of two Chinas.

Notes

1. Dwight D. Eisenhower, *Waging Peace* (Garden City, N.Y.: Doubleday, 1965), p. 692.
2. Text in *American Foreign Policy, 1950-1955* (Washington, D.C.: Government Printing Office, 1957), p. 2468. For a discussion of the American decision

45

and the Chinese Communist reaction to it, see Tang Tsou, *America's Failure in China, 1941 to 1950* (Chicago: University of Chicago Press, 1963), pp. 558-64.

. *New York Times*, November 12, 1950, p. 14.

4. Text in *American Foreign Policy, 1950-1955*, pp. 2470-71.

5. Karl Lott Rankin, *China Assignment* (Seattle: University of Washington Press, 1964), p. 152; *New York Times*, December 7, 1952, p. 72.

6. Stewart Alsop, "The Story Behind Quemoy: How We Drifted Close to War," *Saturday Evening Post* (December 13, 1958), pp. 85-26.

7. Rankin, op. cit., p. 152.

8. Text in *American Foreign Policy, 1950-1955*, p. 2467.

9. Rankin, op. cit., pp. 154-55.

10. Ibid., pp. 167-69.

11. *New York Herald Tribune*, August 12, 1953.

12. Statement by Secretary of State before the Senate Committee on Foreign Relations, February 7, 1955. Text in *American Foreign Policy, 1950-1955*, p. 953.

13. Ibid.

14. Mutual Defense Treaty between the United States and the Republic of China, December 2, 1954, Article XI. Text in *American Foreign Policy, 1950-1955*, pp. 945-47.

15. After the Ichiangshan campaign, no Nationalist warship reached the Tachen Islands until February 7, when a combined American-Nationalist fleet arrived at the Islands to evacuate the Nationalist forces.

16. Congressional Authorization for the President to Employ the Armed Forces of the United States to Protect Formosa, the Pescadores and Related Positions and Territories of that Area, House Joint Resolution 159, Public Law 4, 84th Cong., 1st sess., January 29, 1955. Text in *American Foreign Policy, 1950-1955*, pp. 2486-87.

17. The evidence for this is overwhelming if circumstantial.

18. Dwight D. Eisenhower, *Mandate for Change* (Garden City, N.Y.: Doubleday, 1963), p. 467.

19. "United States Assistance to the Republic of China in the Evacuation of the Tachen Islands," statement by the Department of State, January 5, 1955. Text in *American Foreign Policy, 1950-1955*, pp. 2490-91.

20. Rankin, op. cit., p. 221.

21. Ibid., p. 223.

22. Eisenhower in his memoirs asserts that Robertson and Radford sought only to persuade Chiang to reduce the size of his garrison and not to evacuate the Islands (Eisenhower, *Mandate for Change*, pp. 481, 661-62). Kennedy both before and after his election implied that the purpose of the Radford-Robertson trip was to argue for evacuation (*Washington Post*, October 14, 1960; *New York Times*, June 28, 1962).

23. Eisenhower, *Waging Peace*, pp. 294-95.

24. Ibid.

25. As quoted in ibid., p. 299.

26. "United States-Chinese Nationalist Consultations under Article IV of the Mutual Defense Treaty: Joint Communique Issued at Taipei at the Conclusion of Meetings Between the President of the Republic of China and the Secretary of State, October 23, 1958." Text in *American Foreign Policy: Current Documents, 1958* (Department of State Publication 7322 [Washington, D.C.: Government Printing Office, 1962]), pp. 1184-85.

27. News conference of June 27, 1962, as reported in the *New York Times*, June 28, 1962.

28. Rankin, op. cit., p. 225. The Ambassador feared that making the absolute prediction would lead to an abandonment of Taiwan once the U.S. decided not to defend the Offshore Islands.

29. Eisenhower, *Waging Peace*, p. 692.

The Gaither Committee and the Policy Process*

Despite the extensive government apparatus for policy-making on problems of national security, the American President in the postwar period has, from time to time, appointed groups of private citizens to investigate particular problems and report to the National Security Council.[1] Some of these groups have performed their task without the public's ever becoming aware of their existence; others have in one way or another come to public attention. Among the latter are those which have become known under the names of their chairmen: Finletter, Gray, Paley, Sarnoff, Gaither, Draper, Boechenstein, and Killian. President Truman made use of such groups, and the variety of tasks for which they were appointed grew steadily during the Eisenhower Administration.[2]

Some analysts have seen in this development an indication that the government is exploiting all possible sources of policy recommendations, and have praised the use of such private groups.[3] Others have argued that their use reflects the bankruptcy of the NSC procedure.[4] There is agreement that the committees have often made imaginative and valuable recommendations, but the degree to which such advice can and should be fitted into the Executive decision-making process has been the subject of some dispute.

Perhaps the most publicized and controversial of such groups was the Gaither Committee, which, in 1957, presented a report on the nation's defense requirements. The Report remains a classified document but the effects of the Committee and its work continue to be mentioned in the nation's press. The Gaither Report was probably the most general study of the nation's defense effort to be undertaken by an *ad hoc* civilian group. Much of its contents and the events surrounding its drafting and presentation have become public, shedding a good deal of light on the national security decision-making process.

In this chapter I will attempt to trace and analyze the series of events connected with the Gaither Report. While explicating an important political incident, I will use the Gaither episode to generate hypotheses about the use of civilian study groups, about the Executive decision-making process, and about the role of information in the public debate about national security policy.

Reprinted by permission of Princeton University Press from *World Politics*, vol. XIII, no. 3 (copyright © 1961 by Princeton University Press): pp. 360-384.

*I am indebted to the following for comments and criticisms: Gabriel Almond, Paul Hammond, Paul Nitze, Harry Ransom, Henry Rowen, Thomas Schelling, Warner Schilling, and H. Bradford Westerfield.

I. Drafting the Report

In the spring of 1957 the Federal Civilian Defense Administration (FCDA) submitted a report to President Eisenhower recommending that the government spend 40 billion dollars over a period of several years to erect shelters which would provide protection against the blast-effect of nuclear weapons.[5] The FCDA proposal was discussed by the National Security Council, and the President ordered a study to be made by an *ad hoc* committee of private citizens. The sense of the NSC meeting had been that before the Administration considered spending a sum equal to its annual military expenditure, it should investigate other possible uses of the 40 billion dollars. It was argued that if the government were prepared to increase spending for defense, it should explore the advantages of increasing its active defense effort.

The Eisenhower Administration had come to rely on the use of private consultants and this was the type of situation in which an *ad hoc* group was likely to be most helpful. An alternative would have been to set up a committee of the interested Executive agencies, but such a group would either have been unable to agree or would have drafted a "compromise" split of the proposed 40 billion-dollar expenditure. A committee of private citizens might be expected to take an unbiased look at the situation. The FCDA proposal was too serious to be rejected out of hand and it was too expensive to be adopted. Formation of an expert committee was an effective way of handling the proposal.

Reflecting the NSC discussions, the directive asked the committee to evaluate the shelter-building proposal as part of a study of American active and passive defense capability. It anticipated that the committee would find it necessary to explore other aspects of national security as they impinged on the nation's defense effort. The committee was titled the Security Resources Panel of the Science Advisory Committee to the FCDA, but in fact it was directly subordinate to the NSC and its members were considered NSC consultants.

The President, acting with the advice of his Special Assistant for National Security Affairs, Robert Cutler, called in H. Rowan Gaither, Jr., a West Coast lawyer and chairman of the boards of the Ford Foundation and The RAND Corporation, and asked him to head the Committee. Robert C. Sprague, an industrialist and an expert on continental defense, was asked to serve as co-director of the study. Together they recruited an eleven-man panel which included experts on various aspects of military policy.[6] In addition to Gaither and Sprague, it included William C. Foster, a former Deputy Secretary of Defense and an expert on defense organization; James A. Perkins and William Webster, who had studied civil defense extensively; and, as staff director, Jerome Weisner, an expert on weapons systems evaluation who is now President Kennedy's science advisor. Supplying additional technical competence for the panel were Robert C. Prim and Hector R. Skifter, and rounding out the group were Robert Calkins, John J. Corson, and James Baxter, who provided some of the expertise of the social scientist, particularly in economics and history.

The panel met briefly in the spring of 1957 and set in motion a series of technical studies by the large scientific staff which it had brought together.[7] Much of this work was completed over the summer and the Committee members arrived in Washington in the fall to devote full time to a study of defense policy. At this point the Committee appointed as special advisors Colonel George A. Lincoln of West Point and Paul H. Nitze, a former head of the State Department Policy Planning Staff and now Assistant Secretary of Defense (International Security Affairs).[8]

No public announcement had been made of the existence of the Committee as it set to work in the old State-War-Navy Building on the study which was, in a few months, to come to public attention as the Gaither Report.[9] The first decision taken by the group was to broaden the scope of its inquiry to cover the whole range of defense problems facing the country.[10] This is a phenomenon which seems to typify such *ad hoc* studies. In the absence of agreed American policy on most aspects of national security, it is difficult for any group to evaluate a proposal in any one area without considering other problems. In this case the panel had been asked in effect how the United States could best spend an additional sum for continental defense. But clearly defense is only one part of the deterrence strategy and hinges on how well other parts function. It might very well be true that the greatest payoff for continental defense would come, for example, from investing in ballistic missiles. In the absence of any priority plans for spending additional sums for various systems, the Committee was forced to study the whole problem. In addition, the members were so prominent and had such definite opinions on the problems of American military policy that it was natural for them to decide to use the rare opportunity of drafting a paper for the NSC to present their views on a wide range of topics.

Just as the Committee was beginning its study, Gaither was taken ill and was hospitalized for several weeks.[11] Direction of the study fell to Sprague and Foster, who became co-directors.[12] Each member of the Committee took responsibility for a particular section of the Report, but they all met frequently as a group to discuss each other's work. The Committee drew on the technical studies which had been prepared for it and had clearance to reports of the Defense Department and other agencies concerned with national security.[13] It also held frequent sessions with high military officials, including the Joint Chiefs of Staff. In addition, it consulted with a number of private experts on national security policy and with quasi-public experts, including members of The RAND Corporation.

An advisory panel for the Gaither Committee, appointed by the President, met periodically with the Committee members to fill in gaps in their expertise. Among the panel's eleven members were retired military officers; Frank Stanton, the president of CBS; two prominent Republican financiers, Robert Lovett and John J. McCloy, now head of the United States Disarmament Agency; and I. I. Rabi and Ernest O. Lawrence, two of the nation's top scientists.[14]

As the Committee members sifted through this mass of material, it became clear to them that the top echelons of the government did not fully appreciate the extent of the Soviet threat as it was described by the Pentagon and the CIA.[15] With a real sense of urgency, the Committee set to work to draft a summary report based on the individual studies prepared on various aspects of military policy. Just as the Report was being completed, the nation was shaken out of its complacency by the Soviet Union's announcement on October 4, 1957, that it had launched Sputnik. This event gave the Committee greater hope that the Administration would accept its recommendations.[16] A week later the Report was finished and presented to the President for discussion at an NSC meeting.[17]

II. Presenting the Report

On November 7, 1957, the President presided over one of the largest NSC meetings in history. Over forty people gathered in the White House for the presentation and discussion of the Gaither Report. In addition to the dozen top officials who regularly attended, the civilian secretaries of the services and the Joint Chiefs of Staff joined members of the Committee and its advisory panel and other top government officials. Almost everyone present had read the Report in the three weeks between its completion and the meeting, and chief interest was focused on what the reaction of the President would be.

The briefing on the contents of the Gaither Report was opened by Sprague, and in turn Weisner, Foster, Corson, and Webster came up to the podium to discuss different sections of the Report. Graphs and charts were used extensively to illustrate the points that it made.

The Report presented to the NSC was in many ways not a typical NSC document. Unlike most NSC papers, the Gaither Report did not result from a compromise of the views of a number of departments and agencies. It did not represent an amalgam of considerations, including those of domestic finance. Furthermore, it was not bound by previous government policy decisions and specifically was not within the framework of budgetary limitations laid down by the President. The Report was thus able to call for measures which the Committee thought to be necessary and to present them in a dramatic fashion to the President and his top advisors. It deviated from government policy in a number of ways, but most fundamentally in the estimation of the danger facing the country and the amount of money which the United States should spend for defense.[18]

The Report began with an analysis of Soviet and American capabilities. It compared the economic situation in the two countries, pointing out that the Soviets devoted 25 percent of their GNP to defense, while the United States invested only 10 percent. This meant that both countries were spending the same absolute amount and suggested that, given the faster Soviet growth rate,

Russia would soon be devoting much larger sums to defense.[19] Tables were presented comparing Soviet and American industrial capability and military forces, and projecting relative strength into the future on the basis of present growth rates.[20] The Report contrasted America's armed forces of two and one-half million men equipped and trained only for general nuclear war with the larger Russian army supplied with weapons for both nuclear and conventional warfare.

After drawing this rather grim picture of comparative capabilities, the briefing moved on to an analysis of the situation and a series of policy proposals. The major danger facing the country, according to the Committee, was the vulnerability of the American strategic force.[21] The briefing dwelt at length on the problems of maintaining an effective second-strike force. It was pointed out that what must deter the Russians was not the force which the United States had, but the force which was capable of surviving an all-out Russian attack. The vulnerability of SAC was stressed. The planes of America's strategic force were exposed and concentrated in a way that made it extremely unlikely that they could survive a nuclear attack. The Committee warned that by the early 1960s, when Russia had an operational ICBM, she would be capable of destroying the American retaliatory force.[22]

The Gaither Report argued that the United States must give overriding priority to the development of an invulnerable second-strike force. It urged that for the short run everything possible be done to enable SAC to survive an attack.[23] It also called for an acceleration of the IRBM program.[24] For the longer run the Report urged that the missile production program be greatly accelerated. It warned that there was little value in acquiring missiles which were difficult to fire and which were exposed to enemy bombing. It urged therefore that American missiles be hardened and dispersed.

The Report laid the greatest stress on this point, reflecting the feeling of the Committee members that top Administration officials did not have a complete understanding of the problem of effectively deterring a Russian strategic strike.[25] The Report stressed the need to look at the problem in terms of the vulnerability of the force rather than its initial destructive capacity.[26] This was the problem which most bothered the Committee and gave its members the feeling that the government was dangerously underestimating the gravity of the Russian threat.

The Committee Report reflected the feeling that the vulnerability of the American strategic striking force was *the* great danger facing the country, but it also indicated that this was not the only military danger. The Report advised that, once the United States had recovered its full retaliatory capacity, the military develop a capacity to fight limited wars.[27] The establishment of a nuclear balance would mean that local aggression would be the likely form of warfare. The Committee found that the American military force was unprepared to engage in limited wars. The Report suggested that the Middle East and Asia were the most likely areas in which local wars might erupt and it discussed the importance and the problems of keeping a war limited.[28] The second recommendation of the Committee was therefore that the United States train and equip its forces for conventional local warfare.

The Gaither Committee had considered the FCDA proposal to spend 40 billion dollars for blast shelters, and while conceding that such shelters would save some lives in the event of war, it assigned a very low priority to such construction. In making policy proposals to the NSC, the Committee ranked its suggestions, giving top priority to the need to revitalize the strategic force and improve America's limited-war capability. In the civil defense field, the Report gave first priority only to a comparatively modest proposal to spend several hundred million dollars in the following few years for research on various aspects of shelter construction and other non-military defense measures.[29] The Committee assigned secondary priority to a proposal to spend approximately 22 billion dollars for the construction of radiation (rather than blast) shelters. It was anticipated that any construction program would follow the research phase.

Foster briefed the NSC gathering on the defense reorganization proposals contained in the Gaither Report. He urged that the military command structure be organized to place primary reliance on joint and specified commands. The Report urged that a joint limited-war command be established. It suggested that most planning and research be carried on directly under the Joint Chiefs of Staff. Orders, it was argued, should go from the Secretary of Defense through the Joint Chiefs to the commands, and the services should concentrate on logistics and training operations. The Report also urged that the layers of Pentagon committees be eliminated and the Secretary of Defense be given his own military staff.[30]

Although it was only forty pages long,[31] the Gaither Report also touched briefly on other subjects. It urged the government to increase spending for basic scientific research and stressed the importance to military policy of other areas of foreign policy. It also discussed the potential immediate impact on the American economy of the proposed increase in defense spending. The Report did not provide an exact estimate of the cost of all of its recommendations, but it indicated the need for rapid increases in the military budget to about 48 billion dollars per year in the 1960s.[32]

The entire NSC paid close attention during the presentation of the Report. The President had a copy of the written text balanced on his knee and alternated between following along in the Report and watching the speaker.[33] When the briefing was concluded, a general discussion followed. The President thanked the group and indicated that he was impressed with the arguments contained in the Report and wanted to implement them. However, he expressed a nagging fear that the American people would not be willing to pay the bill.[34] For reasons which I shall explore in the next section, none of the department heads present was willing to give support to the proposals as a whole. In fact, Secretary of

State John Foster Dulles spoke out strongly in opposition to the Report's recommendations. Support came from some members of the Committee's advisory panel. John J. McCloy and Robert A. Lovett, both prominent members of the American financial community as well as former Defense Department officials and active Republicans, argued that the American economy could afford to pay for the vitally needed measures outlined in the Report. They predicted that the people as a whole and the business community in particular would support the President if he urged increased spending for defense.[35]

The session broke up without any sense of the meeting having been arrived at. According to standard NSC procedure, the Report was formally sent to the departments concerned for their information and comments. In general, with reports of this nature nothing further happens. The reports are either used or rejected at the departmental level and the consultants return to their civilian jobs. However, in the case of the Gaither Report, there were significant further developments which throw considerable light on the policy process. Some of the Committee members made a determined effort to have their proposals implemented and at the same time they joined with others in seeking to have the Gaither Report made public.[36]

III. The Effect of the Report

Even in the early stages of their work on the Gaither Report, the members of the Committee were aware of the great discrepancy between the danger which was being described to them by the CIA and the military, and the sense of complacency at the top levels of the government. At least some of the Committee members became convinced that they had an obligation to make a strenuous effort to obtain the implementation of their proposals. Even as they worked on the Report, they were concerned with how best to proceed to secure its adoption by the Administration. In discussions with top civilian and military leaders, the Committee sought support for the types of recommendations it was considering. In the office of the President it attempted to make clear the nature of the problem facing the country.[37]

In seeking to influence national security policy-making at the Executive level, the Committee was dealing with a complex and bewildering decision-making process. It was clear, however, that in seeking to influence policy in a number of agencies, the most direct route was through the President. Some days before the NSC presentation, several of the most prominent members of the Committee and its advisory panel, including Gaither (who had just rejoined the group), Sprague, and Foster, met with President Eisenhower to discuss the content the Report.[38] Again, at the NSC meeting the Committee members had several hours in which to present him with their views.

The difference in tone of two speeches delivered by the President suggests that these briefings had at least a momentary impact on his thinking. On the evening of the NSC meeting of November 7, he gave the first of two scheduled addresses on the state of the nation's security.[39] The tone of this speech was one of reassurance. President Eisenhower stressed the present military strength of the United States:

It is my conviction [he declared], supported by trusted scientific and military advisers, that . . . as of today the over-all military strength of the free world is distinctly greater than that of the Communist countries.

. . . .

It misses the whole point to say that we must now increase our expenditures on all kinds of military hardware and defense. . . .[40]

The President recognized the need "to feel a sense of urgency," but he was determined that the United States not "try to ride off in all directions at once." The speech stressed the need to support a sound economy and to keep down the level of defense expenditure.

A week later in Oklahoma City the President delivered the second part of his talk, entitled "Future Security."[41] While this speech did not directly contradict the first, its tone was completely different. He discussed again the problems of balancing expenditures and receipts and keeping the budget low, but this time he asserted: ". . . now, by whatever amount savings fail to equal the additional costs of security, our total expenditures will go up. Our people will rightly demand it. They will not sacrifice security to worship a balanced budget."[42] The President recalled one of his statements of the previous week, but made a significant addition: "I assure you, as I did last week, that for the conditions existing today they [U.S. military forces] are both efficient and adequate. But if they are to remain so for the future, their design and power must keep pace with the increasing capabilities that science gives both to the aggressor and the defender."[43]

In spelling out the strategic requirements for the future, the President showed most clearly the effect which the Gaither Report was having, at least momentarily, on his thinking. He seemed to be recognizing that the country *did* have to ride off in many directions at once. The first requirement was, he declared, to maintain a nuclear retaliatory force such that an attack by the Soviets "would result, regardless of damage to us, in their own national destruction." In addition, forces were needed to deal with any form of local aggression, and home defense had to be improved. And, the President continued, more money must be spent on SAC dispersal and an acceleration of the missile program. "The answer," President Eisenhower asserted, "does not lie in any misguided attempt to eliminate conventional forces and rely solely upon retaliation. Such a course would be completely self-defeating."[44]

The members of the Gaither Committee quickly realized that the incorporation of some of their ideas into a Presidential speech did not mean that their proposals were about to be adopted by the Administration. The President might forward the Report to his writers with the suggestions that they use some of its ideas, but he was not likely to impose policy decisions on the operating agencies. Under the staff system used by President Eisenhower, policy proposals had to come up through the regular channels before he would act upon them. The Gaither Report had not sufficiently impressed or convinced the President for him to seize the initiative. He was not only reluctant to upset routine staff procedures, but also not eager to embark on the large-scale spending programs urged in the Report. The President was anxious to maintain his image as a man of peace and had no wish to approve a major expansion in the American military forces. He sought from his advisors assurance that the problems were being met rather than programs for new action.

After the failure of the initial attempt to alter Administration policy, the Gaither Committee, led by Foster, considered and to some extent implemented three courses of action. These were: further attempts to reach the President directly, efforts to enlist the support of operating agencies, and measures to arouse the American public and elite groups to the dangers facing the country. The operating agencies were perhaps the most likely allies of the Gaither Committee, and the failure to gain the support of a single department suggests the built-in forces for stability in the process.

The Gaither Report had recommended across-the-board increases in spending. While assigning some priorities, it had not made any really hard choices among weapons systems. Here was seemingly a document which might have been acceptable to everyone. Why then was no support forthcoming?

The Gaither Committee had taken seriously the question which, in effect, had been put to it: how the government should spend vastly increased sums of money. It was clear, however, to the operating agencies who were at the time wrestling with limitations imposed by the Budget Bureau that the "pie" was, in fact, not going to get bigger. The military services, the AEC, and the FCDA could only look upon the Report as a proposal to redivide the pie.[45] As such, they were naturally highly suspicious of its recommendations. The civil defense proposals caused the most difficulty. The FCDA was unwilling to accept a report which rejected its major proposal for blast shelters and which accepted implicitly the notion that civil defense spending should be weighed against possible military uses of the same funds. The military services were unwilling to support a plan which recommended a further splitting of the military-spending pie by including civil defense spending. The Report had given secondary priority to a 20 billion-dollar spending program within the next few years. The military could not have been expected to advocate such spending when their assumption was that it would come out of their funds.

In terms of individual proposals, the Committee members found some support within the services.[46] The Army, for example, was eager to endorse the proposals for a limited-war force. However, the individual recommendations were not new and only provided some additional leverage for the service viewpoints.[47] In addition, the services were reluctant to endorse a paper which suggested that they had been derelict in their duty of keeping the country militarily strong. Although the Army would continue to argue for larger limited-war forces, it would never be ready to agree that it was not in a position to win a limited war. Similarly the Air Force was not willing to concede that its forces were as vulnerable as suggested by the Gaither Report. The military services could not admit the extensive deficiencies outlined by the Report. The formal comment of the Joint Chiefs was reportedly that the study did not contain any new proposals, but was "largely a summation and endorsement of steps under way or under consideration."[48]

The military services were also reluctant to commit themselves to what was in effect a new, more "rational" method of splitting up the defense pie. Under the "political" method the services could pretty well predict what their percent of the defense budget would be. There was no way to tell just what budget-making by outside experts would look like. There is a general distrust among operating officials of this type of advice. In discussing the weakness of private expert committees, Nitze explicated one of the problems facing the Gaither group: "The most serious of these disadvantages is the possibility that the committee may be too far removed from executive branch responsibility to be fully effective. Those members of the executive branch who are actually responsible for carrying out policy . . . feel, perhaps rightly, that such groups are out of touch with the real problems with which the officials, in the end, must always deal. In any case, it is obvious that the committee, once its report has been presented, is in a poor position to help fight its recommendation through the decision stage. *Both of these difficulties characterized the reception of the Gaither Report* two years ago. . . ."[49]

This fear of civilian expertise and the inability of the Gaither group to put any influence back of its recommendations combined with the motives discussed above to explain the failure of administrative agencies to support the Gaither proposals. There were, however, two men in the government who might have been expected to take the over-all view necessary to endorse the recommendations of the Report. For vastly different reasons, however, neither the Secretary of State nor the Secretary of Defense was prepared to do so. Defense Secretary Neil McElroy viewed his job as that of an administrator. He refused to be drawn into strategic discussions or debates about the level of defense spending. He felt that he had been appointed because of his ability to run an organization efficiently and refused to deal with subjects about which he had no expertise.

Secretary of State John Foster Dulles was in no sense reluctant to discuss military matters. He had in fact become closely associated with the policy of massive retaliation which the Report indirectly, but clearly, challenged. Dulles was not prepared to endorse a program which called for large-scale spending and which committed the United States to local defense in the peripheral areas. In addition he felt that a shelter program would frighten America's allies. He feared that the Gaither proposals would use funds that otherwise could be used to increase foreign aid.[50] Dulles' influence with the President on foreign affairs suggests that his opposition must have been a major stumbling block in the efforts to convince the President to implement the Gaither proposals. Both the Treasury and the Budget Bureau were of course opposed to the Gaither recommendations because of the large-scale increase in spending proposed. With the Secretaries of State and Treasury and the Director of the Budget opposed to them and the Secretary of Defense refusing to express an opinion, the Gaither group members had to try either to influence the President directly[51] or to arouse American public opinion.

Following the presentation of their Report, the members of the Gaither Committee discussed possible courses of action among themselves and with experts on American foreign policy and defense. Following these weeks of informal discussions, a dinner meeting was held in Foster's Washington home in mid-December. Joining Foster were Frank Stanton and Paul Nitze, who had worked on the Gaither Report, and others, including Laurance Rockefeller and Elmo Roper.[52] Vice-President Richard Nixon attended on his own initiative but, according to one report, with the approval of the President.[53] Part of the evening was taken up with a further briefing of the Vice-President. In addition, Foster made two proposals to the group. He suggested that it aim at publication of a "sanitized" version of the Gaither Report.[54] He also urged the formation of a committee which would seek to convince the American people of the need for greater sacrifices in light of the grave Soviet threat. Foster argued that the release of the Report was essential to mobilize public opinion to support new programs. At the same time that it was trying to arouse public opinion, Foster suggested that his proposed committee continue the fight within the Executive for the implementation of the Gaither proposals.

In the discussion that followed, a general feeling was expressed of the need to do whatever was possible to alert the Administration and the people. Although Foster's proposal to set up a committee was received with much sympathy, the consensus was that the crucial problem lay with the President. If President Eisenhower could be convinced of the need to take bold action, he would have no difficulty arousing the American people. On the other hand, without the leadership of the President, it was felt that no group, whatever its composition, could reach the public.[55] Other members of the Gaither Committee shared this viewpoint. In testifying before the Jackson Committee, Sprague expressed his own opinion and in effect summed up the feeling of the meeting at Foster's home. In answer to a question as to what could be done to arouse the public, Sprague replied: "Senator, a citizen like myself, *or a group of citizens*, can do very little about this. I think there is one man in the United States that [sic] can do this effectively, and that is the President. I do not think there is anybody else."[56] Sprague's testimony reflected the bewilderment of the Foster group as to the position of the President. The Gaither Committee members were not sure whether the problem was to convince the President that their analysis was correct, or to get him to act on the basis of the information which he now had. As Sprague explained it: "I believe . . . that the danger is more serious than the President has expressed himself to the American public. I do not know whether he feels this or whether he does not. But I do not believe that the concern that I personally feel has as yet been expressed by the President to the American public. This is a complicated matter."[57]

The gathering at Foster's home broke up without a firm decision on whether or not to form a committee, but with a commitment on the part of those present to work for release of the Gaither Report to the public.[58] The efforts of members of the Gaither Committee[59] to have their Report released coincided with the demand of other groups.

IV. The Public Debate

The Gaither Committee had drafted its Report for the President without Congress' or the public's being aware of its existence. When the Report was presented to the NSC on November 7, 1957, the *New York Times* simply stated that an extraordinary meeting of the Council had been held and that members of the President's Science Advisory Committee were in attendance.[60] On November 9 the *New York Times* indicated that a special committee headed by Rowan Gaither had presented a report.[61] The contents of the Report leaked out slowly to the press. On November 23, 1957, the *Herald Tribune* published a fairly complete account of the contents of the Gaither study[62] and on December 20 the *Washington Post and Times Herald* ran a story by Chalmers Roberts which contained the most accurate report of the study's contents that had appeared to date.[63] As the nature of the Report and its sober conclusions came to the attention of the public,[64] a number of groups called for release of the official text. Thus, when the group meeting in Foster's home decided to press for publication of the Report, they were echoing the demand of others.

The group's desire to have the Report released coincided with a similar request from Congressional Democrats and some Republican Senators, including Styles Bridges.[65] The debate over making the Report public attracted wide interest in the press and among the attentive elites. As Senator Clark made clear on the Senate floor, those demanding release of the Report were not concerned with learning its contents. Anyone with this goal had only to turn to one of several newspaper and magazine accounts. To make this task easier, Clark inserted in the *Congressional Record* the Roberts article and assured the readers of the *Daily Record* that it was accurate.[66]

Congressional Democrats, particularly those Senators who had been advocating higher defense spending, viewed the Report as a vindication of their views. The declaration by a group of distinguished citizens, including a number of prominent Republicans, that the Eisenhower Administration had failed to act in the face of a grave danger to the survival of the country was excellent political ammunition. The Democrats had been trying to paint a picture of an inactive President failing to respond to the challenges of the time. Since it would be difficult to publish the Report without creating the impression that its findings were valid, release of the Report by the Administration itself could not fail to bolster this image, with important political advantages for the Democratic Party in the next Congressional election. Apart from the partisan political advantage which they saw in publication of the Report, the Senate Democrats were concerned about the state of the nation's defenses. The Preparedness Subcommittee was conducting extensive hearings and an official request for the Report came from Senator Lyndon Johnson, the majority leader and chairman of the Subcommittee. The Johnson Subcommittee was briefed on the substance of the Report[67] but nevertheless pressed for its publication, apparently feeling that it would aid its case regarding the need for the nation to make greater sacrifices.

The Senate debate over release of the Gaither Report followed the presentation to Congress of the President's budget message. The proposed spending for national defense had greatly disappointed those who held the views outlined in the Report. In his State of the Union Address on January 9 the President had declared that the United States must act "wisely and promptly" to maintain the capacity to deter attack or defend itself, and he had added: "My profoundest conviction is that the American people will say, as one man: No matter what the exertions or sacrifices, we shall maintain that necessary strength."[68] But while the budget message had called for some increase in spending, it was not enough in the opinion of those demanding release of the Gaither Report. The budget called for modest acceleration of the missile and SAC dispersal programs but, while recognizing the need for conventional forces and civilian defense, it called for a curtailment of these programs to save part of the amount needed for the expanded activities. It specifically ruled out a substantial increase in the defense budget.[69]

Once again there was a sharp contrast between what was included in the President's speech and the actual policy position of the Administration. Any possibility that the President would have overruled his subordinates on this issue was eliminated by Eisenhower's stroke. He was not working during most of the period between presentation of the Gaither Report and the submitting of his budget to Congress.

Senators and Representatives urging release of the Report felt it would strengthen their hand in trying to convince the Congress to increase defense expenditures substantially and to generate pressures on the Administration to spend the money which was appropriated. As Senator Clark declared on the Senate floor: "That [Gaither] report should have caused this Administration to have a far greater sense of urgency than it presently gives any indication of having."[70] He urged a reading of the Roberts article in order to "have an understanding of the very critical situation which confronts our country, and which I must say in all good conscience the President's budget does so little to remedy."[71]

Echoing this Congressional demand for release of the Report were newspapers and magazines which argued that the public was entitled to read this study by a group of distinguished citizens.[72] It was pointed out that various distortions had appeared in print, including one that suggested that the Committee had advocated preventive war.[73] Only the full publication of the Report would stop the rumors and give the people an opportunity to evaluate this Report which, it was stressed, had been written by an extremely able group of private citizens. Members of the Gaither Committee pressed for publication of the "sanitized" version of the Report which Foster had offered to prepare. Publication would indicate that the Administration took the Report seriously and was prepared to implement it. It also would be an effective first step in what they hoped would be a Presidential campaign to arouse the American people to meet the crisis facing the nation. Those within the Administration who favored more spending for defense were pressing for release of the Report for the same reasons and leaked its contents. Private citizens concerned about the nation's defense effort were also seeking publication of the Report.

Despite these intense efforts, the President refused to yield. The official Administration position was set forth in a letter to Senator Johnson: ". . . From time to time the President invites groups of specially qualified citizens to advise him on complex problems. These groups give this advice after intensive study, with the understanding that their advice will be kept confidential. Only by preserving the confidential nature of such advice is it possible to assemble such groups or for the President to avail himself of such advice."[74] To publish this Report, the letter concluded, would violate the privacy of this relation and also the standing rule that NSC documents are not made public.[75]

Earlier, at a press conference, the President had made it clear that he considered the Report confidential and had no intention of making it public.[76] A Presidential press release noted simply that "the report is, of course, a highly classified document."[77] James Reston, analyzing the Eisenhower Administration's refusal to publish the study, termed the Report an indictment of Eisenhower's policy and noted that publication would have weakened the President as well as the Republican Party.[78] The desire to withhold political ammunition from the Democrats undoubtedly played a part in the decision not to release the Report, as did the need to maintain the tradition of privacy for such reports. Probably more important, however, was the President's oft-repeated fear that the American people, if panicked, would ride off in all directions and demand spending which would be unwise and would damage the economy.[79] Thus, after Sputnik the President moved to calm the nation and ultimately rejected the fundamental assumption of the Gaither Report that the country was in grave danger. To take the unusual course of releasing the Report would imply that it presented an accurate picture and would increase pressures, which the Administration was fighting, to step up defense spending substantially.

The Eisenhower Administration continually denied that the Gaither Report showed the United States to be weak at the time the document was being written. It asserted that the government was already dealing with the problems outlined in the Report and that adequate measures were being taken on the basis of this and other reports to assure the nation's survival.[80]

Although they failed to have their Report released, many of the Gaither Committee members spoke out in an effort to alert the nation to the imminent dangers. Foster, in particular, appeared before numerous groups to argue the need for greater sacrifices. Sprague told the Jackson Committee that he had spoken to thirty or forty groups since serving on the Gaither panel, but, he continued, "I do not think this is very effective. I have done all that I can."[81] After a while the Committee members gave up the effort to arouse the public, with the realization that they could not compete against the President's words of reassurance.

V. Conclusion

The dispute about releasing the Gaither Report was a short episode in the continuing political debate over American defense strategy and the level of military spending necessary to implement the foreign and military policies of the United States. While the Report did not substantially alter the course of the struggle, it helped to bring some of the issues and pressures more sharply into focus. The fight over the release of the Report reflected almost exactly the larger dispute over defense spending. The American political process may be viewed as a struggle between clusters cutting across governmental structure, political parties, and interest groups and forming and reforming around various causes or specific proposals.[82] The defense debate which followed the launching of the Russian earth satellites brought into action two groups. One, which included the President, members of his Cabinet, some Congressional leaders, and members of the attentive elite, reacted to Sputnik with programs for modest increases in national security spending but continued to assert that no large increase in spending or re-evaluation of strategy or governmental structure was needed. The other group, which included members of the Gaither Committee, Congressional Democrats and some Republicans, directors of mass media, and national security experts, saw in the Sputniks an affirmation of its belief that the United States was faced with a grave threat to its survival and an opportunity to have its views prevail. Its members urged substantial increases in government spending and an awakening to the serious military, economic, and political challenge facing the United States and its allies. The Gaither Committee included a number of men who even before Sputnik had been arguing for substantial increases in defense spending. The other members of the Committee were won over to this view by the intellectual climate of the Committee as well as their review of the military situation. The Gaither Report provided a guide for the "pro-spending cluster,"[83] presenting a rationale for its position and a blueprint for the expenditure of the additional sums which were to be made available. It hoped that the Administration could be pressed to accept the Report drawn up by a committee of the NSC as a guide for a substantially increased military effort.[84]

The Gaither Report was valuable to the pro-spending cluster in a number of ways. Within the Administration it provided an excuse for a further review of the American defense position, and brought before the President and his top advisors in a dramatic fashion the arguments for spending substantially larger sums of money. It contributed to an awareness, on the part of the President and his top advisors, of the vulnerability problem and of the crucial importance of the dispersal of SAC and the development of mobile, hardened missile systems. The Report was instrumental in convincing the Air Force of the need to develop invulnerable second-strike forces. In the longer run it was probably partly responsible for the acceptance by both the Eisenhower Administration and the Air Force of programs for SAC dispersal and missile hardening. It also undoubtedly contributed to the growing acceptance by the Administration of the need to have forces for limited war (although it did not alter the failure to implement this decision in the military budget). It contributed to the pressure which raised military spending slightly.

By leaking the Report, those in the Administration arguing for higher spending aided those with similar views in the legislature and the attentive public. For these groups the Report provided substantiation from a source with access to all government intelligence of the arguments frequently offered by critics outside the government.[85] The Report made it clear that Executive optimism was based not on additional information but on a different reading of the facts available to the public. The data and reasoning of the Gaither Report could be used to bolster the case for increased spending, the need to overcome the missile gap and to develop a limited-war force. In addition, the struggle over publishing the Report was dramatic and helped to publicize the somewhat technical arguments over military strategy and the demands for greater expenditure on defense. Their service on the Gaither Committee substantially increased the prestige and influence of its members. Some continued in advisory capacities in the Eisenhower Administration, and all are looked to as experts on national security problems.

The Report had a significant influence on the analysis of strategic problems by national security experts. The recent emphasis in the military policy literature on the problems of vulnerability and second-strike forces stems partly from the impact of the Gaither Report and the members of the Committee and its advisory panel.

While the Gaither Report served temporarily as a rallying point for those favoring increased spending, the anti-spending cluster was quick to recognize the danger which the Report posed. The President, battling the pressures for greater military expenditures, refused to make the Report public and stressed that it was just one of a number of reports made to him. Senate Republicans opposed to large spending urged that the Report be kept secret, noting with alarm the influence it had already had in increasing the pressures on the Administration. Had the Report been made public, it would have represented a significant victory for the pro-spending cluster and would have probably indicated that that group was gaining the upper hand in the Administration.

The complexities of military planning and strategy are such that public debate (and even the Congressional appropriations process) plays a limited role in making critical decisions. The failure of Congress to have the Gaither Report published indicated the ability of the Executive to limit Congress' role by cutting off vital information. Insofar as Congressional and public debate play a role in the process of national strategy, the Gaither incident was of some value. The public debate had an important educational function in bringing to the attention of the Administration an analysis of the situation different from that provided by operating agencies. By calling attention to problems of vulnerability and limited war, the Gaither Report increased public understanding of these crucial questions.

In part, Congressional activity on defense matters can be viewed as a massive lobbying effort to influence the political decision-making process of the Executive branch.[86] The analysis of the Gaither Committee added to the ability of Congress to influence the process and to press for increased and more rational spending. If the public dispute over the Gaither Report contributed to the political climate which has influenced President Kennedy, it may well have made a vital contribution to the nation's security.

Although when the contents of their reports are leaked or released, the work of civilian *ad hoc* NSC committees is of value to Congressmen and private citizens, such groups are primarily instruments of the President and need to be evaluated in terms of their possible contribution to the Executive decision-making process. Within the Executive the Gaither Report provided a fresh look at the nation's defense posture. It served as an effective communication procedure to bring before the attention of the President and his principal advisors concerns which were being felt at the middle and upper levels of the operating agencies but which had not filtered through to the White House.

The Committee Report provided clear, well-reasoned statements of the problems of vulnerability and limited war, of the role of dispersal and hardening, and of the problems and opportunities of civil defense. It undoubtedly made a major contribution to the understanding of these problems by top officials. The panel was able to point out serious deficiencies where it found them because it was not responsible for past policy action, and the President could receive such advice because he anticipated being able to keep it private. The Committee also advanced a number of new policy proposals, particularly in the field of defense reorganization, which were not likely to come from the armed services themselves.[87]

Having made its proposals, the Gaither Committee found that it lacked the power base to fight for their implementation. But clearly the value and activity of such a group are not measurable in terms of its political influence on the decision process. The Committee furnished the President with a program, which, while perhaps not very precise or well thought-out in detail, could have served as a guide for action. The Committee thus fulfilled its primary purpose of providing an additional source of information for the President, unencumbered by future and past policy responsibility. The operating agencies can only view such committees as threats to their prerogative. But to a strong, vigorous President they could prove to be a powerful tool for overcoming bureaucratic and political opposition to the implementation of new, vitally needed programs.

Notes

1. The first such Presidential Commission was appointed by President Truman in January 1948 to make a general survey of foreign intelligence activities (see U.S. Senate, Subcommittee on National Policy Machinery, Committee on Government Operations, *Organizational History of the National Security Council*, 86th Congress, 2nd Session, Washington, D.C., 1960, p. 10).

2. See the following articles by former NSC staff members reprinted in U.S. Senate, Subcommittee on National Policy Machinery, Committee on Government Operations, *Organizing for National Security, Selected Materials*, 86th Congress, 2nd Session, Washington, D.C., 1960 (cited hereinafter as *Selected Materials*): Sidney W. Souers, "Policy Formation for National Security," p. 32; Robert Cutler, "The Development of the National Security Council," p. 58; and Gordon Gray, "Role of the National Security Council in the Formation of National Policy," p. 65.

3. See the articles by Bowie, Cutler, and Gray in ibid.

4. See the articles by Kissinger, Nitze, and Jackson in ibid.

5. *New York Times*, December 21, 1957, p. 8:4; Chalmers M. Roberts' article in the *Washington Post and Times Herald*, December 20, 1957, reprinted in the *Congressional Quarterly Weekly Report*, xv (December 27, 1957), pp. 1328-30, and in the *Congressional Record*, 85th Congress, 2nd Session, Washington, D.C., 1958, p. 858 (Roberts citations hereinafter refer to the *Congressional Quarterly Weekly Report*).

6. The membership of the Gaither Committee and its advisory panel was released by the White House and printed in the *Congressional Record*, loc. cit.

7. A part of this staff was supplied by the Institute for Defense Analyses (IDA). See *IDA Annual Report II*, March 18, 1958, pp. 6-7.

8. Also serving as advisors to the panel were Albert C. Hill, General James McCormack, and Edward P. Oliver of The RAND Corporation.

9. The only leak regarding the Gaither study had come in August when Stewart Alsop reported that the President had asked Gaither to study the possibility of employing new technological means of defense against atomic attack. He noted that the Committee was attracting "top level" talents, but he warned that "it remains to be seen whether anything solid comes of Gaither's assignment, in the present national mood of complacency" (*New York Herald Tribune*, August 26, 1957, p. 12:7).

10. Interview with Gaither, *New York Times*, December 25, 1957, p. 24:6.

11. Ibid., p. 24:5.

12. Ibid., December 21, 1957, p. 8:4.

13. Press release by Presidential Press Secretary James Hagerty, ibid., December 22, 1957, p. 4:1.

14. The other members of the advisory panel were Admiral Robert C. Carney, General James H. Doolittle, James B. Fisk, General John E. Hull, Mervin J. Kelly, and James R. Killian.

15. Testimony of Dr. James R. Perkins in U.S. Senate, Subcommittee on National Policy Machinery, Committee on Government Operations, *Hearings*, Part II, 86th Congress, 2nd Session, Washington, D.C., 1960, p. 293 (cited hereinafter as *Jackson Hearings*, Part II).

16. Roberts, loc. cit., p. 1328.

17. Perkins testimony, *Jackson Hearings*, Part II, p. 294.

18. The text of the Gaither Report has not been made public. This account relies entirely on published sources. It draws heavily on Roberts' article (see note 5 above), about which Senator Clark declared on the Senate floor: "The importance of the article arises from the fact that it is well known by many Members of this body, including myself, that this newspaper account accurately and clearly states the major findings and conclusions of the Gaither Report" (*Congressional Record*, loc. cit. p. 859). The information in the Roberts article has been supplemented and checked with news and news analysis articles in the *New York Times* and *Herald Tribune*, as well as columns by Arthur Krock, James Reston, Drew Pearson, and Stewart Alsop, and various magazine articles. In addition, speeches by members of the Committee and its Advisory Panel after the Gaither Report was presented, and their testimony at the Jackson Hearings, provided confirmation of the major points made in the Report.

19. Cf. testimony by Robert Sprague, *Jackson Hearings*, Part I, p. 50.

20. Roberts, loc. cit., p. 1329.

21. The Committee's proposals on strategic vulnerability were heavily influenced by a classified RAND report prepared under the direction of Albert Wohlstetter. For a discussion of the RAND report, see Joseph Kraft, "RAND: Arsenal for Ideas," *Harper's*, CCXXI (July 1960), pp. 71-73.

22. Alsop, *New York Herald Tribune*, November 25, 1957, p. 18:7, and ibid., November 23, 1957, p. 1:8; Claude Witze, "Classified Report Says Soviets Can Neutralize SAC by 1960," *Aviation Week*, LXVII (December 2, 1957), p. 28.

23. Such a program would presumably include dispersal of SAC, some planes in the air, and a ready alert for the rest of the command.

24. Drew Pearson, "Gaither Report Release Sought," *Washington Post and Times Herald*, December 18, 1957, D, p. 11:5.

25. Cf. the testimony by Sprague, Baxter, and Perkins in *Jackson Hearings*, passim.

26. For an unclassified but well-informed discussion of the problem of maintaining a stable strategic balance, see Albert Wohlstetter, "The Delicate Balance of Terror," *Foreign Affairs*, XXXVII (January 1959), pp. 211-34.

27. "Leak—and a Flood," *Newsweek*, L (December 30, 1957), p. 14; *New York Times*, November 23, 1957, p. 8:3; *New York Herald Tribune*, November 23, 1957, p. 1:8.

28. Krock, *New York Times*, December 22, 1957, IV, p. 3:2.

29. The Committee's analysis of the civil defense problem reflected the influence of Herman Kahn of The RAND Corporation. The alternative civil defense proposals sketched here are elaborated in *Report on a Study of Non-Military Defense*, RAND, R-322-RC, July 1, 1958.

30. That the Gaither Report included proposals on defense reorganization was indicated by Defense Secretary McElroy (*New York Times*, January 22, 1958, p. 15:4). The proposals were spelled out by Foster in a speech before the Student Conference on United States Affairs (SCUSA), IX, printed in *Proceedings of the Conference*, West Point, N.Y., 1957, p. 9.

31. Cutler testimony in *Jackson Hearings*, Part IV, p. 594.

32. *New York Times*, December 21, 1957, p. 8:4.

33. Charles J.V. Murphy, "The White House Since Sputnik," *Fortune*, LVII (January 1958), p. 230.

34. Roberts, loc. cit., p. 1328; *Newsweek*, L (December 30, 1957), p. 14.

35. Roberts, loc. cit., p. 1328.

36. Some of the Committee members, including Gaither, returned to their civilian jobs and took no part in the campaign discussed below.

37. Sprague testimony, *Jackson Hearings*, Part I, pp. 49-51.

38. Murphy, op. cit., p. 230; Cutler testimony, *Jackson Hearings*, Part IV, p. 594.

39. Reprinted in *New York Times*, November 8, 1957, p. 10.

40. Ibid., p. 10:3, 8.

41. Reprinted in ibid., November 14, 1957, p. 14.

42. Ibid., p. 14:6.

43. Ibid., p. 14:2.

44. Ibid.

45. In considering the reaction of Executive agencies, it should be kept in

mind that the Administration placed very tight restrictions on access to the Report. For example, NATO Supreme Commander General Lauris Norstad did not see it (*New York Herald Tribune*, January 8, 1958, p. 2:2).

46. The recommendations of the Gaither Committee were broken down into groups. The agencies concerned prepared papers on these proposals and they were discussed at a series of NSC meetings. See Cutler testimony, *Jackson Hearings*, Part IV, p. 594.

47. Cf. General Maxwell Taylor, *The Uncertain Trumpet*, New York, 1958, passim. Taylor, in discussing policy papers drafted for the NSC while he was Army Chief of Staff, makes it clear that most of the strategic concepts and recommendations of the Gaither Report were discussed frequently by the Joint Chiefs and the NSC before and after the Gaither Report was presented, although he does not mention the Report itself.

48. *New York Times*, December 21, 1957, p. 8:3. This phenomenon clearly needs greater study. The strait jacket which has confined the military chiefs, preventing them from admitting extensive weakness even while pressing for more funds, has surely been an important restraint on the flow of information to the White House and to Congress. A comparison of the statements to Congress made by Army Chiefs of Staff on, for example, the adequacy of our capability for limited war and the statements they make after retiring indicates vividly the reality of this phenomenon. (I am indebted to Paul Hammond and Louis Kushnick for bringing this point to my attention.)

49. Paul H. Nitze, "Organization for National Policy Planning in the United States," *Selected Materials*, p. 168 (italics added).

50. Cf. Dulles' testimony before the Senate Foreign Relations Committee, *New York Times*, January 10, 1958, p. 1:5.

51. For an excellent discussion of the kinds of problems that President Eisenhower would have faced in seeking to impose the recommendations of the Gaither Report on the operating agencies, see Richard Neustadt, *Presidential Power*, New York, 1960, passim.

52. *New York Times*, December 11, 1957, p. 8:6; *New York Herald Tribune*, December 11, 1957, p. 1:3.

53. *New York Times*, December 12, 1957, p. 11:1.

54. Krock, ibid., December 13, 1957, p. 26:5.

55. This feeling that the President constituted the key to the problem was reflected in a report by Samuel Lubell on a field trip made soon after Sputnik II. Lubell reported that "one thing I found especially striking was how closely the public's reactions corresponded to the explanatory 'line' which was coming from the White House. Relatively few persons repeated the criticisms which were being printed in newspaper editorials or were being made by members of Congress or by scientists. In talking about sputnik, most people tended to paraphrase what Eisenhower himself had said. . . . The public generally tended to follow the President's lead. In no community did I find any tendency on the

part of the public to look for leadership to anyone else—to their newspapers or radio commentators, to Congressmen or to men of science. Nor, with some exceptions, could people be said to be in advance of the President, or to be demanding more action than he was." (Samuel Lubell, "Sputnik and American Public Opinion," *Columbia University Forum*, I, Winter 1957, p. 18.)

56. *Jackson Hearings*, Part I, p. 55 (italics added).

57. Ibid.

58. Ultimately no committee was set up reflecting the view expressed by Sprague. A leak to the press about the gathering and its purpose made further action by the group more complicated and, in addition, embarrassed the Vice—President.

59. Not all of the Gaither Committee joined in this effort. Gaither, for example, told a news conference that "a report like this to the Security Council and to the President is never made public. If all or part of it is made public, it would be an exception, and the first time such a thing was ever done." (*New York Herald Tribune*, December 25, 1957, p. 3:1).

60. *New York Times*, November 8, 1957, p. 10:8.

61. Ibid., November 9, 1957, p. 11:6.

62. *New York Herald Tribune*, November 23, 1957, p. 1:8.

63. See note 5 above.

64. The leaks apparently came both from within the Administration and from members of the Gaither Committee.

65. *New York Herald Tribune*, December 13, 1957, p. 1:3; *Washington Post and Times Herald*, December 21, 1957, p. 1:6.

66. *Congressional Record*, loc. cit., p. 858.

67. *New York Times*, December 23, 1957, p. 6:4.

68. Paul Zinner, ed., *Documents on American Foreign Relations, 1958*, New York, 1959, p. 2.

69. Portions of the budget message relating to national security are printed in ibid., pp. 15-23.

70. *Congressional Record*, loc. cit., p. 860.

71. Ibid.

72. See, for example, the editorials in the *New York Times*, December 13, 1957, p. 26:2; *New York Herald Tribune*, December 23, 1957, p. 16:1; and *Washington Post and Times Herald*, December 30, 1957, p. 14:1.

73. In his column in the *New York Times* on December 20, 1957 (p. 26:5), Arthur Krock inferred from what he knew about the Gaither Report that it recommended a "first strike" strategy and speculated that this was why the Report was being kept secret. Two days later he was able to write that "it is authoritatively stated that this point was not included in the report" (ibid., IV, p. 3:2).

The Communists sought to exploit this and other distortions of the Gaither Report. On December 26, Moscow and Peking broadcasts monitored in

London charged that the "authors of the report are proponents of a limited war which would be fought with all types of modern nuclear weapons" (*New York Times*, December 27, 1957, p. 4:5). Then Soviet Premier Bulganin in a note to President Eisenhower on March 7, 1958, wrote that "the American press has been discussing for the past few weeks the idea of 'preventive war' against the U.S.S.R. which, according to such well-known American commentators as Hanson Baldwin, Arthur Krock and Drew Pearson, was advanced in a secret report to the National Council of Security [sic] by the so-called Gaither Committee" (ibid., March 8, 1958, p. 2:8).

74. Ibid., January 23, 1958, p. 10:4.

75. This was not an unimportant consideration. It undoubtedly heavily influenced the President's Special Assistant for National Security Affairs, Robert Cutler, who argued against the release of the Report. Cf. Robert Cutler, "Organization at the Policy Level," *General Electric Defense Quarterly*, II (January-March 1959), pp. 12-13. For a general discussion of this problem, see Francis E. Rourke, "Administrative Secrecy: A Congressional Dilemma," *American Political Science Review*, LIV (September 1960), pp. 691-93.

76. *New York Times*, January 16, 1958, p. 14:6.

77. Ibid., December 22, 1957, p. 4:1.

78. Ibid., January 22, 1958, p. 10:5.

79. Krock, ibid., December 22, 1957, IV, p. 3:1.

80. Ibid., December 29, 1957, p. 1:3.

81. *Jackson Hearings*, Part I, p. 56.

82. For a similar model spelled out, see Roger Hilsman, "The Foreign Policy Consensus: An Interim Research Report," *Journal of Conflict Resolution*, III (December 1959), pp. 361-82. I am indebted to H. Bradford Westerfield for the model used here.

83. The term "pro-spending cluster" is not meant to imply that its members favored spending for its own sake. While some people supporting the Gaither proposals were willing to back any plan for larger government spending, others (notably Sprague) were reluctant to endorse any spending programs; most of this cluster supported the Gaither proposals without being influenced by the spending implications.

84. NSC 68 provides some interesting parallels to the Gaither Report and suggests the role it might have played if Sputnik had led to an Administration decision to increase the defense budget substantially. NSC 68 was drafted by a joint State Department-Defense Department committee, but it was, like the Gaither Report, prepared without considering domestic economic or political factors and without regard to the budget level set by the President. It included a complete review of the national security situation and called for a large increase in defense spending—providing a blueprint for the use of the funds. The Report was presented to the NSC just prior to the outbreak of the Korean War. It was initialed by President Truman just after the war started and served as the

government's rationale for the expanded defense effort. It enabled the Administration to assert that spending was being guided by a long-range plan drafted prior to the war. See Paul Hammond, "NSC-68: Prologue to Rearmament," to be published in a volume sponsored by the Institute of War and Peace Studies of Columbia University.

85. For example, in the Rockefeller Brothers study on defense problems, whose recommendations closely parallel those of the Gaither Report; see Special Studies Report II, Rockefeller Brothers Fund, *International Security: The Military Aspect*, Garden City, N.Y., 1958 (reprinted in *Prospect for America: The Rockefeller Panel Reports*, Garden City, N.Y., 1961, pp. 93-155).

86. Cf. Samuel P. Huntington, "Strategic Planning and the Political Process," *Foreign Affairs*, XXXVII (January 1960), pp. 285-99.

87. Some of its proposals were adopted in the 1958 reorganization of the Defense Department.

The Gaither Committee
Report (Text)

DETERRENCE & SURVIVAL

in the

NUCLEAR AGE

SECURITY RESOURCES PANEL

of the

SCIENCE ADVISORY COMMITTEE

Washington-November 7, 1957

EXECUTIVE OFFICE OF THE PRESIDENT
OFFICE OF DEFENSE MOBILIZATION
WASHINGTON, D.C.

November 7, 1957

The President
The White House
Washington, D.C.

Dear Mr. President:

We have the privilege of transmitting to the National Security Council, through the Honorable Gordon Gray and the NSC Planning Board, the Report of the ODM Security Resources Panel. This Panel was established by the Science Advisory Committee pursuant to NSC Action 1691-b(2), April 4, 1957.

Formation of the Panel began in May, under the able leadership of Mr. H. Rowan Gaither, Jr., who, regrettably, had to withdraw in September* from further active direction of the undertaking for reason of health, but not before the study program was completely organized and the Panel was well under way in carrying out its responsibilities.

The make-up and organization of the Panel is shown in Appendix G, attached. Including advisors and staff, more than ninety persons of widely varying specialties and experiences participated in its work. Although the membership includes competent scientists and engineers—many with extensive familiarity with military technology—it was early decided that the Panel would not try for invention but, rather, would concentrate on the many studies undertaken by large and experienced groups, within our area of interest, both within and outside the military, and to try to relate them to our assignment.

Not only have these studies been carefully examined, but our working groups have spent considerable time with many of the participants in them, the better to understand the basic assumptions on which they were predicated and the methodology involved in the more important and pertinent war gamings.

Special members of our Panel have received authorized access to particularly sensitive studies and Intelligence information, and the implications of these have influenced our final judgments.

Our membership has had complete cooperation from and full opportunity to question civilian and officer personnel of the Department of Defense, the Office of Defense Mobilization, the Central Intelligence Agency, the Federal Civil Defense Administration, the Treasury, the Bureau of the Budget, and other departments and agencies of the Government.

---

*Mr. Gaither recently rejoined the study as a member of the Advisory Panel.

Thus the Panel, in the preparation of this Report, has benefitted from information sources of extreme scope and depth; and the membership, in full and vigorous analysis and discussion, has assessed the implications of this knowledge and has directed its findings to the problem confronting the Panel. However, the Steering Committee, which includes the Director, the Co-Director, and the heads of the four Working Groups, have full responsibility for this Report.

We are grateful to the many who have worked and cooperated with us.

Respectfully submitted,

Steering Committee
Security Resources Panel

Robert C. Sprague, Director
William C. Foster, Co-Director

James P. Baxter	Robert C. Prim
Robert D. Calkins	Hector R. Skifter
John J. Corson	William Webster
James A. Perkins	Jerome B. Wiesner

Edward P. Oliver, Technical Advisor

Table of Contents*

Letter of Transmittal   75

I.   Assignment   78

II.   Nature of the Threat   78

       A. Economic
       B. Military

III.   Broad-Brush Opinions   81

       A. Measures to Secure and Augment Our Deterrent Power
       B. Measures to Reduce Vulnerability of Our People and Cities

IV.   Related Concerns   84

       A. Improvement of Management of Defense Resources
       B. Strategic Warning and Hard Intelligence
       C. Integration With U.S. Foreign Policy

V.   Costs and Economic Consequences   87

       A. Costs
       B. Feasibility
       C. Economic Consequences

VI.   Public Education and Political Consequences   88

VII.   Deterrence and Survival   89

Appendix   A. Time Table   90
           B. Passive Defense   93
           C. Approximate Increased Costs of Defense Measures
              (1959-1963)   98
           D. Projected Federal Receipts and Expenditures
              (1959-1963)   100
           E. An Early Missile Capability   101
           F. Active Defense   102
           G. Organization and Roster of Security Resources Panel   105

*The page numbers in this table of contents have been changed to reflect the pagination of the Report in this book.

Deterrence & Survival
in the Nuclear Age

I. Assignment

The Security Resources Panel was asked to study and form a broad-brush opinion of the relative value of various active and passive measures to protect the civil population in case of nuclear attack and its aftermath, taking into account probable new weapons systems; and to suggest which of the various active and passive measures are likely to be most effective, in relation to their costs. While fulfilling its assignment, the Panel was also asked to study the deterrent value of our retaliatory forces, and the economic and political consequences of any significant shift of emphasis or direction in defense programs.

The Panel has therefore examined active and passive defense measures from two standpoints: their contribution to deterrence; and their protection to the civil population if war should come by accident or design.

We have found no evidence in Russian foreign and military policy since 1945 to refute the conclusion that USSR intentions are expansionist, and that her great efforts to build military power go beyond any concepts of Soviet defense. We have, therefore, weighted the relative military and economic capabilities of the United States and the USSR in formulating our broad-brush opinions, basing our findings on estimates of present and future Russian capabilities furnished by the Intelligence community.

The evidence clearly indicates an increasing threat which may become critical in 1959 or early 1960. The evidence further suggests the urgency of proper time-phasing of needed improvements in our military position vis-à-vis Russia. A time table distinguishing four significant periods of relative military strengths is given in detail in Appendix A.

II. Nature of the Threat

A. Economic

The Gross National Product (GNP) of the USSR is now more than one-third that of the United States and is increasing half again as fast. Even if the Russian rate of growth should decline, because of increasing difficulties in management and shortage of raw materials, and should drop by 1980 to half its present rate, its GNP would be more than half of ours as of that date. This growing Russian economic strength is concentrated on the armed forces and on investment in heavy industry, which this year account for the equivalent of roughly $40 billion and $17 billion, respectively, in 1955 dollars. Adding these two figures, we get

78

an allocation of $57 billion per annum, which is roughly equal to the combined figure for these two items in our country's current effort. If the USSR continues to expand its military expenditures throughout the next decade, as it has during the 1950s, and ours remains constant, its annual military expenditures may be double ours, even allowing for a gradual improvement of the low living standards of the Russian peoples.

This extraordinary concentration of the Soviet economy on military power and heavy industry, which is permitted, or perhaps forced, by their peculiar political structure, makes available economic resources sufficient to finance both the rapid expansion of their impressive military capability and their politico-economic offensive by which, through diplomacy, propaganda and subversion, they seek to extend the Soviet orbit. (See Figures 1 and 2.)

B. Military

The Soviet military threat lies not only in their present military capabilities—formidable as they are—but also in the dynamic development and exploitation of their military technology. Our demobilization after World War II left them with a great superiority in ground forces, but they had no counter in 1946 for our

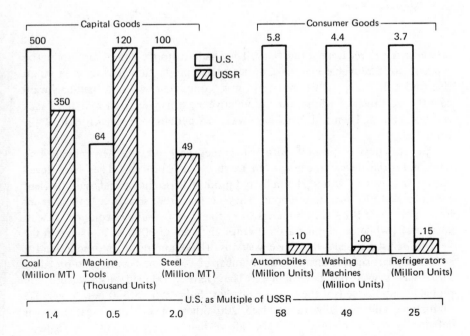

Figure 1. Production of Selected Capital & Consumer Goods: 1956

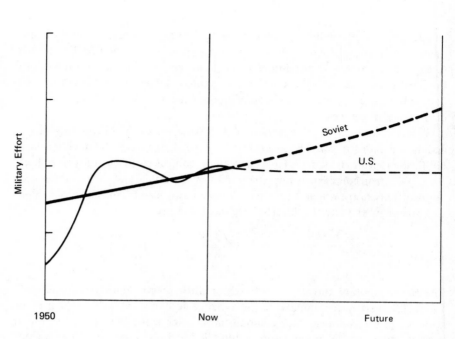

Figure 2. Past and Projected Relationship Between U.S. and U.S.S.R.
Military Effort

Strategic Air Force nor for our Navy. They had no atomic bombs, no productive
capacity for fissionable materials, no jet engine production, and only an infant
electronics industry. This situation was compatible with a then-backward
country, so much of whose most productive areas had suffered military attack
and occupation. Their industrial base was then perhaps one-seventh that of the
United States.

The singleness of purpose with which they have pressed their military-cen-
tered industrial development has led to spectacular progress. They have developed a spectrum of A- and H-bombs and produced fissionable material sufficient
for at least 1500 nuclear weapons. They created from scratch a long-range air
force with 1500 B-29 type bombers; they then substantially re-equipped it with
jet aircraft, while developing a short-range air force of 3000 jet bombers. In the
field of ballistic missiles they have weapons of 700 n.m. range, in production for
at least a year; successfully tested a number of 950 n.m. missiles; and probably
surpassed us in ICBM development. They have developed air-to-surface and
probably submarine-launched cruise missiles; built 250 to 300 new long-range
submarines and partially modernized 200 others. They have created an air
defense system composed of 1500 all-weather and 8500 day jet fighters;
equipped at least 60 sites, each with 60 launchers, for a total of over 3600

launching pads for surface-to-air missiles provided with a sophisticated and original guidance system and a ground environment of 4000 radars. At the same time, they have maintained and largely re-equipped their army of 175 line divisions, while furnishing large quantities of military equipment to their satellites and Red China.*

III. Broad-Brush Opinions

The Panel has arrived at the following broad-brush opinions as to the present situation:

A. In case of a nuclear attack against the continental United States:

1. Active defense programs now in being and programmed for the future will not give adequate assurance of protection to the civil population. If the attack were at low altitude, or at high altitude with electronic countermeasures (jamming), little protection would be afforded. If the attack should come at moderately high altitude and without electronic countermeasures, some considerable protection will be afforded the civil population.

2. Passive defense programs now in being and programmed for the future will afford no significant protection to the civil population.

B. The protection of the United States and its population rests, therefore, primarily upon the deterrence provided by SAC. The current vulnerability of SAC to surprise attack during a period of lessened world tension (i.e., a time when SAC is not on a SAC "alert" status), and the threat posed to SAC by the prospects of an early Russian ICBM capability, call for prompt remedial action.

The Panel has arrived at the following conclusions as to the value, relative to cost, of various measures for protecting the civil population.

A. Measures to Secure and Augment Our Deterrent Power

Since the prevention of war would best protect our urban population, we assign the highest relative value to the following measures to secure and augment our deterrent power. These would protect our manned bombers from surprise attack, increase our forces available for limited military operations, and give us an earlier and stronger initial operational capability (IOC) with intermediate-range and intercontinental ballistic missiles. Basic elements in this program are:

---

*By the very nature of the sources of intelligence information, none of the specific numbers cited above can be precisely known. The approximate size of each number, however, and more importantly the over-all order of accomplishment, are well established by the available data.

1. To lessen SAC vulnerability to a Russian surprise bomber attack in a period of low tension (a present threat):
   a. Reduce reaction time so an adequate number (possibly 500) of SAC planes can get off, weapons aboard, on way to target, within the tactical warning time available. This can be done by promptly implementing SAC's "alert" concept.
   b. Improve and insure tactical warning. Radars in the seaward extensions need to be modernized to assure tactical warning at high and low altitude, and the extensions need to be lengthened to prevent "end runs."
   c. Provide an active missile defense for SAC bases (Nike-Hercules or Talos) against bombers.
2. To lessen SAC vulnerability to an attack by Russian ICBMs (a late 1959 threat):
   a. Develop, to an operational status, a radar early-warning system for an ICBM attack.
   b. Further improve SAC's reaction time to an "alert" status of 7 to 22 minutes, depending on location of bases.
   c. Disperse SAC aircraft, to the widest extent practical, to SAC and non-SAC military bases in the ZI and possibly also to commercial airfields in the ZI.
   d. Protect a large part of SAC's planes by providing 100 to 200 psi shelters, and equivalent protection for weapons, personnel, and other needed supplies and facilities.
   e. Provide SAC bases with an active missile defense against ICBMs, using available weapons such as Nike-Hercules or Talos and the improved long-range tracking radars now existing in prototype.
3. To increase SAC's strategic offensive power (to match Russia's expected early ICBM capability):
   a. Increase the initial operational capability of our IRBMs (Thor and/or Jupiter) from 60 to 240.
   b. Increase the IOC of our ICBMs (Atlas and Titan) from 80 to 600.
   c. Accelerate the IOC of the Polaris submarine IRBM system, which offers the advantages of mobility and greatly reduced vulnerability.
   d. Every effort should be made to have a significant number of IRBMs operational overseas by late 1958, and ICBMs operational in the ZI by late 1959.
   e. Hardened bases for the ICBMs should be phased in as rapidly as possible.
4. Augment our and Allied forces for limited military operations, and provide greater mobility, to enable us to deter or promptly suppress small wars which must not be allowed to grow into big ones. The Panel suggests that a study be undertaken, at the national rather than at a Service level, to develop current doctrine on when and how nuclear weapons can contribute to limited operations.

B. *Measures to Reduce Vulnerability of Our People and Cities*

The main protection of our civil population against a Soviet nuclear attack has been and will continue to be the deterrent power of our armed forces, to whose strengthening and securing we have accorded the highest relative value. But this is not sufficient unless it is coupled with measures to reduce the extreme vulnerability of our people and our cities. As long as the U.S. population is wide open to Soviet attack, both the Russians and our allies may believe that we shall feel increasing reluctance to employ SAC in any circumstance other than when the United States is directly attacked. To prevent such an impairment of our deterrent power and to ensure our survival if nuclear war occurs through miscalculation or design, we assign a somewhat lower than highest value, in relation to cost, to a mixed program of active and passive defenses to protect our civil population.

1. A massive development program to eliminate two major weaknesses in our present active defenses:
   a. The vulnerability of the radars in our ground environment and in our weapons control to "blinding" by enemy electronic countermeasures (ECM).
   b. The small probability of kills against a low-level attack.
2. Further strengthening of our active defenses as soon as their vulnerability to ECM and low-level attack is removed. Current research affords hope that at least our weapons-control radars can be made proof against ECM. Radars can be located at high points to guard against low-level attacks, and a barrage-type defense against low-level attacks from the sea might prove a stopgap. An effective air defense system is so important to ensure continuity of government, and to protect our civil population, our enormously valuable civil property and military installations, that these development programs we suggest should be pushed with all possible speed.
3. A nationwide fallout shelter program to protect the civil population. This seems the only feasible protection for millions of people who will be increasingly exposed to the hazards of radiation. The Panel has been unable to identify any other type of defense likely to save more lives for the same money in the event of a nuclear attack.

   The construction and use of such shelters must be tied into a broad pattern of organization for the emergency and its aftermath. We are convinced that with proper planning the post-attack environment can permit people to come out of the shelters and survive. It is important to remember that those who survive the effects of the blast will have adequate time (one to five hours) to get into fallout shelters. This is not true of blast shelters which, to be effective, must be entered prior to the attack.

We do not recommend major construction of blast shelters at this time. If, as appears quite likely, an effective air defense system can be obtained, this will probably be a better investment than blast shelters. However, because of present uncertainties, on both active and passive fronts, it appears prudent to carry out promptly a research and development program for such blast shelters since we must be in a position to move rapidly into construction should the need for them become evident.

A more detailed statement of the Panel's findings on passive defense is included as Appendix B.

4. A program to develop and install an area defense against ICBMs at the earliest possible date.
5. Increased emphasis on the R&D program to improve the Navy's anti-submarine effort, including defense against submarine-launched missiles. The principal protection against these latter may have to be provided by air and ballistic missile defense systems.

IV. Related Concerns

A. Improvement of Management of Defense Resources

The Panel has been impressed with the supreme importance of effective control and management of the resources allocated to defense.

The new weapons systems, in cutting across traditional Service lines, have caused management problems which have been difficult to resolve within existing legislative and organizational restrictions. We have lost ability to concentrate resources, to control performance and expenditures, and to change direction or emphasis with the speed that a rapidly developing international situation and rapidly developing science and technology make necessary.

We are faced by an enemy who is able, not only ruthlessly to concentrate his resources, but rapidly to switch from one direction or degree of emphasis to another.

A radical reorganization of the Department of Defense might cause such confusion, at least temporarily, as to weaken our defense. However, some immediate steps to more effective control and management of our defense resources are urgently needed and appear practicable.

Some such steps can be taken without new legislation and certainly they would be timely, even before the return of Congress in January. A further step would appear to be a decision within the Executive Branch to seek from Congress the amendment of present legislation, which freezes the organization of the Defense Department along lines that may have been appropriate before the evolution of present weapons systems, but which are clearly inappropriate today and may become intolerable in the near future.

Changes in the Defense organization might take the following lines:

1. An increased focusing of responsibility and authority in operational commands, with missions appropriate to integrated weapons systems.
2. The concentration of research and development responsibilities for the two or three major integrated and complete weapons systems in manageable organizational units.
3. A more effective concentration of the military departments and departmental staffs upon training and logistics.
4. More direct command channels between the Secretary of Defense and the operational commands.
5. A command post-type staff, responsible directly and solely to the Secretary of Defense to assist him, both in the essentially managerial task of control and command, and in the long-term planning his responsibilities require.
   a. Such a staff should be organized as a staff, not as an interagency committee. Policy should be established to encourage the objectivity of officers serving on such a staff; and rotation would enable them to keep abreast of appropriate developments bearing on the mission.
   b. Officers serving on such a staff should be selected and relieved directly by the Secretary of Defense. Satisfactory service on this staff should, as on certain other joint staffs, meet one of the preliminary requirements needed for consideration for promotion.

Through such evolutionary development, the functions of planning, budgetary control, and operational command could increasingly be brought together and responsibility focused and delegated, rather than bucked.

The Panel further believes that coordination in depth between the Defense Department and those responsible for other aspects of our national policy, particularly the State Department, can be improved, especially in the field of forward planning.

Existing plans to protect and care for people in the event of attack have become obsolete as a result of the growing threat, and are therefore ineffective. Provisions for relocating government officials and for evacuating civilians are unrealistic in many respects. The plans of many states and metropolitan areas for handling local police, fire, health, water, sanitation and related problems are primitive in many areas.

Protection of the civil population is a national problem requiring a national remedy. We urge the re-evaluation of the existing organizational structure that distributes responsibilities among the Office of Defense Mobilization, the Federal Civil Defense Administration, the military, and state and local governments.

B. Strategic Warning and Hard Intelligence

Strategic warning—information obtained and correctly interpreted prior to the actual launching of an enemy attack on the United States—would be of immense value to this country. Further, it will become even more valuable as the maximum achievable tactical warning time shrinks to a matter of minutes in the case of a missile attack. At present, however, we have no assurance that strategic warning will be received.

We have too few solid facts on which to base essential knowledge of USSR capabilities and too few solid facts to learn how they are changing with time. From such observations, intentions may often be deduced. More positive and direct intelligence of USSR activities and accomplishments can be obtained by vigorous use of presently known techniques and available methods.

Because of their utmost importance to our actual survival, we urge exploitation of all means presently at our disposal to obtain both strategic warning and hard intelligence, even if some risks have to be taken, together with the vigorous development of new techniques.

C. Integration with U.S. Foreign Policy

The reduction of the vulnerability of the United States and its population should be made part of a broad program to improve the security and political position of the Free World as a whole, in accord with the enlightened self-interest of the United States.

If not so integrated into our foreign policy, any substantial program to reduce the vulnerability of the United States might be widely interpreted as signalizing a retreat to "Fortress America." The USSR would be sure to fully exploit the resulting uncertainties.

Such an integrated program might include:

1. Measures, some of which are already under way, to pool and make more effective the economic, technological and political resources of ourselves and our allies.
2. Supplying NATO with nuclear weapons, to remain in U.S. custody in peacetime, for use in wartime under NATO command—as a means of increasing confidence.
3. Measures designed to assure the uncommitted nations that their national interests are truly a matter of continuing concern to us.

Such an integrated and comprehensive program could significantly raise the level of hope, confidence and strength in the Free World, and could give renewed prospect of securing Russian agreement to safe arms control and regulation.

V. Costs and Economic Consequences

A. Costs

The added defense measures to which the Panel has assigned relative values will probably involve expenditures in excess of the current $38 billion defense budget.

The measures of highest value, to strengthen our deterrent and offensive capabilities, are estimated to cost over the next five years (1959-1963) a total of $19 billions.

Additional measures of somewhat lower than highest value, for the protection of the civil population, include a strengthening of active defenses, a fallout shelter program, and the development of a defense system to protect cities from missile attack. The estimated costs of these items total $25 billions over the next five years.

More detailed cost estimates are shown in Appendix C. To initiate the measures of highest value will cost $2.87 billions in 1959; and $3.0 to $5.0 billions per annum in the following four years. The entire program, including the lower-than-highest-value additional measures, would cost approximately $4.73 billions in 1959, and annual expenditures rising to a peak of $11.92 in 1961 and dropping to $8.97 billions in 1963. Several of these measures will involve further outlays in excess of operating and maintenance costs after 1963.

B. Feasibility

These several defense measures are well within our economic capabilities. The nation has the resources, the productive capacity, and the enterprise to outdistance the USSR in production and in defense capability. This country is now devoting 8.5% of its production to defense, and 10% to all national security programs. The American people have always been ready to shoulder heavy costs for their defense when convinced of their necessity. We devoted 41% of our GNP to defense at the height of World War II and 14% during the Korean War. The latter percentage is somewhat higher than would be required to support all our proposals.

C. Economic Consequences

The additional expenditures for measures of highest value are barely within the estimated receipts from existing taxes in the first three years, and more definitely within estimated receipts thereafter, assuming continued and uninterrupted high employment and growth. To the extent that economies can be achieved in existing defense or non-defense programs, the increase in total expenditures could be minimized. An increase in the debt limit would be necessary. This would be a precautionary measure against the possibility that revenues may initially fall below the estimates based on high employment and because expenditures normally run ahead of revenues during a portion of the fiscal year.

The demands of such a program (measures of highest value) on the nation's economic resources would not pose significant problems. Aside from its psychological impact, increased defense spending would have some influence on capital investment. If a moderate recession is impending, tax receipts would decline, but the increase in Federal expenditures would help to sustain production and employment. Under conditions of full employment, the program would have some inflationary effects, requiring a continuation of monetary and credit restrictions.

To undertake the whole program of active and passive measures would involve outlays of $4.8 to $11.9 billions per annum over the next five years, and further unestimated expenditures thereafter. Except as economies can be achieved in defense and non-defense expenditures, these sums would represent additions to the Federal budget.

Large additional expenditures of this sort are still within the economic capabilities of the United States. They would necessitate, however, an increase in taxes, a somewhat larger Federal debt, substantial economies in other government expenditures, and other curbs on inflation. Additional private investment would be required, especially to carry out the shelter program which would impose heavy requirements for steel, cement and labor. In all probability, this program would necessitate some slow-down of highway construction and other postponable public works.

The early announcement of such a program would be a stimulus to the economy and would have an inflationary influence. Measures to cope with the inflationary problem posed by such an increase in defense spending should be planned as part of the program.

VI. Public Education and Political Consequences

The Panel urges an improved and expanded program for educating the public in current national defense problems, in the belief that the future security of the United States depends heavily upon an informed and supporting public opinion. We have been heartened by the recent announcement that positive steps will be taken to initiate what we hope will be a broad and sustained program of such education. We must act now to protect, for this and succeeding generations not only our human and material resources, but our free institutions as well. We have no doubt of the will and capacity of the American people to do so if they are informed of the nature and probable duration of the threat and if they understand what is required of them. Only through such enlightenment and understanding can we avoid the danger of complacency and the enervation of our inherent strengths.

VII. Deterrence and Survival

The measures advocated by the Panel will help to unite, to strengthen and to defend the Free World, and to deter general war which would expose our cities and bases to thermonuclear attack. They would improve our posture to deter or promptly to suppress subversion or limited war, which may be more likely in the years immediately ahead. No one of these lesser enemy moves might directly threaten our survival. Yet, if continued, they might nibble away the security of the Free World as Germany undermined the superior military power of Great Britain and France between 1936 and 1939.

If deterrence should fail, and nuclear war should come through miscalculation or design, the programs outlined above would, in our opinion, go far to ensure our survival as a nation.

To illustrate the urgency of prompt decision and rapid action, we submit in Appendix A a time table of relative strengths under our present programs and the assumed Russian programs. As this appendix indicates, the United States is now capable of making a decisive air nuclear attack on the USSR. The USSR could make a very destructive attack on this country, and SAC is still vulnerable to a surprise attack in a period of lessened world tension. As soon as SAC acquires an effective "alert" status, the United States will be able to carry out a decisive attack even if surprised. This could be the best time to negotiate from strength, since the U.S. military position vis-à-vis Russia might never be so strong again.

By 1959, the USSR may be able to launch an attack with ICBMs carrying megaton warheads, against which SAC will be almost completely vulnerable under present programs. By 1961-1962, at our present pace, or considerably earlier if we accelerate, the United States could have a reliable early-warning capability against a missile attack, and SAC forces should be on a 7 to 22 minute operational "alert." The next two years seem to us critical. If we fail to act at once, the risk, in our opinion, will be unacceptable.

Appendix A
Time Table

(Under Our Present Programs and Assumed Russian Programs)

Period A—Present Phase (starting now and ending 1959/early 1960)

Characteristics

1. U.S. has an adequate capability to make a decisive* air nuclear attack on Russia.

2. U.S. has an inadequate retaliatory capability if SAC bases are surprised at a time of lessened world tension, i.e., a time when SAC is not in a state of combat readiness. Prompt and agressive implementation of the SAC "alert" concept would cure this defect.

3. USSR has capability to make a destructive attack on the U.S.

4. USSR has an inadequate retaliatory capability if SUSAC bases are surprised at a time of lessened world tension.

5. Although Russia will probably add to her inventory of long-range jet bombers during this period, the small number of these produced in recent months and the apparent lack of air-refueling of her large number of medium jet bombers indicate the Soviets are probably taking a calculated risk during this period and are shifting a large part of their national effort from manned bombers to long-range ballistic missiles.

Effects

1. A surprise attack by either SAC or SUSAC in a period of lessened world tension might almost completely disarm the other's long-range air atomic strike capability, unless and until either side has successfully implemented an adequate "alert" concept.

2. During this period, a surprise attack could determine the outcome of a clash between these two major powers.

3. As soon as SAC acquires an effective "alert" status, the U.S. will be able to carry out a decisive attack even if surprised. *This could be the best time to negotiate from strength, since the U.S. military position vis-à-vis Russia might never be as strong again.*

Period B—(starting 1959/early 1960—ending 1961/1962)

Characteristics

1. The USSR will probably achieve a significant ICBM delivery capability with megaton warheads by 1959.

---

*Decisive is defined as follows: (1) ability to strike back is essentially eliminated; or (2) civil, political, or cultural life are reduced to a condition of chaos; or both (1) and (2).

2. U.S. will probably not have achieved such a capability.

3. U.S. will probably not have achieved either an early warning of or defense against an ICBM attack.

4. SAC will have increased modestly its number of operational bases, but none will be hardened.

5. Rapid increase in USSR stockpile of fissionable material and in weapons technology will substantially increase megaton load that can be delivered by manned bombers in the U.S.

6. In spite of continuing additions to our continental defense net, the attrition imposed on a manned bomber attack at low altitude and/or with electronic countermeasures will probably destroy only a small portion of the attacking force.

Effects

1. SAC could be completely vulnerable to an ICBM attack directly against its bases and weapons stockpile.

2. If the USSR were successful in a missile disarming attack against SAC bases, manned bombers could then deliver a decisive attack against the U.S.

3. This appears to be a very critical period for the U.S.

Period C—(starting 1961/1962—ending 1970/1975)

Assumptions: As a minimum, the SAC missile bases will be hardened, the U.S. will have a reliable early-warning capability against a missile attack; and SAC will have a significant part of its force on a 7- to 22-minute operational alert. These minimum objectives will require much emphasis and effort if they are to be achieved early in Period C.

Characteristics

1. U.S. and USSR will substantially increase their respective ICBM capabilities.

2. USSR will have achieved an early-warning capability to detect ICBM attack.

3. U.S. and USSR will begin to achieve some anti-ICBM defensive capabilities during the middle of the period.

Effects

1. An air nuclear attack by either side against the other could be decisive unless the attacked country had implemented, at a minimum, a nationwide fallout shelter program.

2. If all missile and bomber bases had also been hardened, the retaliatory strike could also be decisive if the attacker had not also implemented, at a minimum, a nationwide fallout shelter program.

Period D—(starting 1970/1975—onward)

Characteristics

1. U.S. and USSR both will continue to produce large amounts of fissionable material and long-range ballistic missiles.

2. Second and later generations of missiles, with solid propellents, CEPs measured in the thousands of feet instead of several miles, and with larger megaton warheads and quicker reaction time, will be put into production.

3. Both U.S. and USSR will develop improved means for detecting and defending against missile attacks.

4. The missiles in turn will be made more sophisticated to avoid destruction; and there will be a continuing race between the offense and the defense. Neither side can afford to lag or fail to match the other's efforts. There will be no end to the technical moves and counter-moves.

Effects

1. The net megaton attack which each side could deliver through the other's defenses might destroy approaching 100 percent of the urban population, even if in blast shelters, and a high percentage of the rural population unless it were protected by fallout and blast shelters. An attack of this size and devastation would result in less than one-tenth the radiation required for world contamination.

2. This could be a period of extremely unstable equilibrium.

3. A temporary technical advance (such as a high-certainty missile defense against ballistic missiles) could give either nation the ability to come near to annihilating the other.

Implications of the Table

The above time table suggests the great importance of a continuing attempt to arrive at a dependable agreement on the limitation of armaments and the strengthening of other measures for the preservation of peace.

Appendix B
Passive Defense

Active defense cannot alone provide adequate protection to the civilian population. Even if most of the attacking weapons could be shot down, there would still be a major hazard from fallout. Passive defense will materially reduce casualties. The precise number differs widely with the type of program, the weight and pattern of attack, and the effectiveness of active defense.

The Panel has considered passive defense as a two-pronged* program: (1) shelters, and (2) survival in the aftermath of nuclear attack. Each aspect is interdependent with the other; and every shelter proposal must be examined in the context of the post-attack environment to see if, after varying conditions of attack, the sheltered population might reasonably expect to emerge into a situation permitting survival and recuperation.

A. Shelters

The many shelter plans examined by the Panel indicate that broad protection can be provided, and that the cost varies fairly directly with the effectiveness of the program. All programs are expensive, as might well be expected, since the cost of a nationwide effort is calculated by multiplying an amount in dollars per person by the two hundred million people we will be protecting in 1966. As a natural consequence, the programs must be kept simple, even spartan, to cut down on the cost per person. Safety, not comfort, is the keyword. Last, we emphasize a common aspect of all programs: none offers absolute protection, and even with a prohibitively expensive program we must anticipate heavy casualties if we are attacked.

We have centered consideration on a series of four programs ranging from fallout shelters alone through combinations of blast shelters and fallout shelters described in Figure B-1. The curves on the chart** show the benefits of the different shelter programs under varying conditions of attack that might penetrate our defenses.† The middle curve (Attack B—medium weight—divided between military and civilian targets—2500 megatons on target) shows that about half the population would be casualties were they completely without protection.

---

*We have also examined such alternatives as evacuation and dispersal; the magnitudes of the costs and problems involved appear, to us, to make these unacceptable alternatives.

**These are not identical with the five plans considered in the Interdepartmental Report but, as evidenced by the chart, the correlation in cost results is extremely close. (Ref: Report to the National Security Council by the Special Committee on Shelter Programs, July 1, 1957.)

†A level of attack, far above any that we believe need be seriously considered at this time, is conceivable in the distant future; and this, if not intercepted at a distance, could lay down such a level of radiation that very large areas could, as a practical matter, be unusable for a period of years.

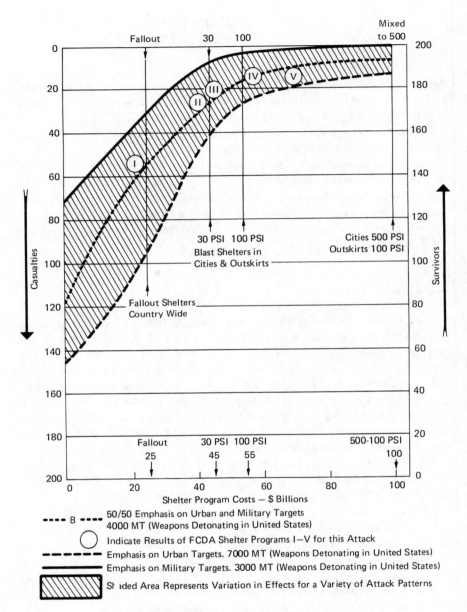

Figure B-1. Shelter Programs: Effectiveness vs. Cost

A program of fallout shelters for everyone would cost about $25 billion and would save nearly half the casualties. Such a program would be equally or more effective in saving lives (perhaps fifty million) under an attack directed entirely at military targets.

It does not appear that any practicable addition to our defense, regardless of cost, can offer so much of a return under as wide a variety of conditions. (For example, their use is not dependent on warning, since they may be entered from one to five hours after attack. Further, fallout shelters are not outmoded by the transition from bomber to missile attacks.) As a bonus, such a program of fallout shelters would have a significant additional advantage of permitting our own air defense to use nuclear warheads with greater freedom.

If an adequate active defense system cannot be devised, we may have to turn to blast shelters to reduce further the severe—and probably unacceptable—casualty list with fallout shelters only. A program that might reduce the casualties under this same Attack B to about 10% of the population will cost $20 to $30 billions more, depending on the level of protection furnished.

Blast shelters present substantially more difficult problems than do those designed for fallout alone. Not enough is known of the design problems, nor is there sufficient test experience, to be able to plan a nationwide system of such structures without further extensive research and development. Typical of the factors that complicate planning for blast shelters are the decisions of locating them*—particularly in view of the shorter time that will be available for the population to reach shelters as ICBMs come into use.

We have examined cost estimates on many shelter programs and find a wide variation. The general figures used herein are comparable to those used in the Interdepartmental Report and seem to represent a reasonably attainable figure at the 1957 price level. The cost given for any of these programs would include provision of over $10 billions' worth of equipment and the supplies to maintain the sheltered population for approximately two to three weeks.

The question of how fast to build any shelters involves balancing the 1959 need against the desire to spread out the expense so as to avoid overloading our construction facilities and our capacity to produce construction materials. Perhaps five years for a fallout program would be an appropriate compromise; any blast shelter program would need to be spread over a longer period.

Any shelter program must presumably be accompanied by:

1. A strong program of organization and management of the construction phases to take advantage of all possible means of reducing costs by proper scheduling of manpower and materials and by efficient production-line techniques.

2. A program providing the necessary trained leadership and trained emotional and physical behavior in the general public requisite for their successful psychological and physical survival under shelter conditions and the aftermath.

B. Survival in the Aftermath

Our investigation of the post-attack environment has involved study of radiation levels, food supply, water, agriculture, transportation, utilities, communications, etc. Unquestionably, conditions may be harsh, increasingly so with each heavier

---

*And the elaborate public training required if they are to be used successfully by a high proportion of the public.

level of attack assumed to penetrate our defenses. It appears, however, for the foreseeable future that sheltered survivors could pull through and remake a way of life in our own country.

Such a prediction presupposes careful planning, training and a strong central organization to handle both the attack and the post-attack situations. And—more important—it presupposes that the pre- and post-attack planning and organization have been done in parallel, with recognition, for example, that industrial preparedness is a necessary complement to any shelter program.

Far too little is really known about the recuperative powers of our industrial economy, and even less of the actual minimum requirements of the population surviving an attack. It is certain that there must be stockpiling of essential survival items to serve the surviving population for six to twelve months. In addition, the construction of additional hardened dispersed plants in a few critical industries (such as drugs and liquid fuels) is imperative. These seem problems of planning and ingenuity rather than items of major expense.

It seems that, for six or eight years, the safeguarding of industrial plant capacity should not be an overriding problem. But in the light of the heavier blows that are conceivable in the later 1960s, and particularly with a well-sheltered population, certain programs should be begun now to protect industrial facilities vital to the survival of this larger surviving population.

We feel it important that, concurrent with other survival plans, a strong program of appropriate medical research be undertaken.This will cost relatively little money; it could have great peacetime value in any case; and, in the event of actual attack, the results of such work might prevent literally millions of casualties from becoming fatalities.

C. Summary

As a consequence of examining various shelter and survival programs, their costs and implications, and of relating these to active defense programs and plans, the Panel believes:

A combination program comprising at a minimum nationwide fallout shelters and augmented air defense will give more protection for a given sum than will either all-out reliance on a maximum shelter program or on an air defense without shelters. This conclusion rests on the assumption that the two major weaknesses in our active defenses can and will be eliminated.

A year from now, the value and cost of still further expansion of air defense can better be weighed against the relative value of blast shelters. Additional active air defense appears now to offer a more favorable prospect of preventing casualties for no more money than a blast shelter program would cost, and, further, would save industry and structures.

In view of the fact that intensive research and development is probably needed before commencing major blast shelter construction, it seems wise to defer any decision regarding blast shelters for a year, during which time a research and development program would be initiated, and presumably the necessary job of augmenting our active air defense would continue.

Of itself, a shelter program would, in the Panel's opinion, forcibly augment our deterrent power in two ways: first, by discouraging the enemy from attempting an attack on what might otherwise seem to him a temptingly unprepared target; second, by re-inforcing his belief in our readiness to use, if necessary, our strategic retaliatory power.

Further, a shelter program might symbolize to the nation the urgency of the threat, and would demonstrate to the world our appraisal of the situation and our willingness to cope with it in strength. It would symbolize our *will to survive*, and our understanding of our responsibilities in a nuclear age.

Needless to say, the benefits that can derive from an intelligent and coordinated passive defense program are realizable only in the context of a superior over-all organization, charged with responsibility for the total job and with authority and means to get this job done.

Appendix C
Approximate Increased Costs of Defense Measures (1959-1963)

Measures	Approximate Increased Costs of Defense Measures 1959-1963 — Expenditures (Billions of Dollars)					
	5-Year Total	1959	1960	1961	1962	1963
A. Highest Value Measures (to strengthen deterrent and offensive capabilities):						
1a. Reduce bomber reaction time (for 1/3 the force) against bomber attack to less than 2 hours, the tactical warning time.		(No significant additional costs)				
1b. Improve and insure tactical warning against bomber attack.	$ .54	$ .14	$ .17	$ .12	$ .08	$ .03
1c. Provide active missile defense of SAC (NIKE-HERCULES of TALOS) against bombers.		(Costed with Item 2e.)				
2a. Develop early warning against ICBM attack.	.30	.05	.15	.10		
2b. Further reduce SAC reaction time to 7 to 22 min. alert status.	3.36	.45	.80	1.17	.47	.47
2c. Disperse SAC to SAC, military, and civilian bases.						
2d. Build 100-200 psi shelters for SAC planes, weapons and personnel.	1.50	.25	.50	.40	.35	
2e. Provide active missile defense of SAC against missiles—NIKE-HERCULES/TALOS (and against bombers, 1c. above) (assumes expenditures to $36 million in FY 1958 and includes R&D and introduction of new systems for 4 bases by end of FY 1963).	2.90	.13	.50	.95	.75	.57
3a. Increase initial operational capability of IRBMs from 60 to 240.	.55	.10	.15	.10	.10	.10
3b. Increase initial operational capability of ICBMs from 80 to 600.	2.85	.30	.75	.70	.60	.50

98

	5-Year Total	Fiscal Years				
		1959	1960	1961	1962	1963
3c. Accelerate initial operational capability of Polaris system (6 subs; 96 missiles).	1.30	.30	.30	.30	.20	.20
3d. Locate IRBMs overseas.	.29	.05	.14	.10		
3e. Harden ICBM bases.			(Included in 3b. above)				
4. Augment forces for limited war capability.[a]	5.50	1.10	1.10	1.10	1.10	1.10
Sub-total	$19.09	$2.87	$4.56	$5.04	$3.65	$2.97
B. Lower Than Highest Value Measures (additional, to protect civil population):						
1. Development program for eliminating major weaknesses in continental air defense (to correct radar "blinding" and improve low-altitude kill probability).[1]	$ 2.40	$ .60	$1.00	$ .80		
2. Further strengthen active defenses.[1]	...	...	...	...	...	...
3. Fallout shelter program including R&D for blast shelters.	22.50	1.20	3.30	6.00	6.00	6.00
4. Develop city and area defense against[2] ICBMs.	.23	.06	.08	.08	.01	
5. R&D anti-submarine defense.						
Sub-total	$25.13	$1.86	$4.38	$ 6.88	$6.01	$6.00
Grand Total	$44.22	$4.73	$8.94	$11.92	$9.66	$8.97

Contingent Estimates:

[1] If development successful to eliminate weaknesses in air defense, implement CADOP Program which would involve additional expenditure of $900 million in FY 1958.

	$11.6	$2.5	$2.2	$2.0	$2.7	$2.2

[2] If development successful, produce initial installation in 1962 and complete national system by 1965.

	5.3	.2	1.0	1.1	1.3	1.7

[a] A minimum estimate, to check declining capabilities.

99

Appendix D
Projected Federal Receipts and Expenditures

(Billions of Dollars)

	5-Year Total	1959	1960	1961	1962	1963
				Fiscal Years		
Gross National Product*		457.0	473.0	490.0	507.0	525.0
Federal Receipts** (present taxes)		76.1	79.0	82.1	85.2	88.5
Federal Expenditures***		73.1	74.3	75.5	76.7	78.0
Surplus		3.0	4.7	6.6	8.5	10.5
I Highest-Value Measures: (to strengthen deterrent and offensive power)	19.09	2.87	4.56	5.04	3.65	2.97
Surplus		.13	.14	1.56	4.85	7.53
II Somewhat Lower Than Highest-Value Measures: (additional, to protect civil population)	25.13	1.86	4.38	6.88	6.01	6.00
Total Program	44.22	4.73	8.94	11.92	9.66	8.97
Surplus and/or Deficit		−1.73	−4.24	−5.32	−1.16	+1.53

*Estimates based on uninterrupted growth in GNP at 3-1/2% per annum with no inflation.

**Receipts from existing taxes rise faster than GNP because of income tax rates.

***Defense expenditures of $38 billions annually; non-defense expenditures increasing at 3-1/2% per annum.

Appendix E
An Early Missile Capability

The early acquisition by SAC of an ICBM capability and the implementation of an IRBM capability overseas will greatly increase this country's offensive posture and deterrent strength.

An integrated program of Atlas and Titan, and an IRBM program including the achievement of a significant operational capability at the earliest possible date, should be given the highest national priority. It does not appear unreasonable nor too great a risk to consider at this time a rapid build-up of IRBMs and their deployment on overseas bases if they can be obtained. With a major effort, it appears possible to have at least one squadron in place during the last quarter of 1958, and 16 squadrons in place overseas before the end of 1960. Such a time scale would require decisions in the near future, some additional funds and an intensive training program in order to provide operational crews as rapidly as the missiles become available.

It appears possible to plan a build-up of ICBMs in the order of 60 squadrons (600 missiles) by the end of Fiscal 1963. The ICBMs will probably become available during 1959. The limiting factor in their deployment (assuming that no major technical difficulties are encountered) will be the rate at which launching sites and crews are made ready. The first site could become operational in 1959. The speed of build-up is adjustable over a wide range if one is prepared to take some risk now.

Except for the initial Atlas group, all ICBM bases should incorporate hardening against the Soviet ICBM threat.

The Polaris submarine-based weapon system, with its great mobility and security from attack, will be a valuable addition to a mixed strategic offensive force. Strong support should also be given to this program in order to speed up the first planned operational capability for 1963 by at least a year, and to increase the planned force of six submarines for 1965 by approximately a factor of three. A mixed offensive force complicates the defense of an enemy and increases his uncertainty.

The Polaris missile will be a solid-fuel rocket which makes it a much more desirable weapon than the early IRBMs for overseas deployment. It appears that the design of this missile for land-based use could be completed by early 1959 if desired. We believe that it is important to achieve this capability at the earliest possible time.

When this missile becomes available it might be phased into the liquid-fuel IRBM program.

Appendix F
Active Defense

An active continental defense system must contend with three different threats: manned bombers, intercontinental ballistic missiles, and submarine-launched missiles. Each of these poses its own peculiar problems for defense, and each requires alerting for optimum operation. Defense and warning systems to contend with the submarine threat and the bomber threat exist, and are scheduled for improvement. However, these now have and, as presently planned, will continue to have limited capabilities. Design concepts exist for a variety of anti-ballistic missile defense and warning systems. But no operational units have as yet been built or tested.

A. Defense Against Manned Bombers

1. Warning

The present and planned system for providing tactical warning of enemy manned bombers approaching the continental United States has serious limitations which can be corrected. This problem has been studied in detail by a subcommittee of the Joint Chiefs of Staff Ad Hoc Committee on Air Defense of North America, and an excellent report presented 30 June 1957.

In general we are concerned that:

a. The early-warning radar network is our principal means of collecting warning data on aircraft to permit two or more hours' warning, which is absolutely essential in the near future (e.g., for the protection of SAC). However, the complete network is not scheduled to be operational until mid-1960; and, even at this date, much of the network will be equipped with obsolete equipment.

b. Even when completed, the presently planned system can be flanked with distressing ease, considering Soviet capabilities.

c. The presently operational seaward extensions have very poor radar coverage. A significant improvement is immediately feasible.

d. Identification and raid-size determination techniques are weak but can readily be improved.

e. Research on warning devices has lacked direction and emphasis. The search for new and improved techniques should be pressed with vigor. Infra-red techniques should receive particular attention.

We have no reason whatsoever to feel complacent about the effectiveness of our warning system. The cost of warning is small, its value is very real, and provision of the degree of warning required is well within our technical abilities.

2. Air Defense System

The continental air defense system as it now exists, and as it is now planned to be, does not and will not provide this country with a significant level of protection. It has a number of "Achilles' heels" which can be exploited by an intelligent enemy. It is ineffective in the face of electronic countermeasures, saturation tactics, and low-altitude attacks. We believe that it is possible, with a determined effort, to improve this situation markedly by 1961, and to have a highly effective air defense system by 1963. It is our belief that it would take only a moderate increase in total Defense Department budget, properly spent, to make a large improvement in the air defense system. But when we examine the history of air defense, we conclude that an effective air defense system is unlikely within the present organization framework. The lack of a clear-cut single assignment of responsibility for weapons development, systems design, and implementation has allowed vulnerabilities to persist long after they were recognized. It is imperative that a competent technical group be given the responsibility for planning a balanced defense system in the light of *continually* changing technology and the *continually* changing threat. By the very nature of the problem we face, this group must be heavily technical with military support, as opposed to the present concept of being heavily military with technical advice.

B. Defense Against the Ballistic Missile

1. Warning

A detection system capable of providing early warning against a ballistic missile threat is technically achievable. Such a system would ideally consist of a number of radars located far in the north, possibly at Thule and Fairbanks. An orderly program is recommended; however, in addition, we now believe that a crash program to provide some warning at the earliest possible time is vital, and we believe it could be attainable early in 1959.

The airborne infra-red detection system (mentioned earlier in this Appendix) may provide the earliest attainable system having the capability of providing ICBM warning. We urge that it be given a careful evaluation in the near future.

2. Interception of Ballistic Missiles

Several systems have been proposed which appear to have capability of intercepting ballistic missile warheads at sufficient distances to prevent their doing serious damage. These systems fall into two distinct categories.

The first group are systems assembled from air defense components such as Nike-Hercules, or Talos, and existing long-range radars. These proposed early systems offer a reasonably high defense capability for points such as SAC bases against the early threat, but do not have the capability needed to provide protection for extended areas. In addition, early ICBM interception would occur at moderate altitudes—on the order of 30,000 feet or less—so there is danger of damage to the population and structures from blast and heat. Because these systems are assembled from existing components requiring only moderate modification, a limited operational capability could be available in early 1960, with complete SAC base defense in 1962. These defenses would also have a capability against bombers and thus would prevent sneak attacks.

The other group of proposed missile defense systems aims to intercept the incoming warheads at much higher altitudes. To do this in the face of decoys poses a number of technical questions, the answers for which require a high-priority research and test program. However, the importance of providing active defense of cities or other critical areas demands the development and installation of the basic elements of a system at an early date. Such a system initially may have only a relatively low-altitude intercept capability, but would provide the framework on which to add improvements brought forth by the research and test programs.

C. Defense Against the Submarine-Launched Missiles

The submarine-launched missile threat is a formidable one for which there is presently no known adequate countermeasure. The SOSUS underwater-sound surveillance system provides some measure of warning of the approach of submarines but the probability of detection of truly quiet submarines is small. We believe that anti-submarine efforts should be greatly augmented, particularly in research and development. For the immediate future it seems that the principal protection against submarine-launched missiles will have to be provided by the air defense and ballistic missile defense systems. The submarine-launched missile threat imposes several additional requirements on the design of such systems. A submarine-launched missile defense system is required to acquire targets over a wide range of angles; and the warning time available to alert the system is considerably less—less even than is available against the ICBM. However, it may be noted that at least one of the missile defense systems mentioned above has been conceived with these requirements in mind.

In conclusion, we feel that planning and performance in active defense are inadequate. However, we believe that an adequate defense is feasible and, furthermore, that active defense is an essential part of the national military posture. The active defense system must be balanced, e.g., even in the ICBM era, the manned bomber will remain an important threat.

Appendix G
Security Resources Panel

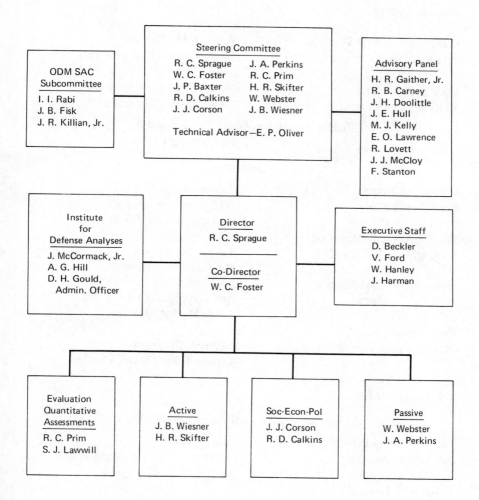

Membership Roster

Steering Committee

Sprague, Mr. Robert C.
Sprague Electric Company

Perkins, Dr. James A.
Carnegie Corporation

Foster, Mr. William C.
Olin-Mathieson Chemical Corp.

Prim, Dr. Robert C.
Bell Telephone Labs.

Baxter, Dr. James P. III
Williams College

Skifter, Dr. Hector R.
Airborne Instruments Labs.

Calkins, Dr. Robert D.
Brookings Institution

Webster, Mr. William
New England Electric System

Corson, Mr. John J.
McKinsey and Company

Wiesner, Professor Jerome B.
Massachusetts Institute of Technology

Technical Advisor—Oliver, Mr. Edward P.
Rand Corporation

Advisory Panel

Gaither, H. Rowan, Jr.
Ford Foundation

Lawrence, Dr. Ernest O.
Radiation Laboratory
University of California

Carney, Admiral Robert B.
Westinghouse Electric Co.

Lovett, Mr. Robert
Brown Bros., Harriman

Doolittle, General James H.
Shell Oil Company

McCloy, Mr. John J.
Chase Manhattan Bank

Hull, General John E.
Manufacturing Chemists Assoc.

Stanton, Dr. Frank
Columbia Broadcasting System

Kelly, Dr. Mervin J.
Bell Telephone Laboratories

Science Advisory Committee—Subcommittee

Fisk, Dr. James B.
Bell Telephone Laboratories

Rabi, Dr. I.I.
Science Advisory Committee

Killian, Dr. James R., Jr.
Massachusetts Institute of Technology

Executive Staff

Beckler, Mr. David Z.
Science Advisory Committee

Ford, Lt. Colonel Vincent T.
United States Air Force

Institute for Defense Analyses Officers

McCormack, General James, Jr.
President

Hill, Dr. Albert G.
Vice President and Director of Research

Project Members

Alexander, Dr. Sidney S.
Massachusetts Institute of Technology

Barrer, Mr. Donald Y.
IDA/WSEG

Berkner, Dr. Lloyd V.
Associated Universities, Inc.

Bissell, Mr. Richard M.
Central Intelligence Agency

Booth, Dr. Eugene T.
Columbia University

Booth, Mr. Richard P.
Bell Telephone Laboratories

Bouricius, Dr. Willard G.
International Business Machines

Bradley, Dr. William E.
Philco Corporation

Butler, Mr. William E.
Chase Manhattan Bank

Carulli, Mr. Leonard
McKinsey and Company

Clifford, Dr. Joseph M.
IDA/WSEG

Contos, Dr. George A.
IDA/WSEG

Cross, Mr. James E.
Center for International Study

Daniel, Dr. John H.
IDA/WSEG

Elliott, Dr. Edwin O.
Operations Evaluation Group

Emberson, Dr. Richard
Associated Universities, Inc.

Frantz, Mr. William J.
Boeing Aircraft Corporation

Fredericks, Dr. J. Wayne
Ford Foundation

George, Mr. Edwin B.
Office of Defense Mobilization

Hall, Dr. William M.
Raytheon Manufacturing Co.

Hansen, Dr. Robert J.
Massachusetts Institute of Technology

Hanson, Dr. Joseph O.
U.S. Information Agency

Hartgering, Lt. Colonel James
Walter Reed Medical Center

Hawkins, Mr. Robert A.
AVCO Manufacturing Company

Higinbotham, Dr. William A.
Brookhaven National Lab.

Horton, Mr. H. Burke
Office of Defense Mobilization

Hutchins, Mr. William R.
Raytheon Manufacturing Corp.

Jones, Mr. Chandler W.
Narragansett Electric Company

Keeny, Mr. Spurgeon M., Jr.
Office of Sec. of Def. (R&E)

Klotz, Mr. John W.
Office of Sec. of Def. (R&E)

Knox, Omar E., Colonel, USAF
IDA/WSEG

Kybal, Mr. Dalimil
Lockheed Aircraft Corp.

Lawson, Dr. Joel S.
University of Illinois

Lawwill, Dr. Stanley J.
Strategic Air Command

Lincoln, Colonel George A.
United States Military Academy

Lindsay, Mr. Franklin A.
McKinsey and Company

Longacre, Dr. Andrew
Syracuse University

Marshall, Dr. Andrew W.
Rand Corporation

McMillan, Dr. Brockway
Bell Telephone Laboratories

McMillan, Dr. Edwin M.
University of California

McRae, Dr. Vincent V.
Operations Research Office

Merritt, Dr. Melvin L.
Sandia Corporation

Michael, Dr. Donald N.
Dunlap & Associates

Minshull, Mr. William H., Jr.
Hughes Aircraft Corporation

Navoy, Mr. Anthony J.
IDA/WSEG

Nelson, General Otto L., Jr.
New York Life Insurance Co.

Newmark, Dr. Nathan M.
University of Illinois

Nichols, Mr. Guy W., Jr.
New England Electric System

Nitze, Mr. Paul H.
School of Advanced International Studies

Pechman, Dr. Joseph H.
Committee for Economic Development

Popenoe, Mr. Oliver
Office of Defense Mobilization

Rodgers, Dr. Franklin A.
Lincoln Laboratory

Rohrbacher, Dr. Bruce W.
McKinsey and Company

Sanchez, Mr. Luis R.
Rand Corporation

Siebert, Dr. William McC.
Massachusetts Institute of Technology

Smith, Lt. Colonel Glen A.
Central Intelligence Agency

Stockley, Mr. Robert
Fed. Civil Defense Admin.

Stone, Dr. Donald C.
Springfield College

Strope, Mr. Walmer E.
U.S. Naval Radiological Lab.

Taylor, Mr. Norman H.
Lincoln Laboratory

Van Atta, Dr. Lester
Hughes Aircraft

Walters, Mr. Lawrence R.
IDA/WSEG

White, Mr. William L.
Stanford Research Institute

Whitmer, Dr. Robert
Ramo-Wooldridge Corp.

Wine, Major Paul H., USAF
NORAD

Wood, Mr. Marshall K.
Office of Sec. of Def. (S&L)

York, Dr. Herbert F.
University of California

Administrative Officer (IDA)
Gould, Mr. Daniel H.

Security Officer
Hanley, Mr. Walter

Technical Librarian
Rosenborg, Mr. Staffan

Technical Editor
Harman, Miss R. Joyce

Draftsman
Miller, Mr. Lowell

Secretarial Staff

Barbera, Miss Grace A.
Beard, Mrs. Kathryn
Crow, Mrs. Laura
Doherty, Mrs. Olive
Droke, Mrs. Robertine H.
Eggers, Miss Ann
Houser, Miss Edwina

Long, Mrs. Mary S.
Mitchell, Mrs. Donna
Sanderson, Miss Vollie
Scruggs, Mrs. Dorothy A.
St. Pierre, Miss Elizabeth
Wilson, Miss Joyce A.
Wolin, Miss Beverly

The Decision to Deploy the ABM: Bureaucratic and Domestic Politics in the Johnson Administration*

Why did the Johnson Administration decide in the late 1960s to deploy a ballistic missile defense system in the United States? In attempting to answer this question we need to seek an understanding of several distinct decisions and actions.[1] The most puzzling event occurred in San Francisco on September 18, 1967, when Secretary of Defense Robert McNamara delivered an address to the editors and publishers of United Press International.[2] McNamara devoted the first fourteen pages of his talk to a general discussion of the strategic arms race, emphasizing the limited utility of nuclear weapons and the fact that neither the United States nor the Soviet Union had gained any increased security from the arms race. With this as background, he turned to a specific discussion of the ABM issue:

Now let me come to the issue that has received so much attention recently: the question of whether or not we should deploy an ABM system against the Soviet nuclear threat.

To begin with, this is not in any sense a new issue. We have had both the technical possibility and the strategic desirability of an American ABM deployment under constant review since the late 1950s.

While we have substantially improved our technology in the field, it is important to understand that none of the systems at the present or foreseeable state of the art would provide an impenetrable shield over the United States. Were such a shield possible, we would certainly want it—and we would certainly build it. . . .

Every ABM system that is now feasible involves firing defensive missiles at incoming offensive warheads in an effort to destroy them.

But what many commentators on this issue overlook is that any such system can rather obviously be defeated by an enemy simply sending more offensive warheads, or dummy warheads, than there are defensive missiles capable of disposing of them.

And this is the whole crux of the nuclear action-reaction phenomenon.

Were we to deploy a heavy ABM system throughout the United States, the Soviets would clearly be strongly motivated to so increase their offensive capability as to cancel out our defensive advantage.

It is futile for each of us to spend $4 billion, $40 billion, or $400 billion—and

Reprinted by permission of Princeton University Press from *World Politics*, Vol. XXV, No. 1 (copyright © 1972 by Princeton University Press): pp. 62-95.

*An earlier version of this paper was prepared for delivery at the Sixty-sixth Annual Meeting of the American Political Science Association, September 8-12, 1970. I have benefited from comments from a number of readers of previous drafts, including Graham Allison, William Capron, Leslie Gelb, Arnold Kanter, Herbert Kaufman, and Jerome Kahan.

at the end of all the spending, and at the end of all the deployment, and at the end of all the effort, to be relatively at the same point of balance on the security scale that we are now. . . .

If we in turn opt for heavy ABM deployment—at whatever price—we can be certain that the Soviets will react to offset the advantage we would hope to gain.

Many listeners undoubtedly expected the speech to end with the Secretary of Defense committing the United States firmly against an ABM deployment. Instead, McNamara immediately turned to another tack:

Having said that, it is important to distinguish between an ABM system designed to protect against a Soviet attack on our cities, and ABM systems which have other objectives.

One of the other uses of an ABM system which we should seriously consider is the greater protection of our strategic offensive forces.

Another is in relation to the emerging nuclear capability of Communist China.

There is evidence that the Chinese are devoting very substantial resources to the development of both nuclear warheads, and missile delivery systems. As I stated last January, indications are that they will have medium-range ballistic missiles within a year or so, an initial intercontinental ballistic missile capability in the early 1970s, and a modest force in the mid-70s.

Up to now, the lead-time factor has allowed us to postpone a decision on whether or not a light ABM deployment might be advantageous as a counter-measure to Communist China's nuclear development.

But the time will shortly be right for us to initiate production if we desire such a system. . . .

Is there any possibility, then, that by the mid-1970s China might become so incautious as to attempt a nuclear attack on the United States or our allies.

It would be insane and suicidal for her to do so, but one can conceive conditions under which China might miscalculate. We wish to reduce such possibilities to a minimum.

And since, as I have noted, our strategic planning must always be conservative, and take into consideration even the possible irrational behavior of potential adversaries, there are marginal grounds for concluding that a light deployment of U.S. ABMs against this possibility is prudent.

The system would be relatively inexpensive—preliminary estimates place the cost at about $5 billion—and would have a much higher degree of reliability against a Chinese attack, than the much more massive and complicated system that some have recommended against a possible Soviet attack. . . .

After a detailed review of all these considerations, we have decided to go forward with this Chinese-oriented ABM deployment, and we will begin actual production of such a system at the end of this year.

Before concluding, the Secretary of Defense returned to his earlier theme and warned of the danger in the deployment he had just announced:

There is a kind of mad momentum intrinsic to the development of all new nuclear weaponry. If a weapon system works—and works well—there is strong pressure from many directions to procure and deploy the weapon out of all proportion to the prudent level required.

The danger in deploying this relatively light and reliable Chinese-oriented ABM system is going to be that pressures will develop to expand it into a heavy Soviet-oriented ABM system.

We must resist that temptation firmly—not because we can for a moment afford to relax our vigilance against a possible Soviet first-strike—but precisely because our greatest deterrent against such a strike is not a massive, costly, but highly penetrable ABM shield, but rather a fully credible offensive assured destruction capability.

The so-called heavy ABM shield—at the present state of technology—would in effect be no adequate shield at all against a Soviet attack, but rather a strong inducement for the Soviets to vastly increase their own offensive forces. That, as I have pointed out, would make it necessary for us to respond in turn—and so the arms race would rush hopelessly on to no sensible purpose on either side.[3]

The apparent contradictions in the speech were a puzzlement to the audience. Some speculated that McNamara had planned to give an anti-ABM speech and was instructed by the President at the last minute to add a deployment decision. However, an examination of the following questions will show us that the speech was planned from the first as it was delivered.

1. Why, in January 1967, did President Johnson ask Congress to appropriate the funds to deploy an ABM, but state that he would defer a decision to initiate the deployment pending an effort to get the Soviet Union to engage in talks on limiting the arms race?[4]

2. Why was the decision to deploy an ABM announced at the end of a speech whose whole structure and purpose was to explain why an ABM defense against the Soviet Union was impossible?

3. Why did the Secretary of Defense describe the system as being directed against China, while the Joint Chiefs of Staff and their congressional allies described it as a first step toward a full-scale defense against the Soviet Union?

4. Why was the system that was finally authorized for deployment one which was designed and deployed as if its purpose was to protect American cities against a large Soviet attack?

Having stated the questions, we must postpone attempting to provide the answers until we have examined in some detail the nature of the process by which the decisions were made. We must ask who the participants in the process were. We must examine the personal and organizational interests that defined their stakes in the ABM debate. We must determine the constraints operating on the process in terms of the decision-makers' shared images of the world, the rules of the game by which decisions were made, and the participation of large organizations. We must also ask what arguments were advanced on each side to secure the outcome desired, and what the consequences were. After thus analyzing the process we will be better prepared to find answers to our puzzling questions.

In seeking to understand why the United States Government makes a particular decision or takes a particular action, we can make no greater mistake than to assume that all the participants in the process looked at the issue in the same way and agreed on what should be done. The reality is quite different.

When individuals in the American government consider a proposed change in American foreign policy, they often see and emphasize quite different things and reach different conclusions. A proposal to withdraw American troops from Europe, for example, is to the Army a threat to its budget and size; to Budget Bureau examiners a way to save money; to the Treasury Department a gain in balance of payments; to the State Department's Bureau of European Affairs a threat to good relations with NATO; and to the President's congressional advisers an opportunity to remove a major irritant in the President's relations with the Hill.

The differences stem from the differing faces of the issue which they see; they depend in part on whether their interests lead them to perceive a threat or an opportunity.

What determines which face an individual sees? What accounts for his stand?

Participants in the process of national security policy in the American government believe that they should take stands which advance the national security of the United States. Their problem is to determine what is in fact in the interest of national security; they must seek clues and guidelines from a variety of sources. Some hold to a set of beliefs about the world (e.g., the Soviet Union is expansionist and must be stopped by American military power). Others look to authorities within the government or beyond it for guidance. For many participants, what is necessary for the nation's security comes to be defined as a set of more specific intermediate interests. For some, these may be personal (e.g., since, in general, I know how to protect the nation's security interests, whatever increases my influence is in the national interest). For others, the intermediate interests relate to domestic political interests (e.g., since a sound economy is a prerequisite to national security, I must oppose policies which threaten the economy).

Many participants define national security according to the interests of the organization to which they belong. Career officials naturally come to believe that the health of their organization is vital to the nation's security. Organizational commitments on the part of outsiders appointed to senior posts vary depending on the individual, the strength of his prior convictions, his image of his role, and the nature of the organization he heads. Some senior officials seek clues less from their organization's interests than from the interests of the President, as they define them.

The proposal to deploy an ABM was seen in different ways by different people and posed different threats and opportunities to their perception of the national interest as well as domestic, organizational, and personal interests. A look at the faces of the issue as seen by the participants, and their calculation of the stakes, is the place to begin to seek a solution to our puzzles.[5]

We will start with the organizations that were exerting pressure upward on the Secretary of Defense and the President. In doing so we will oversimplify: we will talk about the Army, the Directorate for Defense Research and Engineering, etc. Just as the United States Government can be broken down into major departments, and these departments in turn into smaller components, these smaller components themselves have parts with differences of interest, objectives, and perspective. For our purposes in explaining the ABM decision, it is sufficient to go no lower than the main components of the Defense Department, such as the Army and the Directorate of Defense Research and Engineering.

Organizational Stakes[6]

The Army [7]

Throughout the 1950s the Army fought for a role in the preparations for strategic nuclear war. It did so because it recognized that budget funds were moving towards strategic nuclear programs and because it believed that these programs were critical to the security interests of the United States. Most of the Army's efforts, however, were unsuccessful. It did receive partial responsibility for air defense involving warning systems and surface-to-air missiles, but it did not have the tactical fighter component of the air defense system, and it failed to get involved in strategic offensive forces. The Army did receive permission to work on the R & D for medium-range ballistic missiles, but in the end the responsibility for deployment went to the Air Force. Thus, by the late 1950s the Army realized that its role in strategic nuclear forces would be restricted to defense. Because of the limited role of anti-aircraft defenses, those in the Army who were responsible for developing, deploying, and operating air defense systems turned to missile defense. For them it was simply the next step in the same direction.

One of the most publicized aspects of the program budgeting system installed in the Pentagon by McNamara and his Comptroller Charles Hitch was the so-called program package. Under this concept, strategic forces would compete for defense funds with each other, rather than with other programs in the budget of each Service. Insofar as this procedure really affected budgets, the funds for the ballistic missile defense program would come out of the budget for strategic offensive and defensive systems and not out of the Army budget, as it would probably have in the 1950s when budgeting was explicitly done on the basis of Service shares of the budget. Some in the Army undoubtedly opposed the ABM, arguing that in fact each Service still had a limited budget which, in the case of the Army, should be used for its main purpose, viz., ground combat forces. However, this was also a period of rising defense expenditures, with the Services competing vigorously for the larger funds. Thus, the opposition within the Army to seeking a major ballistic missile defense was weakened: proponents could argue that the means would come, not from the existing Army budget, but from new funds which would otherwise go to Air Force and Navy strategic programs.

The Navy

In the postwar period, the United States Navy developed a broader participation in the various roles and missions of the United States Armed Forces than either the Army or the Air Force. The Navy has its own ground troops in the form of Marines, and its own air capability, both for tactical air support of Marine operations and for strategic bombing missions from carriers. In the late 1950s it staked out a major role in strategic offense missions when it got permission to proceed with Polaris submarines with their nuclear missiles. Strategic defense was the only area in which the Navy was not yet active.

The Navy's attitude towards ABM was determined in part by a search for a share in the responsibility. By the early 1960s the Navy had a program aimed at developing a ship-based ballistic missile defense. Naval officials recognized that they could not hope to get exclusive responsibility for ballistic missile defense, since the Army had primary responsibility. The Navy therefore sought to justify its system as a supplement to the Army land-based system. Consequently, the Navy recognized that the only hope of getting permission for deployment was to have the Army go forward first. The Navy, then, wished to proceed with the ABM in a way which kept open the possibility that later additions to this system would include a Navy-controlled, sea-based system.

In return for Army support of continuing development of the Navy sea-based ballistic missile system, the Navy was prepared to support an Army land-based system.

Moreover, the Navy was concerned, as was the Air Force, with maintaining the system of unanimous support by the Joint Chiefs of Staff for Service procurement programs. This issue is discussed in detail below in considering the rules of the game.

The Air Force

The Air Force-Army rivalry in the field of defense has always been intense because of the lack of a clear division of roles in air defense. Both the Army and the Air Force have sought total control over the air defense role, the Air Force viewing it as part of the strategic mission and the Army as related to battlefield defense. In the late 1950s, when the Air Force got exclusive authority for medium-range ballistic missiles, an uneasy truce had been worked out on air defense, under which the Air Force had responsibility for tactical fighters and the Army for surface-to-air missiles. The Air Force did not, up to the end of 1968, make any effort to challenge this division by seeking a role in deploying ballistic missile defense.

Some Air Force officials, particularly those in SAC, were concerned about the proposals from the Office of the Secretary of Defense (OSD) for defending

Minuteman silos with the Army ballistic missile defense system. In part this was a reflex reaction, a desire not to have Air Force missiles protected by "Army" ABMs. In part there was concern that the Air Force would not be funded for a new offensive missile if billions were spent defending the Minuteman missiles with an ABM system. The Air Force clearly preferred that the funds for missile defense be used by the Air Force to develop new hard rock silos or mobile systems.

However, as long as the ABM was an area defense, competing (as the Air Force saw it) with Army funds for air defense and for civil defense, the Air Force was prepared to go along. Area defense also did not challenge any Air Force missions or appear to pose competition for funds for new strategic offensive forces.

Although each of the three Services saw a different face of the ABM issue, in the end they all were prepared to support it. There was no such unanimity within the Office of the Secretary of Defense, to which the Secretary looked for advice and support on this matter. The three offices involved were the Office of the Director of Defense Research and Engineering, headed during this period by John S. Foster; the Office of Systems Analysis, headed by Alain Enthoven; and the Office of International Security Affairs, headed by John McNaughton and then by Paul Warnke. Each of these offices saw a different face of ABM and reached different conclusions.

Defense Research and Engineering
(DDR & E)

The Director of Defense Research and Engineering is the Secretary of Defense's principal adviser on scientific and technical matters. He is also the manager of research and development programs. Foster therefore was responsible for monitoring the progress of ballistic missile defense, both in the Army and in the Advanced Research Projects Agency, which was a part of his office. He had previously been head of an AEC nuclear laboratory, and viewed his role as representing within the higher councils of the Pentagon and within the White House the perspective of the research scientist. Foster took it for granted that technology should be pushed as hard as possible, although he recognized the need to choose from the wide variety of different possible new technologies. He also believed that when technology reached the state where it was militarily effective, it should be deployed.

For Foster, the ABM issue was relatively simple and straightforward. At stake was the continued effectiveness of the weapons laboratory and the scientific research teams of American industry. Having developed an ABM system that was technically well designed, that community would expect it to be deployed. Its morale would be adversely affected by a decision not to deploy a system considered technologically "sweet." As the decision to deploy the ballistic missile defense system was delayed far beyond the time Foster thought to be justifiable on scientific and technical grounds, he began to fear that the laboratories involved would break up as the scientists became convinced that the United States would under no circumstances deploy a ballistic missile defense. He also feared that rising costs due to the delay in opening production lines would make it harder to justify a later decision to deploy. Furthermore, Foster believed that the Russians, in deploying an ABM while we did not, could develop a technologically more efficient system. As far as he was concerned, national security required that we maintain the vigor of our R & D establishment in order to maintain military superiority.[8]

Thus, Foster was for deployment of the ABM. The move from research and development to deployment was more important to him than how the decision was rationalized publicly.

Systems Analysis (SA)

Systems analysis was perhaps McNamara's major innovation in Pentagon organization and decision-making. Organized by Enthoven in 1961, the SA office was responsible for preparing for McNamara a series of Draft Presidential Memoranda (DPM), including one on strategic offensive and defensive forces. This document laid out McNamara's rationale for procuring strategic forces and indicated his decisions on particular force posture issues.

Enthoven believed that we were spending too much on strategic forces and strongly resisted Service-proposed programs to build a new bomber, a new missile, a new submarine, or to increase expenditures vastly on strategic forces. He doubted whether strategic superiority gave the United States any significant advantage.

In deciding whether an ABM system should be deployed, Enthoven and his colleagues examined the possible role of the system as compared to other methods of accomplishing the same objectives. With regard to city defense they expressed doubts about whether the system would function effectively; they pointed out that the Russians could respond at much less cost and negate the value of any larger ABM system. Defense against China was difficult to evaluate in terms of systems analysis. SA could only calculate the cost of the system relative to the possible savings in lives in the event of a Chinese attack; it could not judge whether the cost was justified. For the defense of Minuteman silos, SA calculated the cost of ABM protection by comparing it to the cost of moving into much harder rock silos or to that of a mobile land-based missile. In terms of these comparisons, the choice of whether or not to proceed with a ballistic missile defense was always a marginal one. In the end, however, the advantage of heading off Service pressures for new strategic offensive systems tipped the balance in Enthoven's mind toward support of ABM defense for Minuteman silos.

International Security Affairs (ISA)

ISA has no budget, no relations with outside laboratories, industry, or foreign governments, and is committed to no specific method of analysis. Hence, the approach it takes tends to be dominated by the views of the Assistant Secretary. John McNaughton and Paul Warnke brought to this position a strong commitment to arms control, both in terms of a United States-Soviet agreement on strategic forces and a nuclear non-proliferation treaty. Both saw American ABM deployment as a threat to these interests and opposed it.[9]

Secretary of Defense Robert S. McNamara

During the course of his seven years as Secretary of Defense, McNamara became more and more concerned with the problems of getting the strategic arms race under control. He came to believe by 1965 that, early in the Kennedy administration, the United States had bought a far larger strategic force than was necessary for deterrence of the Soviet Union, in turn stimulating a Soviet build-up which was now threatening to force the United States to step up the arms race once again. He believed that what he called the "mad momentum of the arms race" had to be brought under control in order to prevent nuclear war and to create a climate in which political relations between the United States and the Soviet Union might be improved. McNamara appears to have viewed the ABM as in some sense a symbol of the arms race. If the United States could take the decision not to deploy an ABM, then it might be possible to negotiate an agreement with the Russians or to reach a tacit understanding with them which would permit a leveling off of the strategic expenditures on both sides and, ultimately, their reduction. On the other hand, the decision to deploy the ABM—a system which McNamara, unlike Foster, believed was technologically unlikely to work—would symbolize our determination to buy whatever was available and to continue the search for a superiority which McNamara felt was unattainable and much less useful than many believed. Perhaps more than any other participant in the process, McNamara saw very high stakes for the national interest in the decision whether or not to deploy an ABM system; and he had no doubt that the correct decision, on grounds of national security, was *not* to deploy.

McNamara, as Secretary of Defense, was keenly conscious of his accounts both with the military and with the President. He believed that he could overrule the Joint Chiefs of Staff on matters about which they felt strongly on only a limited number of occasions, and he carefully chose the issues. He recognized that on such occasions the Chiefs might go directly to the President, and that they would almost certainly go to the Hill to seek to enlist their supporters in bringing pressure to bear on the President to overturn his decision. Nevertheless, he expected to get (as he did on most occasions), the President's backing, but this depended on not seeking presidential support too often and never on issues on which the President was strongly committed to the other side.

ABM was for McNamara a vital issue, and he was prepared to overrule the Chiefs and to seek the President's support. At the same time, he was not prepared to push the issue to the point of a break with the President.

Walt W. Rostow

Serving as the President's National Security Assistant, Walt W. Rostow was potentially in a position to play a major role. However, Rostow never had the mandate (which both Bundy and Kissinger have had) to involve himself heavily in the substance of all major foreign policy issues, particularly those pertaining to defense. Furthermore, McNamara tended to deal directly with the President, and to get involved in between on an issue concerning McNamara and Johnson would have meant a substantial cost to Rostow. Since the two apparently were in disagreement on the issue, he could only lose by stating a position. In this relationship, Rostow tended to save his own influence for Vietnam and a few other issues about which he felt very strongly.

Rostow's own stakes in the decision were not very high compared to the cost of involvement. He thus remained outside and did not play a key role, either in providing information for the President or in seeking to influence his decision directly.

Congressional Leaders

Under the rules of the game in the United States, military leaders have not only the right but the obligation to state their personal views on defense issues to Congress when asked by members of the Armed Services or Appropriations Committees. Thus, it was routine for Congress to be informed that the Joint Chiefs of Staff were unanimously in favor of a ballistic missile defense system and to hear the arguments for such a deployment from senior military officers. In addition, there may well have been private discussions between military leaders and senior Senators and Congressmen.

Congressmen tend to defer to expertise, and the leaders of these committees viewed the military rather than the civilians in the Pentagon as the experts on national security. They were prepared to support programs which the military believed were vital to the improvement of American military capability. In particular, they found it difficult to understand why we should not deploy something which would save American lives in the event of a war. As Richard Russell said in explaining his position, if only two human beings were to survive a nuclear war, he wanted them to be Americans: as he saw matters, an ABM would clearly increase this possibility. In general, the legislators were suspicious of Soviet motives and believed that the United States should maintain strategic superiority. Many of them also derived advantages, in terms of defense industries in their states and districts, from increased defense spending. Finally, they felt that the Secretary of Defense was seeking to substitute his judgment for that of the military, and that this was dangerous. For congressional leaders like Russell, Stennis, Jackson, and Thurmond, the stakes were the national interest as defined by the military.

President Lyndon B. Johnson

President Johnson assumed the Presidency of the United States without any strong commitments to particular foreign policy positions. His own concerns and interests were tied up mainly with domestic issues.

Johnson does not appear to have seen any major national security stakes in the decision whether or not to deploy the ABM. Because it was an issue that generated intense passion in others, he was concerned, but he did not ascribe to it any intrinsic importance in terms of his conception of American security or America's role in the world. He was apparently wary of possible Chinese irrationality, having recently received a number of reports that the Russians believed the Chinese to be dangerous. Therefore an ABM against China, while not imperative, made sense to him. As will be discussed below, Johnson was interested in Strategic Arms Limitation Talks (SALT) with the Russians, but evidently did not share McNamara's fear that an American ABM deployment would impede agreement.

The issue for Johnson tended to be defined in terms of his relations with the other participants, including the Secretary of Defense, the Joint Chiefs of Staff, and congressional leaders concerned with defense matters—particularly those on the Senate Armed Services, Joint Atomic Energy, and Appropriations Committees. He was also, of course, sensitive to the implications that any decision might have for the 1968 presidential election.

Johnson's relations with McNamara had become uneasy during this period because of their growing disagreements about the conduct of the Vietnam war. Though prepared to overrule McNamara on Vietnam issues, Johnson was—at least until he made the decision to move him to the World Bank—interested in keeping McNamara on board, and he recognized that this meant supporting him on a number of other issues. Johnson could have had no doubt that McNamara felt strongly that a ballistic missile defense system should not be deployed, certainly not a large area defense system against the Soviet Union.

If the Chiefs' assertion of vital interests was not enough to settle the issue, neither was it something to be dismissed out of hand. Johnson clearly viewed the Joint Chiefs of Staff as a separate entity. He did not believe that he could leave the job of managing them to the Secretary of Defense. In general, he was reluctant to overrule the military; he viewed them as a group to be bargained with, in large part because of their power and influence on the Hill. He also was not prepared totally to discount their views on issues of national security. If the Chiefs said that an ABM was vital to the security of the United States, Johnson was not prepared to dismiss that as the rhetoric of the military who always want every new system.

For Johnson, certain of his former colleagues in the Senate constituted a major reference group on national security matters. He had had a close relation with Richard Russell, who was then the Chairman of the Senate Armed Services Committee, as well as with such men as John Stennis and Henry Jackson. Johnson did not like to challenge their positions. He also took their views on national security seriously, and knew that they all felt very strongly that the United States should deploy a ballistic missile defense designed to deal with a Soviet attack against the United States.

The domestic political stakes could not be ignored by the President. There could have been little doubt in his mind that the Republican nominee, whether he be Richard Nixon or Nelson Rockefeller, could well make defense a major issue in the campaign. At the urging of his Secretary of Defense and under intense budget pressures, Johnson had permitted the non-Vietnam portion of the defense budget to decline, at least in real terms, and he was regularly rejecting proposals from the Joint Chiefs to develop and deploy a whole array of new strategic systems (for instance, a new manned strategic bomber) and new general-purpose systems. Opposition to his defense program was building, particularly among leaders of the Senate and House, and the Republicans were beginning to sense the possibility of a defense issue in the next presidential election. The ABM was rapidly becoming a symbol of defense preparedness. Johnson had to recognize that, if he did not deploy an ABM, he was open to the charge that he had failed to take a step which would save American lives in the event of a war. Although political scientists may point out that issues of defense procurement rarely swing votes in an election, Presidents are not so certain. Kennedy had apparently scored effectively against Nixon in 1960 on the missile-gap issue, and Johnson was reluctant to run the risk that the "defense-gap" issue would be used effectively against him.

Thus, Johnson saw the stakes largely in terms of his relations with the Secretary of Defense, with the military, and with the senior members of the Congress concerned with defense, especially inasmuch as implications for the 1968 election were involved. As the President saw it, McNamara was strongly against a deployment (as was Secretary of State Dean Rusk), while congressional leaders and the military were strongly in favor. All claimed to be reasoning from the point of view of national security. Johnson's own instincts would have led him to search for a compromise which would minimize the damage to his relations with his advisers.

The other participants were maneuvering and putting forward arguments in an effort to alter his perception of domestic or international consequences. The way in which they struggled to define an issue for the President and to seek the outcome they desired was biased by the images that are taken for granted in the top hierarchy of the United States Government, the rules of the game, and the fact that the deployment of the ABM could be carried out only by the United States Army and only by the use of existing procedures.

Rules of the Game

The most important rule of the game which affected the nature of the ABM debate in the executive branch was the one requiring the President to make budget decisions once a year and to defend his decision publicly. This is a rule that derives from the system of government and applies to any President. Since the ABM had aroused great congressional and public interest, the President could not duck the issue in his budget messages. Instead, he had to discuss the subject and state clearly why he was for or against an ABM. This meant that the option of trying to keep the issue away from the President was not open to the opponents of the ABM. Because it was an annual budget issue, proponents of the deployment of an ABM system had no difficulty reaching the President, and opponents had to persuade the President not only to rule against deployment but to take a public stand. Thus, at each budget cycle McNamara had to devote considerable effort and energy to developing a rationale against deployment which the President would be prepared to accept and to embrace publicly as his own.

Other rules of the game were peculiar to the Johnson administration. The nature of the President's relationship with his Secretary of Defense affected the outcome of the ABM debate. McNamara tended to deal privately with the President on issues of major concern to him. Formal memoranda, which he would clear throughout the Defense Department and send to the President, were prepared only after he and the President had privately agreed on a position. The President's meeting with the Joint Chiefs on the budget tended to be a routine and formalistic opportunity for the Chiefs to appeal the Secretary of Defense's decisions. McNamara's annual meeting with the President's National Security Adviser, Science Adviser, and Budget Director was equally formalistic. Although this procedure eventually broke down on Vietnam, it did not do so on defense-budget issues. This meant that there was no open debate within the administration. Because of the private nature of McNamara's relation with the President, other agencies such as the State Department, ACDA, and the President's Science Adviser were not able to make inputs to the decision in an orderly way before McNamara and the President had reached tentative agreement.

The rules of the game under which the Joint Chiefs of Staff operated also influenced the outcome of the ABM question. During the 1950s the Joint Chiefs of Staff tended to split on major issues, particularly on those affecting the deployment of systems for one Service. Each Service tended to support its own deployment, and except where specific deals were made, to oppose controversial deployments for the other Services—particularly expensive ones which might upset the existing arrangement allocating shares of the defense budget. Because they did not see any threat to their autonomy from the Secretary of Defense in the 1950s, the Chiefs were prepared to deal separately with the Secretary and with the President. Robert McNamara's approach changed the procedures dramatically.

Unlike his predecessors, McNamara saw himself as a decision-maker on strategic issues and not simply as a business manager who left policy to the military. The Joint Chiefs discovered that when they split, McNamara would use their disagreements to reject programs supported by just one of the Services. In order to counterbalance this influence, the Joint Chiefs developed a policy of compromise—to unite in support of each Service. Thus, by 1965 the Army was able to make a strong enough case for an ABM to get the support of the other Chiefs. The Navy was apparently brought along by Army support for a development of the concept of a ship-based ABM system and some other Navy programs. The Air Force appears to have been brought along by Army support for Air Force strategic programs, and by the Army's willingness to forego ABM protection of Minuteman silos. As a result of these arrangements, the Secretary of Defense and the President were confronted by the Joint Chiefs' unanimous position that ballistic missile defense was vital to the security of the United States, even though really only the Army favored it strongly. Congress was informed that the Chiefs unanimously supported a deployment.

Shared Images

The debate within the executive branch was founded on a set of widely shared images about the role of the United States in the world and about the nature of the threats to its security. All participants in the debate accepted the notion that the Soviet Union and China were potential enemies of the United States who would engage in military threats and who might use military force, if not against the United States, at least against our allies, unless the military power of these countries was counterbalanced by that of the United States.

There was also the widespread belief that nuclear power was an important component of national power. It was widely accepted that the United States had to maintain strategic superiority over the Soviet Union and China since these countries were aggressive and expansionist and the United States was defensive and peaceful. It was also assumed that any military capability which would enhance the ability of the United States to survive a nuclear war should be procured; many believed that the United States should procure any weapons system which the Russians had.

Although McNamara began to argue against some of these beliefs beginning in the mid-1960s, they were by and large accepted by most of the participants, and the debate was carried out within these terms. McNamara was forced to construct his arguments largely within the framework of the images held by the rest of the participants. The proponents of ABM deployment found that the shared images biased the debate in their direction.

Arguments

Within these constraints, proponents and opponents of an ABM deployment put forward arguments designed either to convince other participants or to demonstrate that a decision reached because of organizational or political interests could effectively be defended before domestic audiences.

Arguments in Support of Deployment[10]

1. *This will save American lives.* Supporters of the ABM argued that in the event of a nuclear war the ABM system would shoot down incoming Soviet missiles and hence would save American lives. The extreme form of this argument, as has already been mentioned, was presented by Senator Richard Russell. Others pointed out that even if 60 million Americans were killed in a nuclear attack, the expenditure on ABM would be worth saving a possible 120 million other Americans.

2. *The Russians have it.* Throughout the postwar period the United States has felt obligated to match Soviet deployments. It has been argued that if we let the Russians have something that we do not have, they would gain a psychological or political advantage in dealing with us. Similarly, if the Russians were to develop something while we did not, they would gain a technological lead. Thus, in the public debate, and even with the bureaucracy, the argument that "we need it because the Russians have it" has carried great weight.

3. *It works.* Proponents of the ABM sought to counteract technological arguments against deployment by asserting its effectiveness. They pointed to tests in which a single ABM had intercepted a single incoming warhead, and they

expressed confidence that the entire system would in fact work in the event of a nuclear attack. If it worked, it should be deployed.

Arguments Against Deployment

It was more difficult to find clear and simple arguments against the deployment of the ABM system that would appeal to the President and be persuasive in dealing with Congress and the public. Over time, the Secretary of Defense developed a series of arguments against an ABM deployment, and specifically against a large-scale deployment directed against the Soviet Union, which was the system that the Joint Chiefs of Staff and the senior congressional leaders were proposing.

1. *The system is not technologically ready.* Up to 1963, McNamara was able to argue, with wide support from the technological community, that the Army-proposed Nike-Zeus system simply could not be effective against the kind of decoys and other penetration aids that the Soviets were fully capable of producing.[11] If we went ahead with a deployment, he argued, we would wind up with a second-rate system. On the other hand, if we waited, we had hopes of developing a new and more effective system. By 1963 this argument was no longer valid because a new and more technologically efficient system had been developed, and it appeared unlikely that additional breakthroughs would occur in the foreseeable future.

2. *This will bring less return than expenditures on other systems.* After 1963, the Secretary of Defense introduced arguments of cost effectiveness. He pointed out that a large ABM system designed to protect American cities would be aimed at reducing American casualties in a nuclear war. He suggested that one had to examine alternative ways of reducing casualties and determine which would be the most effective for any given sum of money. McNamara examined a number of alternative ways of reducing casualties, including air defense and civil defense. He argued that the studies made clear that the installation of a nation-wide system of fall-out shelters would produce the largest saving. Thus, if the United States were to commit itself to a "damage-limiting" program designed to save lives in the event of a nuclear war, it should build a shelter system. Only after the shelters were completed should one consider spending money on other measures, such as ballistic missile defense.[12] The civil defense argument was a complicated one. It depended on people understanding marginal utility and accepting that one should always proceed in the most efficient way. McNamara appears to have put this argument forward not to make a case for civil defense, but to make one against ballistic missile defense.

3. *There will be an equal and opposite reaction negating the value of the system.* McNamara next turned to the argument of the equal and opposite reaction.[13] As he explained it to Congress, if the United States deployed a large

ABM system which would cost between $20 and $40 billion, it would, against the *currently expected* Soviet threat, save a number of American lives in the event of a nuclear war. McNamara then proceeded to show that the Russians could offset our ABM deployment at substantially smaller cost, and casualties would return to the previous level. Thus, he argued, our ABM system would bring an equal and opposite reaction from the Soviet Union which would totally negate the value of the ABM system—producing the same amount of casualties at a higher expense to us. Although sophisticated critics were able to point out that there was nothing in the history of the arms race to suggest that in fact an equal and opposite reaction was inevitable or even likely, McNamara's argument was a simple and effective one. It summarized in a crude way the truth that over time the Soviets would build decoys and MIRVs if the United States built an ABM, and that in the end there would not be the savings in lives that ABM proponents suggested.

4. *We must resist the mad momentum of the arms race.* In his speech announcing that the United States would deploy a light area defense directed against China, McNamara introduced a new argument against an ABM deployment directed at a large Soviet attack. He talked about the history of the arms race and argued that the United States on a number of occasions had built a larger force than it needed for deterrence. He suggested that in turn this had stimulated the Soviets to build more. Such an interaction, which he called "the mad momentum of the arms race," was, he said, a danger to the security of the United States, and therefore the United States should take the initiative in exercising restraint.

5. *We must negotiate arms limitation with the Soviet Union.* Encouraged by Johnson's interest in strategic arms limitation talks, McNamara sought to utilize this presidential concern to delay the decision to deploy ABM. He argued that a public call for talks would serve as a reasonable rationale for delaying deployment. He also argued that an American commitment to deploy ABMs would decrease the likelihood of Soviet agreement.

Puzzles and Tentative Solutions

Having examined the stakes as the participants saw them, as well as the constraints and the arguments that were used, we can now consider in detail the questions we posed at the outset.

1. Why, in January 1967, did President Johnson ask Congress to appropriate the funds to deploy an ABM, but state that he would defer initiating the deployment pending an effort to get the Soviet Union to engage in talks on limiting the arms race?

As preparations for the budget for the fiscal year 1968 neared completion in the closing months of 1966, time appeared to be running out on McNamara's efforts to prevent deployment of a Soviet-oriented ABM system. A number of pressures seemed to be coming to a head, including the following:[14]

Technological improvement. The technology of ballistic missile defense had improved drastically in the preceding few years. Those responsible for the program in the scientific community, in DDR & E and its operating arm, the Advanced Research Projects Agency (ARPA), as well as in the Army, were now arguing that an effective ABM system could be built and could ultimately be improved to handle even a large Soviet attack. In previous years, the testimony of these scientists had effectively served to offset the pressure exercised by the Joint Chiefs of Staff and had enabled McNamara to persuade the President and the Congress that the technology was not yet ripe for an ABM deployment. They were no longer prepared to play this role.[15]

Soviet ABM deployment. There was growing evidence that the Soviet Union was beginning to deploy an ABM system around Moscow. In the past the intelligence community had been split as to whether the so-called Tallinn system being deployed across the northern part of the Soviet Union was in fact an ABM system. (Although some military intelligence agencies were pressing the view that Tallinn was an ABM system, the majority of the intelligence community believed that it was an air defense system.) However, there was no dispute at all that the system being deployed around Moscow was an ABM. This added to pressures to begin an American deployment in order to avoid an ABM gap.

JCS pressure. In part because of the changes in technology and the Soviet ABM deployment, the Joint Chiefs of Staff were no longer willing to concur in delaying ABM deployment; they were determined to go firmly on record before Congress in favor of a deployment *now*, and in particular for a deployment that would develop into a large anti-Soviet system.

Senate pressure. Pressure was also mounting from Senate leaders for initial ABM deployment. Among others, Russell, Jackson, and Thurmond had spoken out in favor of an early ABM deployment. The general expectation in the executive branch was that Congress would put great pressure on the President to agree to a deployment if he did not include it in his budget message.[16]

Republican pressure. It was also becoming evident that the Republican Party planned to make a campaign issue out of an alleged ABM gap. Governor George Romney of Michigan, then believed to be a leading Republican candidate for the presidential nomination in 1968, had, on a "Meet the Press" broadcast in November, talked of an ABM gap and made it clear that this would be an issue in the campaign. Moreover, the GOP Congressional Policy Committee led by Melvin Laird had decided to make the ABM a vehicle to challenge Lyndon Johnson's strategic policies. Senator Strom Thurmond, a leading Republican expert on defense matters, had also attacked the failure to deploy an ABM.[17]

There was no doubt that JCS demands for an immediate ABM deployment would be made known to leaders on the Hill, as would the growing evidence of a Soviet ABM deployment around Moscow. Congress had in the previous year included funds for the ABM deployment which the President had not requested; the stage was set for a confrontation should Johnson again accept the advice of his Secretary of Defense and delay an ABM deployment.

The President's choices seemed to be rather narrow. He could reject ballistic missile defense, embrace McNamara's arguments against deployment, and prepare to take his case to congressional leaders and the public. Alternatively, he could proceed with a ballistic missile defense deployment at the cost of overruling his Secretary of Defense. The odds were high that the President would proceed with the ballistic missile defense deployment being pressed on him by the Joint Chiefs and the Senate leaders. Only if he could find another option did McNamara stand any chance of again delaying a presidential commitment to ballistic missile defense.

It appears that McNamara first discussed the subject with the President at meetings held on his Texas ranch on November 3rd and 10th. These discussions were reported to focus on the ABM and the question of extending the bombing to additional targets in North Vietnam.[18]

Following the meeting with the President on November 10th, McNamara reported at a press conference that the Soviets were now believed to be deploying an ABM system around Moscow. McNamara's initiative in releasing this information made it possible for him to preempt an inevitable news leak and, at the same time, to air his view that the Soviet ABM deployment required improvements in American offensive capability rather than a matching deployment. McNamara noted that the United States was moving ahead with Minuteman III and Poseidon, and therefore was fully confident of its ability to deter this Soviet ABM. He declared that it was too early to begin deployment of an anti-Chinese system, and that no decision had been made on other possible reasons for a deployment.[19]

The decisive meeting with the President appears to have been held on December 6th. At this meeting—attended by McNamara, his Deputy Secretary Cyrus Vance, all the members of the Joint Chiefs, and the President's Special Assistant Walt Rostow—the Joint Chiefs were given the opportunity to put forward their argument for what was then called Posture A, a full coverage of the United States with a system designed for defense against more than a Chinese attack. The Joint Chiefs made it clear that they intended to see that Posture A would develop into Posture B, a larger anti-Soviet system designed to reduce casualties in the United States in the event of a large Soviet attack, and that they would accept nothing less. McNamara countered by presenting the arguments against an anti-Soviet system emphasizing that the Soviets would eventually have an offensive capability which would fully offset the value of the ABM. At this point he appears to have presented the President with two possible compromises. The first, which he was ultimately able to persuade the President to accept, called for a procurement of production items requiring a long lead-time, with no specific decision as to what system, if any, would be deployed; this was to be accompanied by an effort to begin arms limitation talks with the Soviet Union. The second option was to begin deployment of a small anti-Chinese system. The meeting ended with Johnson agreeing that the State Department should begin to probe the Soviets on the possibility of talks, but apparently withholding any decision on ABM deployment.

The State Department thus proceeded to explore the possibilities of arms limitation talks with the Soviets. At the same time McNamara wrote up and presented to the President a Draft Presidential Memorandum (DPM) summarizing his arguments against an anti-Soviet system, but suggesting that an ABM defense against China might prove useful.

To demonstrate that he was not the only opponent of a large Soviet-oriented ABM system, McNamara arranged for the President and the Joint Chiefs of Staff to meet early in January 1967 with past and current Special Assistants to the President for Science and Technology and Directors of Defense Research and Engineering. None of the scientists present dissented from the view that an ABM to defend the American people against a Soviet missile attack was not feasible and should not be built. There was some discussion of a Chinese-oriented system and some divergence of views, but a majority was opposed to deployment.[20]

Following this meeting, McNamara was apparently able to persuade Johnson to delay any deployment, whether anti-Russian or anti-Chinese, and to pursue the option of procuring long lead-time items, and to concentrate on the effort to open arms limitation talks with the Soviet Union.

The proposal for such talks seemed to be a vehicle for the pursuit of a number of presidential objectives. Johnson was haunted, as all of his postwar predecessors had been, by the specter of nuclear war. He was anxious to try to do something to bring nuclear weapons under control. Moreover, here was an issue on which the President could appeal to the desire of the general public for peace, and specifically to the left wing of the Democratic Party, which was becoming increasingly disaffected on Vietnam. It was also an issue that could make history for Johnson as the man who had made the decisive move to end the nuclear arms race which threatened mankind's doom. Johnson was quick to sense these possibilities.

McNamara was able to argue that a decision to proceed with ballistic missile defense would hamper arms limitation talks with the Russians, since one of the main purposes of such talks would be to seek an agreement by both sides to avoid any ballistic missile defense deployments. Further, he could argue that a dramatic act of restraint by the United States would increase the probability that the Russians would respond favorably, and that the talks would begin. In any case, a bold gesture for peace on the part of the President would undercut much of the opposition to his decision not to proceed right away with a ballistic missile defense deployment.

At the same time, by asking for funds for ballistic missile defense and implying that he would be prepared to spend them if talks did not get under way, the President was able to avoid making the argument that the United States should unilaterally forego deployment of a ballistic missile defense. Johnson would be able to tell the Joint Chiefs and the senior congressional leaders that he had certainly not ruled out a ballistic missile defense; that in fact he had taken a major step toward such a deployment, but that he was postponing the actual deployment pending an effort to get an arms control agreement with the Soviet Union. Though the military and congressional leaders might be somewhat uneasy about the further delay, they could not effectively mount a campaign against an effort to seek agreement with the Soviet Union, given the widespread popularity of such efforts.

Thus, the proposal to link the two issues enabled McNamara to gain a further delay, which he hoped would last indefinitely as the talks continued. The President could avoid paying any major price in his relations with McNamara, the Joint Chiefs, or the congressional leaders who favored an ABM deployment. He could put off a hard choice and open up the possibility of arms control negotiations which would substantially enhance his domestic position and solidify his prospects for a favorable place in the history books.[21]

2. Why was the decision to deploy an ABM announced at the tail end of a speech whose whole structure and purpose was to explain why an ABM defense against the Soviet Union was impossible? 3. Why did the Secretary of Defense describe the system as being directed against China, while the Joint Chiefs of Staff and their congressional allies described it as a first step toward a full-scale defense against the Soviet Union?

What has been said thus far should make it clear that the answers lie in the bargaining between McNamara and Johnson, with each taking account of the positions of the Joint Chiefs and the congressional leaders.

The effort to get the Soviets to agree to set a date for arms limitation talks was unsuccessful. When President Johnson met with Soviet Premier Kosygin at Glassboro, New Jersey, on June 23rd and 25th at a hastily arranged summit conference, there was still no Soviet agreement to talk. Johnson brought McNamara along; while the two leaders ate lunch, the Secretary of Defense gave them a lecture on nuclear strategy, previewing his San Francisco speech and emphasizing the value of an agreement to both sides. The Soviet leader was unyielding; he described ABM as defensive and unobjectionable and was not prepared to agree to talks.[22]

Following the Glassboro Conference there could be little doubt that talks would not be under way before the President's next budget message in January

1968. Almost immediately Johnson informed McNamara that some kind of ABM deployment would have to be announced by January at the latest.[23] At that time the President would have to account for the disposition of the ABM contingency funds he had requested and state whether he was seeking additional sums for deployment of an ABM system. Given his stakes as we have defined them, and given the implicit commitment that he had made in January of 1967 to go forward in the absence of arms limitation talks, the President's decision was not difficult to predict. January of 1968 would be Johnson's last chance to announce the deployment in a budget message before the presidential elections in November. To hedge again, stating that he was still seeking talks, would have seemed unconvincing since Johnson had been unable to secure Kosygin's agreement to talks at the Glassboro meeting. The intermediate options had run out. The President was determined to go ahead, even if it meant paying a price in his relations with the Secretary of Defense. Apparently, Johnson also felt that by beginning to deploy an ABM he might convince the Soviets to enter into arms limitation talks.[24]

Having decided to proceed with an ABM deployment, Johnson was obviously concerned about reducing the cost in terms of his relations with McNamara. He was willing to let the Secretary announce the deployment in any way he chose. For the sake of military and congressional acceptance, the President may have insisted that the deployment be such that others could describe it as the first step toward an anti-Soviet system.

McNamara's primary goal remained to prevent deployment of a large system directed at the Soviet Union. If the United States were to go forward with any ABM deployment, it was important to do whatever possible to create in the public mind a clear difference between the system being deployed and a large system, at the same time vigorously putting forward the case for not deploying a large system against the Soviet Union. It was therefore in McNamara's interest to be able to explain his view of the arms race, explain his opposition to a large anti-Soviet system, and *then* announce an ABM deployment. The apparent contradiction in the speech was designed by McNamara as a way of emphasizing that this was not a large ABM deployment against the Soviet Union. He may also have hoped that his speech would generate substantial public opposition to an ABM deployment.

McNamara had recognized several years earlier that he might lose the battle against deploying any kind of ABM system and had begun laying the groundwork for a fall-back position in the form of a small ABM system directed against China. In February 1965, he publicly raised the possibility of ABM protection against a small nuclear attack from China, but argued that even on those grounds the decision was not then needed because "the lead-time for additional nations to develop and deploy an effective ballistic missile system capable of reaching the United States is greater than we require to deploy the defense."[25] In the following year McNamara indicated that the ABM system now being developed would not be effective against a larger attack, but could deal with a small Chinese threat.[26]

Thus, in September of 1967, McNamara could announce that the lead-time for an ABM deployment was now about the same as the lead-time for the Chinese deployment of an ICBM system of significant size. Therefore, it was now prudent to proceed with this deployment which he had been discussing for several years. And McNamara appears to have been convinced that, in its own terms, ABM defense against China was, as he described it in his speech, "marginal" but nevertheless "prudent." In announcing the decision to deploy an ABM system against China, McNamara was putting forward arguments which he believed.

Even more important was the fact that McNamara's major concern was to try to prevent a large deployment directed at the Soviet Union which would force the Soviets to respond, setting off another round of the arms race. An anti-Chinese system could be limited more easily than a small system directed against the Soviet Union. One alternative was to describe the system as one designed for protection for Minuteman installations, although it would be difficult to justify on grounds of cost effectiveness. Moreover, a system deployed only around missile sites would have been resisted by the Joint Chiefs and the Senate leaders; it did not pave the way for a larger system against the Soviet Union and could not be described as the beginning of one. It is not clear whether McNamara himself or the President ruled out this alternative.[27]

4. Why was the system authorized for deployment one which was designed and deployed as if its purpose was to protect American cities against a large Soviet attack?

Once a presidential decision is made on a policy issue, the details of implementation must be turned over to an individual or organization. In the case of the ABM, there was no choice but to assign responsibility to the Army. Although McNamara could and did attempt to monitor how the Army would deploy the system, he was unable or unwilling to direct that the system be designed and deployed so as to minimize the possibility of growth. The Army's freedom may have been enhanced by the fact that McNamara's scientific and technical advisers themselves tended to favor keeping open the option for growth into a large ABM system. Deputy Secretary of Defense Paul Nitze, to whom general responsibility for much of the day-to-day administration of the Pentagon fell as McNamara devoted more and more of his time to Vietnam, also tended to favor keeping open the option for a large system.

But there was a more fundamental problem. Once the decision had been made to proceed with a ballistic missile defense directed against China, there was strong pressure to move forward quickly. The President could not admit at that point that we had no hardware for such a system and that three or four years of research and development would be necessary before deployment would begin: one had to start with deploying the components that were already developed, even though they were not the optimum ones for a defense system against China that could be kept from growing into a large ABM system against the Soviet Union.

Geography also worked against a limited system. Both Russian and Chinese ICBMs approach the United States through the same corridor over the pole. The same radar could be used for an anti-Chinese system and an anti-Russian system, and long-range missile launchers would be useful against both threats.

DDR & E, which favored a large Soviet-oriented system, had no incentive for using its ingenuity to develop components that could be effective against China but had little potential for a large anti-Russian system. And, in making precise decisions about the location of radar and missile-launching sites, the Army in fact opted for sites close to cities, to permit the eventual deployment of a large anti-Russian system.

McNamara's control over the implementation of this decision was simply not great enough to prevent these developments. His attention was increasingly absorbed by Vietnam and he was clearly on his way out. He did not have the support of the President in seeking to limit the system. His principal assistant did not share his desire to reduce the possibility of growth, and the Army, charged with deployment, favored a large anti-Soviet system. Thus, despite McNamara's efforts in his statements to distinguish sharply between an anti-Chinese and an anti-Russian system, the Army was able to tell the Congress that actual deployment was not different in any significant way from the projected first stages of an anti-Russian system, and that the system being deployed was expected to grow.

Conclusions

The decision of the Johnson administration to deploy an ABM system, the way in which it was announced, and the preparations for deployment which followed illustrate the pulling and hauling of many different players with different interests that is characteristic of the foreign policy process in the United States. No single player's views, including those of the President, of what should be done, dominated, although the President's views played a major role in shaping the general direction in which American actions moved.

Two independent decisions were involved, with different actors influencing the course of each. The first decision was simply whether or not to deploy the ABM at all. This was necessarily a presidential decision; there was no end run around him. As the ABM decision illustrates, the President is qualitatively different—not simply a very powerful player among less powerful players.

The second decision related to the timing, substance, and shape of deployment, given the previous decision that there was to be an ABM of some kind. In this latter decision the President played a much less central role, and other players were somewhat more influential. Johnson was both less interested and less in control.

The decision to announce some sort of deployment by January of 1968 can thus best be explained by exploring the multiple constituencies and interests that the President had to balance. The foreign policy interests of all postwar Presidents have come to focus on relations with the Soviet Union as they affect the nuclear balance and the need to avoid nuclear war. These concerns, while from time to time stimulating interest in arms control, have mainly led to support for defense efforts. At the same time, the Presidents have all been concerned with their image in history and have developed a desire to go down as men who contributed to a peaceful international environment. All of them felt, as Johnson did, the responsibility to avoid a nuclear holocaust that would destroy civilization.

Moreover, no President can ignore the pressures exerted by the bureaucracy, especially the military and the senior cabinet officers, or by senior congressional leaders and the public, when a presidential campaign is around the corner. All of these pressures came to bear on Lyndon Johnson as he faced the ABM decisions during the course of 1967. Johnson appears here in the characteristic presidential role of conciliator: a man who attempts to give as much as he can to each of a number of his principal subordinates and the permanent bureaucracies while seeking a position that avoids any conflict between his own various interests and constituencies beyond the government. The limited ABM which Johnson ultimately directed be deployed could be described by Robert McNamara as anti-Chinese and therefore not a danger to Soviet-American relations in general or future arms talks in particular. At the same time, the Joint Chiefs and Senate leaders had their own payoffs. Despite McNamara's statement, they could describe it as a first step towards an anti-Soviet system. Moreover, the small anti-Chinese system which Johnson approved was much larger than the system the Soviet Union was deploying around Moscow. Given these ambiguities and the simplified nature with which the public views such questions, the Republican Party had effectively been deprived of a missile gap issue. That was the President's payoff.

Johnson was also able to reconcile his own concern, to seek an end to the nuclear arms race with the Soviet Union, with the need to maintain American military strength. Early in 1967 he was prepared to go along with McNamara's proposal that arms talks with the Soviet Union be sought before a firm final decision was made to proceed with an ABM deployment. After talking with Kosygin, he concluded that the Soviets would not enter talks under the current circumstances. He believed that perhaps the pressure that would be put upon the Soviet leaders by the beginnings of an American deployment would constitute a leverage on the Russians to agree to talks. In ordering the deployment, Johnson was not abandoning his efforts for arms talks and an arms agreement with the Soviet Union; rather, he was structuring the issue, making an American ABM deployment a way to get the very talks that both he and McNamara desired.

If the decision to order a deployment can be most clearly understood in terms of the conflicting pressures on the President, the precise nature of the deployment can be understood largely in terms of pressures within the bureaucracy below the President, constrained by the operating procedures of the Army and of the Pentagon as a whole. Although McNamara himself favored no deployment or a limited deployment, the staffs on which he had to depend to monitor and implement the President's decision were unanimous in their belief that an ABM system should be built that could grow into a large anti-Soviet system. His science adviser, John S. Foster, who would have to have the major role in monitoring both the research on the ABM system and its development and production, believed strongly that the option for a large system should be left open, as did Paul Nitze, McNamara's Deputy Secretary of Defense (following the departure of Cyrus Vance who more closely shared McNamara's views). The Army itself favored a big system. No imaginative thought had gone into the design of components for a specifically anti-Chinese system. In fact, the implementers were straining as hard as they could to design and deploy a system that could be expanded as far as possible. McNamara's power, as suggested above, was weak in this game; he lacked strong presidential directive as well as strong staff support to keep the system small. His primary attention was focused on Vietnam, and his days as Secretary of Defense were obviously numbered.

One of the truisms of bureaucracy is that it resists change. Innovation, when it occurs, must generally be explained. The history of the ABM appears to be an anomaly. McNamara, the defender of the status quo, had to take the initiative to prevent an ABM deployment, since the system seemed to be grinding inevitably towards it. The explanation for this lies in the fact that the system was heavily biased toward the deployment of new weapons systems under certain conditions; ABM deployment was not seen as change. A number of components of the rules of the game, the shared images, and the organizational procedures of the American government produced a situation from the time of the Korean War through the end of the 1960s in which the procurement of new systems was part of the routine.

As has already been noted, the budgetary process itself creates a unique set of pressures. The fact that ABM decisions had to be recorded in the budget meant that the issue would reach the President without any effort on the part of its proponents. This was particularly true because of the rule giving the JCS the right to appeal to the President any decision of the Secretary of Defense or the Budget Director. No other career service enjoys this right. Moreover, the President had to make a decision and announce it publicly, in keeping with a deadline brought about by the budget. To urge him to delay was equivalent to urging him to take a public stand against an ABM deployment at that time.

The operating rules of the Joint Chiefs of Staff, as well as their access to congressional leaders and congressional committees, also produced a bias towards deployment of weapons systems that were favored strongly by one of the Services. Given strong Army support for an ABM, and given the judgment of scientists that it was technically feasible, unanimous JCS support for the system was forthcoming under the logrolling rules which the Chiefs had begun to use in the McNamara period. The fact that they would report their views to the Congress when asked meant that the President could not keep differences hidden and, in order to prevent a deployment, would have to challenge the JCS in public.

The sequence of the private decision-making process involving negotiations of the President and the Secretary of Defense with the Joint Chiefs also biased decisions toward deployment: the normal desires of the Budget Bureau to avoid expensive weapons systems, the skepticism of the scientists on the President's Science Advisory Committee, and the opposition of some parts of the State Department to a deployment could not be brought into play early enough in the process to affect presidential decisions.

Shared images which, according to official belief, dominated American society also biased the system towards an ABM deployment. There was a widely accepted view that the United States needed to have strategic superiority over the Soviet Union and that the United States needed to match any system the Soviets deployed. The general view was that the United States should deploy any strategic system which worked well and which appeared to have the prospect of reducing damage if war should occur. The existence of these shared views made it difficult to put forward arguments within the bureaucracy against an ABM deployment, and even more difficult to shape arguments which the President would consider to be effective with the Congress and with the public. Given this situation, the President had to be concerned with the domestic political effects—particularly on his prospects of re-election in 1968—if he appeared to be opening an ABM gap, failing to match the Soviet system, and giving up American nuclear superiority.

The organizational procedures of the Pentagon also tended to bias toward a decision to deploy. Research, both in the Army and in the Advanced Research Projects Agency, was dominated by scientists who believed that any feasible system should be deployed. Moreover, the focus tended to be on the greatest conceivable threat, and hence on designing a system against a large Soviet attack. In addition, the desire to make an effective case for deployment led to underestimates of cost and overestimates of feasibility.

McNamara seemed to recognize that, because of the constraints within the system, success was unlikely. Thus his effort had to be directed as much toward changing the long-standing strategic nuclear biases as toward devising a delaying action against deployment. Although he lost the short-run battle to prevent deployment or to deploy a system that could not grow into a large anti-Soviet system, his efforts to change the terms of the debate within the bureaucracy, with the Congress, and with the public were considerably more successful.

By 1969, President Nixon accepted nuclear sufficiency rather than superiority as the American goal. He also embraced, as his own, McNamara's arguments against an anti-Soviet system. He announced that the United States had no intention of deploying such a system, not only because it was technically infeasible, but also because such a system would threaten the Soviet deterrent. While he proceeded with a system that was against China and in defense of Minuteman sites, Nixon directed that it be designed so that it could not grow—nor appear to the Soviets that it could grow—into a large anti-Russian system. In part as a result of the arguments McNamara had made in his speech announcing the deployment, as well as of his posture statements, the attitude of the Senate changed dramatically on this range of issues.

Perhaps the most successful conversion was that of the Russians. Kosygin had argued at Glassboro that ABMs were purely defensive weapons and that the American effort to prevent their deployment was immoral. However, by 1971 the Russians were pressing for an agreement at the strategic arms talks simply to limit ABMs. Even the fact that the talks were under way at all can be attributed to McNamara's efforts to prevent an ABM deployment.

Changes in the rules of the game and the shared images of the bureaucracy, the Congress, and the public have altered the biases of the system. However, the actions of the Nixon Administration can only be explained by considering the new set of players and their interests. It is a new tale, but one not unaffected by this one.

Notes

1. The framework of analysis used here is drawn from the author's ongoing study of Bureaucratic Politics and Foreign Policy.

2. Robert S. McNamara, "The Dynamics of Nuclear Strategy," *Department of State Bulletin*, October 9, 1967, 443-51.

3. Ibid.

4. Lyndon Baines Johnson, "Annual Budget Message to the Congress, Fiscal Year 1968, January 24, 1967," *Public Papers of the President of the United States, 1967: Book I* (Washington 1968), 48. "In 1968, we will: continue intensive development of Nike-X but take no action now to deploy an anti-ballistic missile (ABM) defense; initiate discussions with the Soviet Union on the limitation of ABM deployments; in the event these discussions prove unsuccessful, we will reconsider our deployment decisions. To provide for actions that may be required at that time, approximately $375 million has been included in the 1968 budget for the production of Nike-X for such purposes as defense of our offensive weapons systems."

5. The discussion of the interests of the participants is based in part on knowledge gained by the author as a participant in the process, as Deputy Assistant Secretary of Defense (ISA). Some of the observations are based on

guesses about positions taken. Many of the same insights can be derived from a reading of congressional testimony, speeches, etc. See also Edward Randolph Jayne II, "The ABM Debate: Strategic Defense and National Security," MIT Center for International Studies, Center Paper C/69-12, 669-712. This study, based largely on interviews, confirms many of the stands described here. To be fair to the reader (and to add to his confusion), it should be noted that the present author was one of those interviewed by Jayne.

6. On Service interests, see Morton H. Halperin, "Why Bureaucrats Play Games," *Foreign Policy*, No. 2 (Spring 1971), 70-90.

7. On the Army's interest in ABM in particular, see Herbert York, *Race to Oblivion* (New York 1970), 214.

8. Industrial groups and contractors shared these concerns, as did research organizations such as the Stanford Research Institute, which worked on the ABM for the Army. However, the influence of these groups was limited to supplying arguments for ABM supporters in the administration and helping to arouse congressional concern. AT&T, the prime contractor, is much less dependent on defense contracts than the prime contractors of most large systems; nevertheless, AT&T was eager for the contract because it used its involvement in air defense and missile defense to help prevent an anti-trust suit to split Bell Labs, the research group, and Western Electric, the manufacturing unit, from the Bell system.

9. The Arms Control and Disarmament Agency, the State Department, and the President's Science Advisory Committee shared many of these concerns. None of these organizations played a major role in the decisions. Cf. the comment of Herbert Scoville, who at the time was an Assistant Director of ACDA: "ACDA was at no time a participant in any of the senior-level discussions leading up to it [McNamara's speech]." Herbert Scoville, Jr., "The Politics of the ABM Debate: The View from the A.C. & D.A."; paper prepared for the APSA Annual Meeting, September 1970, 4. The rules of the game, as explained below, limited the involvement of these organizations as well as that of the Budget Bureau. Secretary of State Rusk's role involved direct and private communication with the President.

10. See Senate Debates, *Congressional Record*, CXIV, Part 22, 529169-90, 90th Cong., 2nd sess.; testimony of General Earle Wheeler, Chairman, Joint Chiefs of Staff, *Hearings Before the Preparedness Investigating Subcommittee of the Committee on Armed Services*, 90th Cong., 2nd sess., April 23, 1968.

11. Robert S. McNamara, *Testimony Before the Subcommittee of the Committee on Appropriations*, U.S. House of Representatives, 87th Cong., 1st sess., April 6, 1961, 17. For a summary of McNamara's arguments against deployment as presented to various congressional committees from 1961-1967, see Benson D. Adams, "McNamara's ABM Policy, 1961-67," *Orbis*, XII (Spring 1968), 200-225.

12. Robert S. McNamara, *Statement of the Secretary of Defense Before a*

Joint Session of the Senate Armed Services Commmittee and the Senate Subcommittee on the Department of Defense Appropriations on the Fiscal Years 1965-69 Defense Program and the 1965 Defense Budget (multilith), 42.

13. Robert S. McNamara, *Statement of the Secretary of Defense Before a Joint Session of the Senate Armed Services Committee and the Senate Subcommittee on the Department of Defense Appropriations on the Fiscal Years 1968-72 Defense Program and the 1968 Defense Budget* (multilith), 39, 40.

14. The documentation for this section is drawn from Jayne (fn. 5).

15. Ibid., 309.

16. See, for example, *Baltimore Sun*, November 21, 1966 and December 3, 1966; *Washington Post*, November 24, 1966.

17. Jayne (fn. 5), 346.

18. These meetings are described by Jayne (fn. 5).

19. *New York Times*, November 13, 1966.

20. The scientists present were Science Advisers James R. Killian, Jr., George B. Kistiakowsky, Jerome B. Wiesner, and Donald F. Hornig; and Directors of Defense Research Herbert York, Harold Brown, and John S. Foster, Jr. The meeting is described in York (fn. 7), 194-95.

21. On the tendency to make the minimum decision necessary, see Warner Schilling, "The H-Bomb Decision," *Political Science Quarterly*, LXXVI (March 1961), 24-46.

22. Jayne (fn. 5), 366-69.

23. Ibid., 372.

24. Ibid., 373.

25. Robert S. McNamara, *Statement of the Secretary of Defense Before a Joint Session of the Senate Armed Services Committee and the Senate Subcommittee on the Department of Defense Appropriations on the Fiscal Years 1966-70 Defense Program and the 1966 Defense Budget* (multilith), 49.

26. Robert S. McNamara, *Statement of the Secretary of Defense Before a Joint Session of the Senate Armed Services Committee and the Senate Subcommittee on the Department of Defense Appropriations on the Fiscal Years 1967-71 Defense Program and the 1967 Defense Budget* (multilith), 70.

27. In his San Francisco speech McNamara stated, with regard to Minuteman defense, that "the Chinese-oriented ABM deployment would enable us to add—as a concurrent benefit—a further defense of our Minuteman sites against Soviet attack, which means that at modest cost we would in fact be adding even greater effectiveness to our offensive missile force and avoiding a much more costly expansion of that force." A short time later, in an article in *Life* (September 29, 1967, pp. 28 A-C), elaborating on the speech, he stated unequivocally that the Minuteman defense would be deployed. However, following a trip to Europe for a meeting of the NATO Nuclear Planning Group, McNamara declared that no decision had been made as to whether the option to defend Minuteman sites would be exercised.

Part III: Proposals

The President and the Military

All Presidents are dependent on the permanent bureaucracies of government inherited from their predecessors. A President must have the information and analysis of options which the bureaucracies provide in order to anticipate problems and make educated choices. He must, in most cases, also have the cooperation of the bureaucracies to turn his decisions into governmental action. A bureaucracy can effectively defuse a presidential decision by refusing to support it with influential members of Congress or to implement it faithfully.

The President's dependence on the bureaucracy and his limited freedom to maneuvre are acute in all areas. The military, however, poses a unique set of problems for him. These arise in part from the limitations upon the President when he is seeking military advice. When the National Security Council or other presidential sessions are convened to discuss high-level foreign and national security matters, the President has a great deal of influence on the selection of all those who will attend, except the Chairman of the Joint Chiefs of Staff, who must be chosen from a small group of senior career military officers. Compare also the President's ability to appoint noncareer people to subcabinet and ambassadorial posts with the limitations on his range of selection for appointments to senior military positions or overseas military commands.

One dilemma for the President is finding alternative sources of military advice. The military, for example, has a virtual monopoly on providing information to the President about the readiness and capabilities of U.S. or even allied forces. Other groups and individuals can provide advice on many "military" questions, but their access to information is limited. The President may call for judgments from his Secretary of Defense, but the Secretary's analysis must rely on the basic factual material and field evaluations provided by the military.

Judgments about the likely effectiveness of American combat operations are also the exclusive province of the military. In assessing the potential effects of a diplomatic move, the President can turn not only to career Foreign Service Officers, but also to businessmen, academics and intelligence specialists in other agencies. On the other hand, if he wishes to know how many American divisions would be necessary to defend Laos against a Chinese attack, the legitimacy of

Reprinted by permission from *Foreign Affairs*, January 1972. Copyright 1971 by Council on Foreign Relations, Inc.

advice from groups other than the military is distinctly reduced. The military's influence on the information and evaluation of options which reach the President is further enhanced by the important role it plays in the preparation of national intelligence estimates.

Yet another source of leverage for the military is the prestige and influence that military leaders have enjoyed, at least in the past, with leading figures in Congress. Until quite recently, this influence limited presidential effectiveness with Congress and the general public. Even now, military influence continues to be strong with the leaders of the Armed Services Committees and appropriations subcommittees. Legislation clearly gives the military the right to inform congressional committees directly of their differences with administration policy, when asked. Senior military officers frequently exercise that right. In addition, military views on matters of major concern to the services often become known to the press. Thus, Presidents have shied away from decisions that they believed the military would take to the Congress and the public, and have frequently felt obliged to negotiate with the military.

For example, both Presidents Truman and Eisenhower carried on extensive negotiations with the military to secure its support for defense reorganization programs which appeared to have little chance of getting through Congress without military acquiescence. Later Presidents have shied away from defense reorganizations requiring congressional approval, at least in part because of the difficulty of gaining military concurrence, or congressional action without the concurrence. The backing of the military has also been vital to Presidents in other important programs. Truman, for example, relied heavily on the military to endorse his Korean War policies, especially in his disagreement with General Douglas MacArthur over limiting the war. MacArthur, who then commanded the U.N. forces in Korea, wanted to expand the war to China and to use nuclear weapons. The Joint Chiefs were not in favor of the expansion and Omar Bradley, Chairman of the Joint Chiefs and a much decorated World War II hero, strengthened Truman's position enormously when he stated publicly that MacArthur's proposal would lead to "the wrong war, in the wrong place, at the wrong time."

The political influence of the military has been substantially reduced in the last few years. The fact that the Joint Chiefs favor a particular proposal is no longer a guarantee of congressional support and may in some cases be counterproductive. For example, the Joint Chiefs were not asked by the Nixon administration to play a major role in defending the Safeguard ABM. Nevertheless, the fact that the Joint Chiefs still wield influence with certain members of Congress and some parts of the public may inhibit the President, particularly if he fears a right-wing attack or needs a two-thirds vote to get a treaty through the Senate.

The implementation of presidential decisions by the military works both for and against the Chief Executive. The military tradition of discipline, efficiency and a clearly delineated chain of command increases the probability that precise orders will be observed and carried out with dispatch. However, the fact that the military implements decisions according to standard procedures may cause presidential orders to be misconstrued through oversimplification. The Joint Chiefs will defer to the field commander and not monitor his compliance carefully. Moreover, Presidents find it difficult to develop alternate means to secure implementation of decisions in the domain of the military. For example, the President may use special envoys in place of career Foreign Service Officers to carry out delicate negotiations while he can hardly send a retired businessman to land American forces in Lebanon or to command a nuclear missile-carrying submarine.

Presidents also have great difficulty convincing the military to create new capabilities, which they may need in the future but which might tend to alter the traditional role of a particular branch. The services emphasize the forces which conform to their notion of the essence of their role and resist capabilities which involve interservice cooperation (*e.g.* airlift), noncombat roles (*e.g.* advisers), and élite forces (*e.g.* Green Berets). At least until recently, they have also resisted the maintenance of combat-ready nonnuclear forces.

II

This is not to suggest that the President's problems with the military are greater than, for example, those with the Department of Agriculture or other agencies with strong links to domestic constituencies and congressional committees. Nor is it to suggest that the information and advice given the President by the military has over the years been less valuable than the advice of others. The point is rather that within the foreign policy field the greatest limitations on the President's freedom of action tend to come from the military. None of our Presidents has been content with his relations with the military.

In fact, Presidents have used a number of devices to overcome limitations on their power, to get the information and advice they want and to find support for implementing their decisions. Presidential strategies have varied, depending on the type of issue and depending on whether they were seeking: (1) information or options, (2) political support or (3) faithful implementation.

Their techniques include the following:

1. *Reorganizations.* The Nixon National Security Council system and the appointment of the President's Blue Ribbon Panel on Defense Reorganization (Fitzhugh Panel) suggest a return to the emphasis on reorganization which tended to dominate thinking in the early postwar period and, indeed, through 1960. Reorganization efforts within the Pentagon have aimed at securing coordinated military advice, rather than separate advice from each service. Presidents have, in general, pressed the Joint Chiefs to transcend service biases

and to come up with agreed positions based on a unified perspective. Eisenhower was particularly adverse to JCS splits. But the success of these efforts has been relatively limited. Most observers conclude that JCS papers still tend to reflect particular service views, either by way of deference or compromise, rather than the unified military judgment of a "true" Joint Staff. Secretaries of Defense have not looked upon the Joint Staff as part of their own staff.

The reorganization of the National Security Council system beginning in 1969 appears to have been designed to bring to bear a variety of different views on military problems. The evaluation of alternate military forces is centered in the Council's Verification Panel. This group first considered the Strategic Arms Limitation Talks (SALT) and then the prospects and problems of mutual force reductions in Europe, thereby going beyond traditional military and intelligence channels. The Defense Program Review Committee was designed to apply expertise to a review of budget decisions from the Budget Bureau and the President's economic advisers, as well as the State Department and the Arms Control and Disarmament Agency. The NSC system itself was designed to take into account the views of the State Department and other government agencies about military commitments, bases, overseas departments and military assistance. At the same time, these efforts assured the military of orderly consideration of its views, reflecting the judgment that the military is more willing to participate faithfully in the implementation of a decision where it has been overruled if it feels that military views have been fully taken into account.

2. *Military adviser in the White House.* President Franklin Roosevelt relied heavily on Admiral William Leahy as the Chief of Staff to the Commander in Chief. Truman for a brief period continued to use Leahy and then, on a part-time basis, relied on General Eisenhower for advice on budget issues, while Eisenhower was President of Columbia University. Truman later turned to the Chairman of the Joint Chiefs.

Eisenhower, his own military adviser in the White House, had only a junior military officer in the person of Colonel Andrew Goodpaster who functioned in effect as a staff secretary, collecting and summarizing for the President intelligence materials from the State Department and the CIA, as well as the military.

Kennedy, after the Bay of Pigs operation, brought General Maxwell Taylor into the White House as the military representative of the President, and Taylor advised the President on a broad range of issues involving all aspects of national security policy. When Taylor moved over to become Chairman of the Joint Chiefs, a JCS liaison office was created in the White House, working primarily with the President's Assistant for National Security Affairs.

President Johnson relied primarily on other mechanisms but did use General Taylor as a White House consultant after his return from Vietnam. Taylor functioned in relation to the Vietnam issue, providing an alternate source of advice and information to the President on options open to him in Vietnam operations and negotiations.

President Nixon recalled General Goodpaster briefly during the transition period and the very early days of his administration, but since then has not had a senior military adviser in the White House. Henry Kissinger's deputy is an army major-general. He ensures, along with the JCS liaison office, that Kissinger and the President are aware of JCS concerns, but he does not serve as an alternate source of military advice.

3. *A civilian adviser in the White House.* There has been a growing trend in the postwar period toward presidential reliance on White House staff assistance in both domestic and national security policy. In the National Security field, civilian assistance has been used not only as a source of additional information, advice and options, but also as an aid to the President in seeing that his decisions are carried through.

Truman tended to rely on his cabinet officers and the uniformed military, but there were episodic interventions by civilians in the White House. Under Truman, Clark Clifford became heavily involved in the negotiations leading to the Defense Unification Act and the National Security Council system. Later he contributed to the creation of the Atomic Energy Commission and the continued control of atomic weapons by the Commission. Averell Harriman, who became Truman's national security adviser just before the Korean War, functioned briefly during the early stages of the war as a spokesman for the President's position; his tasks included a visit to General MacArthur to explain the President's policies to him and seek his compliance.

Eisenhower had no single national security adviser in the White House. His Assistants for National Security Council Affairs were involved only in the very limited number of issues that were handled in the rather stylized machinery of the National Security Council system as then constituted. Eisenhower brought in several advisers for specific issues, including Nelson Rockefeller, but these advisers tended to interact and overlap with Secretary of State Dulles rather than with the Department of Defense. They were responsible for some new initiatives, such as Eisenhower's "open skies" proposal in 1954, but the instances are few.

The regularization and institutionalization of a civilian adviser in the White House on national security matters came with President Kennedy's appointment of McGeorge Bundy. Bundy, following the Bay of Pigs fiasco, moved to increase the independence of the White House in securing information by arranging to get a good deal of the raw material directly from the field, including State, Defense and CIA cable traffic. Bundy also assumed primary responsibility for briefing the President. Despite the expanded role which involved them in many foreign policy matters with military implications, neither Bundy nor Walt Rostow, Johnson's adviser for national security affairs, were heavily engaged in Defense budget matters. Under President Nixon, Henry Kissinger has been as active in Defense Department matters as he is in those for which the State Department has primary responsibility. Nixon appears to rely upon Kissinger as an alternative source of information and options on the broad range of military and national security matters, and as a channel for various kinds of military advice.

4. *Reliance on the Secretary of Defense.* Truman and Eisenhower tended to rely on their Secretaries of Defense primarily to secure the implementation of their decisions, particularly Defense budget decisions. They expected the Secretaries to bear the weight of military objections to ceilings on defense spending and to force the services to develop forces within those ceilings. Even in this role the Defense Secretaries were of limited value to the President since they tended to become spokesmen for the military desire for increased spending.

The appointment of Robert S. McNamara brought to fruition a trend which had been developing gradually and had accelerated during the brief tenure of Secretary Thomas Gates. This called for the Secretary of Defense to become in effect the principal military adviser to the President, superseding the Joint Chiefs. Over time Kennedy and Johnson, at least until the Vietnam war accelerated in late 1965, tended to look to the Secretary of Defense for advice on commitments, bases, overseas deployments and military aid, as well as budget decisions. The Secretary's job included absorbing the advice tendered by the military and combining that in his recommendations to the President. Both Kennedy and Johnson did, of course, continue to meet with the Chairman of the Joint Chiefs in formal sessions of the National Security Council and in other meetings, but by and large they received military judgments and advice through the filter of the Secretary of Defense. As the Vietnam war heated up, JCS Chairman General Earle Wheeler was included in Johnson's regular Tuesday lunches and began to act as an independent vehicle for reporting JCS views to the President, at least on the range of issues discussed at those meetings. Defense Secretary Laird has continued the tradition of taking positions on substantive issues of military policy and operations, as well as defense budget issues, although the President seems to regard him simply as a second source of advice on military questions. The Secretary and the Joint Chiefs have a co-equal role in the National Security Council and in all of its subordinate institutions.

5. *Reliance on the Secretary of State.* No President has given the Secretary of State a dominant role in decisions regarding combat operations or the defense budget. Truman did call on General Marshall—when he was Secretary of State—for support in keeping the Defense budget down, and Nixon has brought the Secretary's staff into the Defense budget process through the Defense Program Review Committee. However, on issues concerning commitments, bases, overseas deployments and military aid, Truman tended to rely largely on Acheson's judgment, and Eisenhower depended to a large extent on Dulles. Secretary Rusk played a major role in these issues along with Secretary McNamara.

6. *Reliance on scientists.* Although scientists have occasionally been used to evaluate combat operations, by and large their role has been limited to issues reflected in the Defense budget. Eisenhower depended, particularly in the later years of his administration, on the chief scientist in the Pentagon (the Director of Defense Research and Engineering) and on his science advisers. Kennedy also

looked to his science adviser, Jerome Wiesner, for alternate advice on the Defense budget, as well as on arms-control matters, particularly relating to the nuclear testing issue. The role of the science advisers seems to have declined precipitously under Johnson and Nixon, with their energies going largely to non-Defense matters.

7. *Reliance on the Bureau of the Budget.* The role of the Budget Bureau (now Office of Management and Budget) in Defense decisions has been very limited. Truman and Eisenhower relied upon the Budget Director to help set a ceiling on Defense spending, but the Bureau did not get involved in deciding how that money would be spent. Under Eisenhower, Kennedy and Johnson it became a matter of tradition that the Budget Director would have to appeal Secretarial decisions on the Defense budget to the President, the reverse of the situation in all other departments. Press reports suggested that initially Nixon had reversed this process, but he now appears to have returned to this traditional pattern. The Budget Director sits on the Defense Program Review Committee, but the extent of Budget Bureau influence is difficult to determine.

8. *Ad hoc techniques.* Presidents have used a number of ad hoc or special techniques to secure information and options on military questions. One technique frequently used during the Truman and Eisenhower periods was the President-appointed commission. Nixon's Fitzhugh Panel may mark a return to the use of this technique, although it has thus far been limited to organizational rather than substantive questions.

Occasionally, Presidents have sent special representatives into the field to investigate military questions. Kennedy, for example, sent an old friend and military officer to the camp preparing the Cuban guerrillas for the Bay of Pigs operations, and Richard Nixon sent British guerrilla war expert Brigadier General Thompson to Vietnam for an independent assessment.

Now and then a President has been fortunate enough to have the concurrence of the military on a particular policy, without having to bargain. That the Joint Chiefs of Staff opposed expansion of the Korean War and felt that General MacArthur had indeed been insubordinate was of critical importance to Truman in securing public acceptance of this policy. However, in most cases, the President has been forced to bargain for the public support of the Joint Chiefs. Truman had to accept the case for German rearmament in order to gain JCS approval to send American forces to Europe. Kennedy and his Secretary of Defense engaged in long hours of bargaining with the Joint Chiefs before they were able to devise an acceptable safeguard program of standby preparations for nuclear testing that made it possible for the Joint Chiefs to give their reluctant support to the Nuclear Test Ban Treaty. Johnson felt obliged to have the Joint Chiefs of Staff on board before he would order the cessation of the bombing of North Vietnam in 1968.

In some cases, the President has sought to use the prestige and power of his office to accomplish his objectives in the face of military opposition. This tactic has a better chance of success when the decisions involve only executive department action; when the Chiefs are split; and particularly when the decisions do not require the use of armed forces in combat operations. But it can be done in other cases. For example, on the matter of civilian control of atomic weapons and the creation of a civilian-dominated Atomic Energy Commission, Truman appealed to the public and Congress over the objections of the military, and was able to win. Eisenhower in the same way (although less successfully) enlisted the support of the American business community in his effort to reorganize the Defense Department against the judgment of the military.

Presidents have had the greatest success in bypassing the military on Defense budget limitations, because military demands are essentially open-ended and always have to be overruled. However, the appeal to fiscal conservatism and alternative demands for resources have also tended to check defense expenditures.

III

Techniques used to improve the information and options reaching the President can also be applied to the implementation of decisions. For example, civilian advisers in the White House have been used to monitor compliance with presidential decisions, and other Presidents have tended to rely on the Secretary of Defense to see that their decisions were carried out.

In addition, Presidents have sometimes resorted to selecting military officers who they felt shared their views and therefore would act to implement them properly. The most dramatic case came in 1953 when Eisenhower replaced all of the Joint Chiefs of Staff and appointed Admiral Radford, a known supporter of his policy of massive nuclear retaliation, as the Chairman of the Joint Chiefs and chose service chiefs who by and large were prepared to comply. After the Cuban missile crisis, Admiral George Anderson, who had not cooperated fully with the President, was not reappointed to the post of Chief of Naval Operations. However, there are severe limits to the value of such actions: General Ridgway and later General Taylor, the Army Chiefs of Staff appointed by Eisenhower, resisted the reduction in the size of the Army and the Administration's reliance on massive nuclear retaliation. When their views were ignored they resigned and protested publicly. In response to Admiral Anderson's reassignment as Ambassador to Portugal, Congress legislated statutory terms for the members of the Joint Chiefs.

Another technique that has been used to increase compliance with presidential decisions is the creation of new organizations which reflect new desires. The most successful such effort was to create within the Navy a Special Projects Office to monitor the Polaris submarine and to alter promotion procedures so that command of a Polaris submarine would permit promotion to senior grades.

The least successful effort was Kennedy's attempt in the early 1960s to give the military a greater flexibility in dealing with counterinsurgency operations by creating the Green Berets.

IV

The decline of the prestige of the military over the past several years has given President Nixon and his successors greater freedom to determine how advice from the military reaches them, and to accept or reject that advice. The experience of the postwar period suggests two basic changes which the President could institute now that would increase his leverage vis-à-vis the military—one involving the channel by which he receives advice from senior military officers and the other concerning the role of civilian advisers.

The experience of the last 25 years suggests that the effort to reorganize the Pentagon and then to demand "unified" military advice from the Joint Chiefs of Staff has been a failure. As noted above, most observers who have had the opportunity to view the product of the Joint Chiefs would argue that unified JCS papers reflect either a compromise among the services, a form of logrolling in which the proposals of all services are endorsed, or deference to the service or field commander most concerned. As long as the function of the Joint Staff is to come up with a paper that will be endorsed by all of the Chiefs, there does not appear to be any way to alter the situation fundamentally, although some progress has been made in the last several years in increasing the flexibility and independence of the Joint Staff.

More radical changes must be effected if the President is to get good military advice. The key to improving the situation is to separate the Chairman of the Joint Chiefs of Staff and the Joint Staff from the Service Chiefs. The President and the Secretary of Defense would in this case solicit the separate views of each of the Service Chiefs and of the Chairman of the Joint Chiefs, and where appropriate, the views of the relevant unified and specified commanders (*e.g.* commanders in Europe and Asia and the head of the Strategic Air Command). These latter views might be chanelled to the Secretary through the Chairman of the Joint Chiefs. The Chairman would, in turn, be the officer in the line of command through the President and the Secretary of Defense to the commanders (bypassing the Service Chiefs) for carrying out operations in the field.

The basic rationale behind this change in procedure is that the Service Chiefs and the unified and specified commands constitute the highest level at which reliable (first-hand) information and advice are available. The Joint Staff, when it needs information, must solicit either the service staffs in Washington or the field commanders. In fact, JCS information and advice presented to the President and the Secretary usually come from the services and the subordinate service commands in the field. For example, most of the positions taken by the

Joint Chiefs of Staff on questions relating to Vietnam simply involved a JCS endorsement of the recommendations of General Westmoreland or General Abrams, the army commanders in Vietnam, and Admiral Sharp, Commander in Chief of the Pacific, who had particular responsibility for the bombing operations.

On questions of requirements for overseas bases, to take another example, the Joint Chiefs in most cases simply endorse the position of the Service which utilizes the base. On budget issues, the Chiefs tend to endorse all of the programs desired by each of the services. When forced to choose on an issue of policy the Chiefs compromise among the different Service positions rather than attempting to develop a position based on a unified military point of view.

Under the proposed change of procedure the President and the Secretary of Defense would be made aware of differing positions which might otherwise be compromised. In addition this would leave the Chairman of the Joint Chiefs and the Joint Staff free from the job of developing a compromise position and therefore able to present the Secretary of Defense with a military judgment separate from the interests of the Services. If this process is to succeed the President and the Secretary will have to choose a Chairman of the Joint Chiefs with whom they can work. Then, if the system is developed properly, the Chairman and the Joint Staff would come to be seen as part of the Office of the Secretary of Defense, providing him and the President with military advice which could be weighed against the advice of the operators—the Service Chiefs and the unified and specified commanders. The influence of the Chairman would come from his record of persuasiveness with the President and the Secretary of Defense. They will take his judgments seriously if his choice is shown to be based on a broader range of considerations than the advice of the Service Chiefs.

Such a procedure would increase the probability that imaginative and innovative proposals would reach the President. It would also make it more likely that the President would become aware of the wide diversity of military opinions on a question and not act on an erroneous assumption that there was a unified view.

One of the few instances on record in which the President did seek separate opinions from the several Chiefs came in 1961 when President Kennedy was contemplating an invasion of Laos. Partly because of the Bay of Pigs episode in which the doubts of individual Chiefs about the military feasibility of the landing in Cuba never reached him, Kennedy asked each Chief separately for his views in writing and then met with them as a group. He discovered by this process that each one had a slightly different position on what should be done, what troops should be committed, and what the likely outcome of American intervention would be. Receiving this conflicting advice, it was harder for Kennedy to make a decision to intervene but it also meant that he did not make a decision under a mistaken impression that there was a unified military view either for or against the intervention.

The proposed procedure would also increase presidential flexibility in accepting or rejecting military advice because he would no longer be confronted with a unanimous but misleading statement of JCS views. He would be able to choose among service and command viewpoints rather than having to develop a new position which in essence overrules all of the military, in as much as JCS opinions now represent all the services.

In order to increase the President's freedom to choose and the likelihood that he will get faithful implementation and political support for his actions, a procedure should be developed which provides for military access to the President on issues of importance to the military. Access should be provided not only for the Chairman of the Joint Chiefs, but also for the Service Chiefs and the unified commanders most concerned. When he finds it necessary to overrule the military, the President should justify his decision on broad political grounds; he should be seen doing so personally; and he should do so in writing with a clear memorandum stating his position. All of these acts would increase military willingness to go along with presidential decisions and to implement them faithfully.

The military takes seriously the President's role as Commander in Chief and also recognizes that he has broader responsibility concerned with both domestic and international political situations. They are much more amenable to being overruled on these grounds than to being told that their military judgment is questioned. (For this reason the military resented McNamara's reliance on civilians, particularly in the Office of Systems Analysis, for judgments on what they took to be purely military questions, *i.e.* statements of military requirements.) They also implement decisions faithfully when assured that their position has been heard by the President and it has not been lost in the filter of Secretary of Defense memoranda.

Securing separate advice from the Service Chiefs and other military commanders will require that the President, or at least his White House staff, spend more time digesting the separate positions. However, this seems a price worth paying to increase the flow of new ideas or doubts about proposed courses of action to the White House.

Military compliance with presidential decisions would also be enhanced by avoiding the practice of using the military to seek public support for presidential decisions. The value of such action has become considerably reduced in recent years, and such use of the military tends to legitimize and increase the importance of their opposition when they choose to oppose policy.

V

Implicit in the new procedures as suggested is a reduced role for the Secretary of Defense from that which he assumed in the 1960s. His scope would also be affected by another proposed change—that decision-making on matters concerning Defense budgets and the use of military force be moved outside of the Pentagon and into a broader arena involving officials from the White House and other agencies.

The Nixon administration has moved rather significantly, at least in form and to some extent in substance, to change the locus of decisions. The creation of the Washington Special Action Group (WSAG) brings into existence for the first time a forum in which detailed contingency planning for the actual use of military force is carried out beyond the Pentagon. WSAG is chaired by the President's Assistant for National Security and includes senior State Department and CIA officials as well as civilian and military representatives of the Pentagon. It provides a forum where the military, diplomatic and intelligence evaluations of likely use of American military forces can be brought together in a systematic way, something which was not done in the past. This institution needs to be strengthened, probably with the addition of some White House staff assigned specifically to this task.

A second institution of significance is the Defense Program Review Committee (DPRC), which is also chaired by the President's Assistant for National Security and includes representatives not only from State but also from the Arms Control and Disarmament Agency, the Council of Economic Advisers and the Office of Management and Budget. The implications of this institution are enormous. If it is functioning effectively, decisions not only on the total size of the Defense budget but also on the major Defense programs will be made outside the Pentagon in an interagency forum where White House influence is dominant. The President would be receiving advice on Defense budget issues from several different perspectives. While the institution has been created, it does not appear yet to have either the staff or the necessary top level direction to get into a wide range of Defense issues.

For this purpose and also to make WSAG more effective, the President's Assistant for National Security probably needs a Senior Deputy who would take some of the responsibility for White House direction for budget and combat decisions, and who would be explicitly charged with bringing to bear the broader concerns of the President.

The procedures suggested here in no sense imply a downgrading of military advice. Instead they are designed to assure that the President receives the full range of the existing military opinions rather than what filters through a JCS compromise procedure or a Secretary of Defense responsible for presenting military views to the President. They also aim to give the President critical commentary on military proposals from civilian officials with a different and somewhat broader range of responsibilities. In the end, good decisions will depend on the wisdom and judgment of the President. What he decides, however, is greatly influenced by the information presented to him, as well as by his sense of freedom to choose regardless of strong military and other bureaucratic pressures.

The Good, the Bad, and the Wasteful

There is no clear way to determine how much is enough to spend on defense. Conceptually the question is: How much value do we get on the last defense dollar we spend as compared to the value we might get by other governmental or private expenditures?

No methodology exists to compare the payoff from expenditures on, for example, strategic programs with those on general purpose forces; nor is there any way that we can compare the value of either of these programs with the value of domestic programs or of returning the money to the taxpayers to permit additional private consumption. Thus the question of the size of the defense budget is—within wide limits—essentially arbitrary.

Even at the present relatively high level of U.S. defense expenditures, there is no doubt that additional money spent wisely would increase security. At the same time, there is no question that if we cut wisely and carefully we can make substantial reductions in defense expenditures that have little detrimental impact on our security. Moreover, because we do not always spend wisely, *some* increases in expenditures could detract from our security by increasing risks and *some* reductions might actually increase our security.

How Much For Defense?

There have been a number of attempts to come to grips with the problem of the size of the defense budget by proposing changes in our foreign or defense policy.[1] However, alterations of American policy will not necessarily bring about reductions in defense spending. Changing foreign policy or defense policy does not automatically lead to changes in defense expenditures.

For example, the Nixon Administration has announced a change in our general purpose forces requirements from the so-called two and a half war strategy to the so-called one and half war strategy. While to some this means that a substantial reduction in defense expenditures is possible, the view of many military men is quite different. A number of military planners conclude that there is now simply a smaller gap between the forces required to meet our stated objectives and the forces we have available. They still believe that we need a substantial increase (rather than a reduction) in general purpose forces. The

Reprinted, with permission, from *Foreign Policy*, Number 6, Spring 1972, © 1972 by National Affairs, Inc.

uncertainty about the forces required to meet any contingency is, in fact, far greater than the difference between planning for two and a half wars and planning for one and a half wars. Thus a change of doctrine does not *per se* lead to any change in the over-all defense budget.

To take another example of a narrower change in doctrine: there is much discussion of the so-called triad, that is, the three separate strategic systems—land-based missiles, sea-based missiles and bombers—designed to deter a Soviet nuclear attack on the United States. Many have advocated that we go from a triad to a dual or even a single strategic system concentrated on submarine-based nuclear weapons. Once more, however, a change of this kind will not translate directly into a change in the budget. If we decided to go from three to two systems, maintaining the bombers along with the sea-based missiles, there would be increased pressure to go forward with accelerated production of the B-1 Bomber and of an ABM system to protect bomber bases. These steps could more than wipe out the saving from phasing out land-based missiles. Similarly if we went to a single sea-based system the pressure to proceed immediately with ULMs[2] would be very great and there would undoubtedly be a substantial increase in anti-submarine warfare (ASW) research and development.

Cancellation of specific weapons programs does not lead automatically to reductions in the defense budget. Of course, in any given year the over-all budget can be cut by cutting particular programs, but the reductions will not be permanent. The Navy budget for tactical air illustrates this point. The cancellation of the F-111B in 1968 might have been expected to lead to substantial savings. In fact it led to an accelerated F-14 program, which over a five year period will not yield any net reduction in Navy expenditures. Even when the trade-off is not that direct, there are numerous programs within the defense budget which military planners believe are under-financed and which would soak up funds saved from any particular program *unless* at the same time an over-all budget ceiling were enforced.

Thus, the size of the defense budget is substantially independent of decisions over policy, doctrine, and specific weapons programs. One is forced to the conclusion that an arbitrary ceiling on defense budget authorizations and annual expenditures is necessary to control the size of defense spending.

All of our postwar Presidents and Secretaries of Defense have concluded that the only way they could control the size of the defense budget was to provide the military services with an arbitrary ceiling based on Presidential calculations of revenue and domestic needs. Presidents Truman, Eisenhower and Nixon have explicitly provided the services with budget ceilings. During the 1960s there was an attempt to deny that ceilings existed; however, a close look at how the defense budget was developed reveals that there was an implicit ceiling provided to the Secretary of Defense by Presidents Kennedy and Johnson. If Secretaries of Defense and Presidents have concluded that the only way to get a handle on the total size of the defense budget is to provide an arbitrary ceiling, then the case for the same approach is even stronger for congressional committees and for the general public.

To establish a sensible ceiling, one needs first to make an evaluation of expected government revenues at full employment and an estimate of required expenditures for domestic programs. Then and only then can one estimate revenues available for defense. On this basis, it would be useful if the Congress would on an annual basis identify trends in defense spending and give an indication of the ceilings which it believes should be imposed on defense funds. A group of senators and congressmen have sought to impose a spending ceiling for fiscal year 1972 of $68 billion. All things considered, this appears to be a reasonable limit.

For What Forces?

A second and equally important question is the shape of the defense program. Setting a dollar ceiling is not enough. We must also be concerned about how the money within that ceiling is spent. Here our problems are no simpler. There is no known way to calculate the precise impact of different force structures on our security, the probability of war, or the outcome if war occurs. Such decisions depend primarily on intuitive judgments which military officers and civilian analysts are no better equipped than others to make. Hence we cannot leave these decisions entirely to the military, or to bargaining between civilian and military leaders in the executive branch.

The experience of the post-World War II period, and in particular of the last two or three years, suggests that giving authority to the military services to determine how the defense budget will be spent will produce three or four separate military strategies and force structures rather than an over-all structure based on a unified view. Each service—Army, Navy or Air Force—will emphasize programs related to what it sees as the essence of its own unique role. Each will tend to emphasize sophisticated hardware for combat operations, at the cost of manpower. Each will tend to ignore the capabilities of other services and to neglect inter-service programs. For example, in determining requirements for carrier-based air the Navy will tend to ignore Air Force tactical air and the reverse will be true for the Air Force. Both services will tend to give little attention to the lift requirements of the Army. These problems, which were well understood in the 1950s, seem to be emerging again with the tendency to delegate authority for the shape of the defense budget to the military services. Such delegation will not produce the most effective military capability within any given budget ceiling.

Allowing the shape of the budget to be determined by bargaining between senior officials of the executive branch and the military is nearly as unsatisfactory as leaving such decisions entirely in military hands. Certainly this is true when, as at present, the civilian leadership has explicitly abdicated to the Services the primary responsibility for determining the allocation of resources within a fixed ceiling. But even if civilian leaders in the Pentagon and the White House are closely reviewing particular programs, Congress and the public can and should make their own evaluations. The experience of the military and the analytic techniques of the civilians are not, separately or even together, an adequate substitute for political judgment. Congress and the public must make their own assessments of the great uncertainties involved, and determine which risks the American people should run.

In thinking about the shaping of the defense budget I believe it is useful to identify in one's own mind three categories of weapons which, at the risk of sounding frivolous, I will label the "good," the "bad," and the "just plain wasteful."

By "good" I mean those programs which have a high marginal return in that they reduce the probability of war, programs which should be maintained even if defense budgets are cut. The military services may attach less importance to them than would someone with a broader perspective. They also must be protected against the danger that Congress will cut them because they are visible. For example, substantially reducing military forces in Europe would, in my view, be cutting out the part of the defense budget which brings perhaps the highest return for our security.

The "bad" refers to those programs which make a negative contribution to our security. For example, many believe that the MIRV and ABM programs, by stimulating the strategic arms race, in fact increase the danger of nuclear war rather than reduce it.

The "wasteful" refers to those programs which, at current levels, appear to be excessive to our needs and hence could be cut. However, they are not programs which seem to reduce our security by increasing the probability of war or by stimulating an arms race.

In seeking to cut the over-all size of the defense budget, it is important to be sure that cuts in over-all spending do not lead the Services or the Congress to cut out programs which are good. But reductions in defense spending do not always lead to the elimination of programs that one considers "bad." For example, President Nixon in 1969 substantially reduced spending on strategic programs and nevertheless continued the MIRV and ABM programs, which reduce our security. Some weapons programs may be relatively inexpensive and yet threaten stability. Programs to improve the accuracy of our missiles are not costly, but by threatening the Soviet deterrent they could stimulate a further arms race. Thus, in considering the shape of the defense program one needs to focus particularly on (1) those "good" programs which need to be protected as the budget is cut; (2) those "bad" programs which need to be eliminated even if their cost is small; and (3) "wasteful" programs.

The rational insights available to us in evaluating specific programs are quite limited. In general, we are not in a position to say with any precision how changes in defense policy, or in the design of our forces, will affect our security. For example, if we first decide that we want a manned bomber force through the 1970s, then we can compare the B-52 with the B-1. Such analyses are important but concentration on them can lead to ignoring more fundamental questions. In considering our requirements for general purpose and strategic forces we need to keep in mind the main objectives—the probability of war or the results if war occurs—and our limited understanding of what affects them.

Deterrence depends on influencing the decisions of other governments. We have a very poor understanding of how our force structure is perceived by potential adversaries and how it affects their decisions.

War outcome calculations are fraught with uncertainties. In the case of strategic forces, the calculations of war outcome used to test their adequacy assume an unlikely scenario: that the Soviets will fire all of their weapons at American forces and that we will then respond by firing all of our weapons at their cities. In the case of general purpose forces, there is no agreed methodology for *any* calculations. We simply do not know how war outcomes are affected by alternative force structures.

A closer look at both general purpose and strategic forces will serve to illustrate this range of uncertainty.

General Purpose Forces

General purpose forces, excluding expenditures for Vietnam, account for approximately 65 percent of the 1971-72 defense budget. Since these forces are designed to protect countries other than the United States, the requirement for these forces depends basically on political decisions about which nations we wish to be in a position to defend against what threats. Fundamental changes in our answers to those questions could lead to big changes in the defense budget. If the United States made a firm decision that it would never fight again on the Asian mainland (or would fight only in Korea) this could (but need not) lead to a major reduction in force requirements. Short of such fundamental change, alterations in foreign policy have very little impact on the required size of the defense budget.

At a slightly less general level of defense policy, there are a number of key issues (identified in a recent paper by Arnold Kuzmack) requiring judgment which can have substantial impact on the requirements for general purpose forces. Some of these are:

1. Tactical Nuclear Weapons

During the Eisenhower Administration American defense policy was derived from a decision to rely on the use of tactical nuclear weapons in the event of any combat which involved large numbers of American forces. If the United States were to return to such a position, and if we were to conclude that tactical nuclear weapons could be used effectively against larger enemy attacks in likely contingencies, then it would be possible to slash the size of general purpose forces. Spending for such forces could be considerably reduced from its current level of $50 billion.

The major uncertainties here concern both the political implications of using tactical nuclear weapons and the likely effect of their use particularly in circumstances in which the potential opponent also has nuclear weapons available. The evidence of the past two decades is that there may be military pressure to use nuclear weapons but there will also be enormous political pressures against the use of nuclear weapons in any limited war situation; thus it would appear reckless to rely on a Presidential decision that such weapons would be used. Moreover, continuing analysis of the problem suggests that even "tactical" nuclear weapons could cause enormous damage to friendly territory, that they are less effective than some may have believed, and that there is no particular advantage to the United States in using them in a situation in which the potential opponent also has access to nuclear weapons.

2. Simultaneity of Requirements

The decision to go from a two and a half war to a one and a half war strategy did not reflect a determination to prepare for war only in Europe. Rather it was a decision not to prepare for war in Europe and Asia at the same time. The judgment was apparently made that war in Europe and Asia were not likely to begin simultaneously in view of the substantially reduced possibility that there would be a coordinated Chinese and Soviet attack. Decisions about simultaneity are by themselves significantly less important than other factors being discussed here in determining the size of the general purpose force budget. They are also essentially arbitrary.

3. Length of War

The Department of Defense does not appear to have made a firm and clear decision about how long a war it is preparing for in either Europe or Asia. On the central front in Europe most of our allies seem to assume that a conventional war would be over in a very few days. American planning, particularly for the procurement of ammunition, seems to be based on the assumption that a war in Europe might last as long as 90 days but no longer. However, other components of our forces are procured as if a war in Europe might go on indefinitely. For example, an Army division of 16,000 fighting men requires an additional 16,000 men for initial support for a period of up to 90 days but requires a second increment of 16,000 men for sustained support over an extended period of time. Both increments are maintained for all of our NATO-oriented divisions. Our requirements for naval forces are also based on an assumption that a war in Europe might go on indefinitely. A serious decision to act on the assumption that a conventional war in Europe could not possibly last more than 90 days would permit substantial savings. On the other hand, if we took seriously the need to be able to fight indefinitely in Europe, and sought to get our allies to agree, there would be requirements for substantially increased expenditures. The costs involved in not preparing to fight for more than 90 days must be weighed against the effect, if any, on deterrence and possible outcomes if war occurs.

4. Mobilization Lead Time

Our emphasis in the post-World War II period has, by and large, been on forces available on the day that a war begins. In the past, of course, the United States relied very substantially on mobilization to develop needed capabilities in wartime. If the political judgment was reached that a war in Europe or Asia would develop only slowly after a period of political warning, the United States could reduce its number of active divisions and rely on mobilization of reserve divisions for combat. Here again, the decision involves a broad political judgment: Will our leaders be able to determine war probabilities in advance and will they be prepared to act on the basis of such a warning?

5. Forward Defense

Another critical criterion which affects the required size of general purpose forces is where we wish to hold ground. For example if, in the event of a Soviet attack in Europe, we want to hold at the Eastern German border—or in the case of a Chinese attack on Thailand, on the Thai-Chinese border—requirements for general purpose forces, particularly forces in being, are much larger than if we are willing to plan on holding an alternative line which involves some retreat. We would, in the latter case, plan to mobilize and counterattack. Would such a posture increase the risk of war? How do we weigh peacetime costs of preparing to hold a forward line against the increased wartime costs of capturing lost territory?

6. Confidence Levels

Military planning to develop requirements for any particular contingency is generally based on very conservative assumptions about the limited capability of allied forces against a "maximum" capability of enemy forces. The "requirements" also assume that our objective is to have high confidence that we can defeat the enemy and defend the territory under attack. An alternate possible criterion is to view the problem as one of deterrence. If we need sufficient forces to deter the enemy from launching an attack, it is possible that we need only to deny the enemy any substantial confidence that his attack can be successful. Such a change in planning definitions would focus on forces large enough so that the enemy could not calculate that victory was likely in any finite period. This approach could lead to large reductions in the need for general purpose forces.

Judgments about simultaneity, length of war, mobilization lead time, forward defense, and confidence levels can lead to specific decisions in some narrow areas such as ammunition stockpiles. However, their impact on determining over-all force requirements is limited because of a lack of any agreed method for determining the relationship between opposing force structures and war outcomes. For example, the question of the relative balance of forces on the Central Front in Europe has been studied more often, more intensively, and by more groups than any other defense question. Yet the differences of opinion remain enormous—ranging from the view that NATO forces are in all important respects equal to those of the Warsaw Pact to the view that the Soviets could sweep across Western Europe in a few days. To take another example, we have recently been warned of the dangerous growth of Soviet naval power. Comparing the two navies, we find that the United States continues to spend the bulk of its naval funds to procure, maintain, and defend aircraft carriers while the Soviets have only two small helicopter carriers. Would likely war outcomes be improved by switching to a force which imitated that of the Soviet Navy? Few U.S. Naval officers would favor such a move and yet they remain concerned about the Soviet forces.

Even more uncertain is the relationship between force structures and deterrence of attack. We do not know what the Soviet evaluation of forces on the Central Front is, nor how it would be affected by possible changes in force structure. In Asia, where we have several potential opponents, the relation is even less clear. Certainly the substantial American build-up of our capability to intervene in conventional and insurgency warfare in the early 1960s did not deter enemy moves in Vietnam.

Overspending or spending on the wrong general purpose forces raise questions of "waste" rather than of "bad" consequences since larger American general purpose forces do not appear to stimulate an arms race or increase the probability of war.

Strategic Forces

Strategic forces raise crucial questions of good and bad consequences. The amount of money which can be saved by likely and reasonable alterations in strategic programs is not very large in the context of the total defense budget. More than half of the costs of strategic forces are indirect costs for intelligence and communications, Research and Development (R&D), and support. Direct costs amount to only $7.6 billion of the $19.7 billion total for fiscal year 1972. It is difficult to relate reductions in indirect expenses to changes in the direct costs. The range of plausible strategic budgets would appear to go from $13 billion for a single weapons system with limited modernization to perhaps $22 or $23 billion for a triad with extensive modernization and a new bomber and a nation-wide ABM system.

Our major objective in designing strategic forces is to reduce the probability of a Soviet nuclear attack on the United States. In order to do calculations about this, U.S. defense analysts make two major simplifying assumptions. We assume that the Soviet leaders' decision to launch nuclear war will depend on the amount of damage the United States can inflict on the Soviet Union after a Soviet first strike. We also assume that the Soviets calculate war outcomes in the same way that we do. Although the SALT discussions have to some extent clarified Soviet views, we still have no real basis for determining how our strategic force decisions affect the probability of nuclear war. Our calculations do not take into account at all the damage which our airplanes based in Europe, or on carriers, could inflict on the Soviet Union. Yet the Soviet leaders are sufficiently concerned about these forces to insist that they be included in any comprehensive arms control agreement. Nor do we really know how to calculate war outcomes, if indeed such calculations have any meaning in a war in which more than 40 million Americans would be killed.

Despite the changes made by the Nixon Administration in developing the concept of "sufficiency," the cornerstone of strategic policy remains the notion of Assured Destruction—confidence in our ability to kill many Russians after a Soviet first strike. We maintain three separate strategic systems—the land-based ICBMs, sea-based ballistic missiles, and intercontinental bombers, each separately capable of inflicting massive damage on the Soviet Union amounting to at least 25 percent of the population and 50 percent of Soviet industry. Each of the three forces is now invulnerable to a Soviet attack. The Soviets have no way of locating and destroying American Polaris submarines. Their intercontinental missile force is neither large enough nor accurate enough to destroy our fixed land-based missiles. Our bombers are capable of getting up in the air in less than 15 minutes and hence they can be airborne upon receiving warning of Soviet ICBM attack. As the Soviet fleet of submarines carrying ballistic missiles increases, a large part of our bomber force will be subject to destruction on the ground since they would get less than 15 minutes warning. In the long run if the Soviets develop accurate MIRVs for their SS-9 missiles the Minuteman force could also become vulnerable to destruction.

These threats to the bomber and land-based missile forces have raised the question of whether or not the United States needs to continue to maintain a "triad." The argument for the triad is that it adds to our confidence that we can deter Soviet attack and prevents the Soviets from concentrating their R&D in a single area in order to achieve a breakthrough which would make any single force vulnerable. On the other side it is argued that there is no prospect of the submarine force becoming vulnerable and that destruction that can be done by even a small number of surviving submarines is sufficient to deter a Soviet attack.

Against these uncertainties, the best way to proceed would be to rely primarily on the Polaris missile force as the backbone of the American deterrent, while maintaining the other two systems without spending substantial sums on their modernization or improvement.

Conclusion

The choices that need to be made are difficult ones and the consequences serious. If we spend on "bad" forces the results could be catastrophic regardless of the size of the budget. Increased spending thus may not be an effective hedge against uncertainty. Cutting the budget, while it frees funds for domestic programs, could be dangerous if we cut the "good" or fail to cut the "bad."

As complicated as the problems are and as fateful the consequences, choices must and will be made. We should not assume that the President or his principal advisers have access to information that enables them to make better decisions than members of the Congress and the public. The decisions turn largely on matters of judgment and choice as to what risks we should run. The question of security is above all a *political*, not a *technical* question. And in a democracy it is no less a matter for public debate and decision than how much to spend on schools and policemen, farmers and pensioners. Indeed, when it comes to determining the size of the budget a knowledge of the rot of our cities and the domestic despair of many Americans is as important and relevant as the esoterica of military analysts.

Notes

1. See Paul C. Warnke and Leslie H. Gelb "Security or Confrontation: The Case for a Defense Policy," *Foreign Policy* No. 1. (Winter 1970-71) pp. 6-30; and Graham Allison et al., "Limits to Intervention" *Foreign Affairs* (January 1970).

2. Undersea-Launched Missile Submarine (ULMS) is a proposed new submarine to replace those that now carry the Polaris missiles. It would carry a new larger missile.

8

Secrecy and Covert Intelligence Collection and Operations*

We aim in this chapter to assess the effects of secrecy on the conduct of American covert intelligence collection and covert operations, and the effects of those programs on American society and foreign policy. We begin with a description of the structure by which the executive branch plans and carries out covert intelligence collection and operations and then briefly discuss covert activities in which the United States has engaged since World War II. This is followed by an analysis of the costs of such operations, with particular emphasis on the decision-making within the executive branch, the effect on American society, and the effects on American foreign policy. We conclude with an analysis of the covert operations and intelligence programs and some specific recommendations.

I. The Structure of Covert Intelligence and Operations

The only Congressional authorization for covert intelligence operations is contained in the Congressional Act of 1947, which created the entire national security system as well as the Central Intelligence Agency. The Act listed the primary functions of the CIA as advising the National Security Council on intelligence matters and correlating and evaluating intelligence related to national security. The fifth item listed under the functions of the CIA, under the direction of the National Security Council, was: "to perform such other functions and duties related to intelligence affecting the national security as the National Security Council may from time to time direct."

Based upon this very general Congressional authority, Presidents have authorized the CIA to engage in covert intelligence collection and covert operations. Over the years, a structure has grown up within the American government for devising such programs and for implementing them.

At the heart of the covert operations is the CIA. Within the CIA such operations are centered in the "Plans Directorate," under the Deputy Director of

From *None of Your Business: Government Secrecy in America*, edited by Norman Dorsen and Stephen Gillers. Copyright © 1974 by the Committee for Public Justice. Reprinted by permission of The Viking Press, Inc. This article was presented at a conference on government secrecy sponsored by the Committee for Public Justice and the Arthur Garfield Hays Civil Liberties Program of the New York University School of Law.

*Coauthored with Jeremy J. Stone.

the CIA for Plans (known as the DDP). Under the DDP there is an assistant in charge of each region of the world and operators dealing with particular countries or areas. These officials are drawn largely from a career service of covert operators within the CIA. This group is distinct from the career intelligence analysts, who serve only in Washington and only in the evaluation of intelligence material. The covert operators (who have a "cover" identification indicating that they work for the Department of Defense, the State Department, or some other agency or private organization) alternate between assignments in the CIA headquarters in Langley, Virginia, and assignments overseas.

American embassies have a separate section staffed by career covert intelligence operators from the CIA. The head of this unit, who is one of the senior officials of the embassy below the ambassador, is known as the CAS (apparently standing for Chief at Station). This unit maintains its own communications systems with Washington. In friendly countries, its members often operate as liaison with the local intelligence services, but in all cases they are available for the planning of covert intelligence collection and operations.

The only other resources known to be in the field to conduct covert intelligence operations are the military attachés attached to most American embassies. In addition, the service intelligence divisions operate intelligence-collection stations on land, and aboard ships and airplanes. Many of these operations are under the auspices of the National Security Agency, the group charged with the collecting of communications signals and their evaluation.

The National Security Council Act provided that other activities should be conducted only when the National Security Council shall direct them from time to time. In fact, procedures have grown up which provide for continuing authorization to the CIA to conduct covert operations and which put the initiative in the hands of the CIA to come forward with proposals. Beginning in the late 1950s, covert intelligence collection and operations have been approved by a committee chaired by the Special Assistant to the President for National Security Affairs. The existence of the committee and its membership have never been publicly announced, and its name (or rather the number by which it is designated) has changed from time to time. It is now apparently known as the Forty Committee, because its duties were redefined in National Security Decision Memorandum number 40.

In addition to the Assistant to the President for National Security Affairs, the members of the Forty Committee are the Deputy Secretary of Defense, the Chairman of the Joint Chiefs of Staff, the Under Secretary of State for Political Affairs, and the Director of Central Intelligence. Each member is staffed by his own department or agency. For the Director of Central Intelligence, the staffing is done by his Deputy Director of Operations and staff; for the Under Secretary of State, by a small group under an Assistant Director of the Bureau of Intelligence and Research in the Department of State; for the Chairman of the Joint Chiefs, by the Special Assistant to the Chairman for Counter Insurgency and Special Activities (SACSA). Until very recently, the Deputy Secretary of Defense was staffed simply by one of his military assistants, who relied primarily on the evaluations from the Joint Chiefs of Staff. It is possible that this function has more recently been taken over by the new Assistant Secretary of Defense for Intelligence. The Chairman of the Forty Committee, the President's Assistant for National Security Affairs, has in the past been staffed simply by a liaison officer assigned by the CIA.

Proposals for covert intelligence collection or operations normally come from the section of the DDP charged with the relevant geographic area, and, after informal discussion among the staffs of the members of the Forty Committee, they are approved by the Committee itself. In some cases, the proposals come from other members of the committee.

Evaluation of the proposals is limited to the members of this Committee and the staffs designated for this purpose. Under normal procedures, a proposal for a covert operation in Latin America, for example, would not be cleared by the State Department desk officer dealing with that Latin American country or by the Deputy Assistant Secretary, or even, in some cases, the Assistant Secretary for Latin American Affairs. Likewise, it would not be cleared by the Regional Deputy Assistant Secretary in the Office of International Security Affairs in the Pentagon, or even by the Assistant Secretary or the military officers in the Joint Staff charged with planning and policy toward the particular Latin American country. Within the CIA itself, proposals for covert operations are normally not staffed by the Intelligence Branch of the CIA charged with collating and evaluating intelligence materials from all sources. In exceptional cases, particular people from these various organizations may be brought in to consult on a particular problem, but only at the sufferance of the officials formally involved.

Covert operations and intelligence-gathering is conducted, then, under a cloak of what we will call Super Secrecy. Executive Order 10501 specifically prohibited any classification other than the three categories it set out ("top secret," "secret," "confidential") and others authorized by law (such as those involving cryptology and atomic energy). Nevertheless, covert operations carry additional classification markings, and access to them depends on an additional set of clearances whose very existence is classified. Thus, information about them is limited very severely, even within the executive branch. Most of this chapter is devoted to an analysis of the consequences of this Super Secrecy for executive-branch decision-making, for the American constitutional system, and for the conduct of American foreign policy.

II. The Range of Covert Intelligence
Collection and Operations

Covert intelligence operations are of many different kinds and raise quite different issues. The best known concern covert intelligence-gathering. At the beginning of the cold war, the United States had planes engaged in short dashes into Soviet territory. Later, the U-2 flights overflew the territory and a special technology was developed for just this purpose. Stationed around the "Communist bloc," there are planes and ships gathering electronic intelligence—information on the planes flying through Soviet airspace, transcripts of the conversations of the pilots in them, characteristics of Soviet radars, information on Soviet space and missile firings, and so on. The *Pueblo*, captured off North Korean shores, was such a ship. More information comes from satellites encircling the globe and transmitting or dropping information to earth. From satellites, very good pictures of the ground can now be developed.

Covert intelligence gathering also involves the more traditional spy, although the relative effectiveness of spying has greatly decreased. Spies run the gamut from agents injected into a foreign territory, to foreigners recruited for this purpose, to paid informers in friendly or neutral governments, to sympathizers of many kinds and degrees. The Soviet colonel Oleg Penkovsky is probably the best-known example of a spy.

Beyond covert intelligence-gathering lie the activities in support of political groups in a foreign country. Here a line is crossed between efforts to get information and efforts to manipulate. Political parties, labor unions, student groups, and military officers, etc., may be given funds, information, or other help in an effort to win influence over them and to advance shared aims. The first such operation was apparently the massive American intervention in the 1948 Italian election. Later, the United States apparently sought to buy votes in the French National Assembly to secure ratification of the European Defense Community Treaty.

Still greater involvement occurs when insurgent movements get covert support. Here, the United States takes a hand in active struggle. Examples include Indonesia in 1948, Tibet after 1949, Cuba under Batista, China immediately after the Communist revolution, and Katanga. In Iran, the United States sponsored a countercoup to restore the Shah.

Still greater support is involved when the United States seeks to give covert aid to foreign military forces. Here we have assistance to the South Vietnamese against the North, to the secret army in Laos, and to the King of Jordan.

At the end of this spectrum lie major covert military operations. In 1949 the United States air-dropped hundreds of agents into Albania in an effort, much like that of the Bay of Pigs (another example), to overthrow the Albanian government. Tipped off by the Soviet spy Harold Philby, the Albanians had no trouble putting down the revolution.

Sometimes, covert operations involve domestic manipulations, and foreign operations abroad require domestic covers. Travel organizations, student organizations, businesses, foundations, and American labor unions may all be asked to help in providing a base for covert CIA operations. Alternately, they may be infiltrated—with few, if any, of their own higher-ups being aware of it.

Lastly, the United States government cannot credibly deny involvement in dramatic attacks or incidents abroad. A coup in Cambodia or an Israeli attack on Lebanon promptly brings charges of CIA involvement.

III. Distortions in Decision-Making

The Super Secrecy system under which decisions about covert operations are made increases the chances that such operations will be chosen over more desirable alternatives, reduces the effectiveness with which they are designed and carried out, distorts decision-making within the executive branch, and reduces the effectiveness of intelligence evaluation.

The Super Secrecy of covert operations increases the chances that the President will choose covert action rather than other, desirable options, which might be adopted given a free and open debate within the executive branch—and even more clearly if the Congress and the public were involved.

American Presidents face multiple audiences. Whatever the President does is seen not only by the foreign group against which he may be directing his action but also by leaders and active groups in other countries, by the Congress, and by the American public. One of the major attractions of covert operations is that with them one avoids the multiple-audience problem. If something is conducted in secret, then one can avoid the fight over means (as well as ends) which erupts when other audiences perceive an ongoing operation. For example, when President Nixon was asked in the summer of 1970 why the United States had been willing to send military forces to Vietnam to prevent the Communist take-over but was not willing to send American military forces to Chile to prevent a Marxist government from coming into power, he replied that the United States could not send military forces to Chile without provoking an adverse political reaction in the rest of Latin America. Though he did not make it clear at the time, it was later revealed that the United States government had engaged in *covert* operations in Chile. These operations avoided the political outcry which would come from an overt step, such as the introduction of American forces.

As compared to alternatives, the necessary approval for covert operations is easier to obtain. The President himself can often usually authorize them without having to go to Congress for funds or to make a public justification. They also seem cheap and easy because they can usually be disavowed, if necessary. Indeed, the working definition of a covert operation appears to be that it is one which can be disavowed with impunity. As with many other aspects of covert operations of this extreme optimism seems to accompany the evaluation of this factor. Thus, in the cases of both the U-2 and the Bay of Pigs, an explicit element of the calculation leading to the authorization of the plan was the belief that it could be disavowed with a cover story if it was discovered.

The mechanism of decision-making also tends to bias the system toward the choosing of covert options. When the United States government is faced with a problem, meetings are held to discuss the range of overt possibilities; they are weighed against each other in an adversary procedure that will permit critics of one proposal to be heard while the proponents of that proposal are present. Covert operations are not discussed at such meetings, but are considered separately at meetings from which advocates of other proposals, and critics of covert operations, are excluded. Indeed, participants in meetings considering overt options are often not aware that covert alternatives are being considered at other meetings. Those advocating covert operations can bring them up through the mechanism of the Forty Committee, and thus do not have to compete for the time and attention of top-level decision-makers.

These same factors serve to reduce efficiency in the design and execution of covert operations. The Super Secrecy increases the probability that covert operations will be designed and implemented poorly and with little regard for the realities of the external world or for appropriate principles of American behavior. Many problems arise precisely because the circle of people involved in covert operations is kept so very small and is limited to people who tend to be sympathetic to such operations.

Other aspects of covert operations add to the general difficulties of getting any operation evaluated by the people responsible for devising it and later responsible for its execution. For example, the "play god" aspect of covert work—involving as it often does intervention in the internal affairs of other nations—tends to attract people who are likely to be insensitive to the difficulties of the work and to its implications for American constitutional procedures. Moreover, the cabalism—the close working relationship between the small number of people involved—substantially reduces the chance that any insider will object to somebody else's favorite scheme. Officials involved from other agencies are often simply on loan from the CIA or intimately connected with CIA operations.

As in all policy areas, the responsible officials have an interest in keeping the number of participants down and to exclude those who are likely to be critics. In covert intelligence operations, a special tool facilitates such exclusion: the special clearances required for such operations. A "top secret" clearance is not sufficient; one must get special clearances the existence of which are not even known to officials who do not have such clearances. Moreover, authority to grant them is in the hands of the officials who manage the programs, who can use this tool to exclude anyone they fear might be skeptical or critical.

Normally, an official observing an ongoing policy which he sees as a threat to his organization's interests, or to the national-security interest as he defines it, would attempt to fight his way into the process. He would argue that he has a special expertise to contribute or that the interests of his organization are involved. In covert operations, Super Secrecy makes it extremely difficult for this to occur.

First of all, the official usually does not know that the activities are under consideration or being implemented. The existence of the special clearances makes it difficult to assert a right to be involved, since one is asserting the need for a clearance whose existence one is not supposed to know and which is supposedly kept to a small number of people. Thus, someone attempting to fight his way into the evaluation of a covert operation faces not only the normal difficulties of getting into a new policy arena but special problems of appearing to be jeopardizing security requirements.

As a result, a person who finally does get cleared for a particular operation is likely to feel that he has been admitted on the sufferance of the planners. He knows he will continue to be involved only if he accepts the basic principles involved and presents his criticism on the edges of the operation. Someone who is skeptical about covert operations in general, or covert operations in a particular area, is likely not to get the necessary clearances. If he does, he may feel that he must mute his views or find himself isolated and, ultimately, have his clearance withdrawn.

With the circle of those "in the know" kept so small, those in it tend to discount the views of other government officials who are not aware of the details of covert operations. For example, expert estimates of the unlikelihood of a successful anti-Castro operation in Cuba in 1961 were discounted by the officials who knew about the Bay of Pigs operation. These officials knew they were the only ones receiving all the reports from our covert operations in Cuba; intelligence analysts in the CIA and State Department were discounted because they had not received some of the reports from covert agents operating within Cuba.

The process by which proposals for covert operations move up through the narrow group of those with necessary clearances reduces the likelihood that the senior officials on the Forty Committee will examine them critically. Proposals that come before the Committee are usually unanimous because of the close working relationships of the staffs involved, and they tend to be rubber-stamped by the committee. Presumably, they are also rubber-stamped by the President when they are brought to his attention. The lack of vigorous dissent, so common with other proposals of a controversial nature, leads to routine approval.

The inability of top officials to maintain control is particularly acute when an operation is very large. For then the danger of adverse political consequences exists if the operation is halted after it is well on its way. In the case of the Bay of Pigs, President Kennedy was confronted with statements from Allen Dulles that if the operation were to be canceled, Cuban refugees who had been recruited would talk about it and cause political problems because of the intense anti-Castro feeling then rampant in the United States.

One form of monitoring is often entirely absent in the case of covert activities. The press provides one critical aspect of the monitoring system over the President and other top officials. This does not occur with a covert operation unless it reaches such proportions that the press in the field begins to learn of it.

(Paradoxically, in such cases the press may serve to alert other parts of the United States government to what is going on. This appears to have been the case in Laos through the 1960s, where covert activities came to the attention of many government officials through press reports from Laos.)

Super Secrecy also reduces the possibility of effective monitoring within the American government. The acknowledged need for flexibility in covert operations often makes it easy to justify discretionary authority for officials in the field to implement an approved plan. Ambassadors who sometimes provide effective monitoring or control often do not know, and do not want to know, about CIA operations in their countries. Moreover, the CIA controls its own money, people, and communications channels to Washington, often enabling it to move without normal internal executive-branch monitoring, bypassing skeptics who might otherwise try to persuade the President that it was an error and should be abandoned.

Super Secrecy of decision-making and execution of covert operations also casts a shadow over executive-branch decision-making in general on national security matters. Creating a special class of those with a "need to know" for covert operations tends to give those people a sense that on all matters they are better informed than others.

Moreover, within the government, lying becomes an accepted habit. In order to protect the existence of additional clearances and of covert operations, officials with access to information about these things must routinely deceive other officials. This lying breeds cynicism and contempt for those who are lied to, and this must influence the entire pattern of decision-making.

The most obvious demonstration of how Super Secrecy distorts executive-branch decision-making is in the CIA itself. The CIA was envisioned by President Truman, who called for its creation, and by the Congress that authorized it, primarily if not exclusively as an intelligence-evaluation organization. Prior to its creation, President Truman received intelligence reports from each of the armed services and from the State Department. He felt the need for a single agency which would collate and evaluate these reports and which would do so without the bias that an operating agency had in favor of its own programs. Thus, Truman wanted a professional and independent intelligence capability.

This conception of the CIA's role differs markedly from reality because of covert intelligence operations. The CIA has always been dominated by officials whose primary concern has been covert operations rather than intelligence or evaluation. The only career officials to be named heads of the CIA—Allen Dulles, Richard Helms, and William Colby—rose through the covert side of the agency, and Helms and Colby were former DDPs before becoming Directors. The dominance of covert operations within the CIA has diminished the quality of personnel on the intelligence side. The officials who work on intelligence evaluation recognize that they are not operating in a totally hospitable environment and are unlikely to rise to the top.

Moreover, because of its involvement in operations, the CIA is not the neutral intelligence-evaluation organ that President Truman and others envisioned. It has a policy ax to grind concerning its covert operations. The Director of Central Intelligence is reluctant to put out intelligence reports that contradict a view that the CIA is pressing in the Forty Committee or in other covert intelligence channels. Super Secrecy of covert operations also reduces the quality of its intelligence over-all in that the evaluators are often uninformed of covert operations and of matters that would enhance their ability to make sensible intelligence inputs.

Thus, the covert operations staff dominating the CIA weakens it in its primary function of providing objective intelligence evaluation of ongoing problems. The Vietnam war illustrates this well. The Pentagon Papers reveal that intelligence analysts in the CIA frequently produced much more sensible estimates of the situation in Vietnam than other parts of the intelligence community did. What the Pentagon Papers do not indicate, because they did not draw on the files of American covert operations, is that the DDP was as wrong on Vietnam as any other part of the government. The CIA was heavily involved in covert operations in Vietnam, including the training and arming of ethnic minorities. The CIA operators were optimistic about the success of their programs, and the great weight of the CIA effort within the government was to defend these programs rather than to push the consequences of the pessimistic intelligence evaluations.

IV. How Covert Operations Distort the American Constitutional System

The American constitutional system is fundamentally distorted by secrecy—although the different branches of government are affected in different ways.

The executive branch thrives on secrecy because secrecy frees it from Congressional, judicial, and public oversight. But the Congress suffers from secrecy because its power is based on the ability to expose, to rally public opinion, to maintain a dialogue between constituents and elected officials and with the press. When a Congressman is told that CIA operations are Super Secret, self-interest makes him prefer not to know anything about it. These secret operations are dangerous to him—he may be accused of having breached secrecy if the matter gets out, yet the information is of no political use to him unless it can be made public. Only a sense of duty can sustain his willingness to participate in hearings on such matters. Indeed, in the House of Representatives, the CIA subcommittee of the Appropriations Subcommittee has a membership that is secret. The Congressmen do not want it known who they are!

The Congressmen risk being asked whether they knew of covert operations. In 1971 Senators John Stennis and Allen Ellender—the Chairmen of the Armed

Services and Appropriations committees, as well as of their CIA oversight subcommittees—said that they knew nothing about the CIA-financed war in Laos, surely the CIA's biggest operation. It is hard to know whether to believe these denials, which would suggest enormous laxity in oversight.

Covert operations are especially difficult for Congressmen to come to grips with because they involve, or seem to involve, men in the field—"our boys." Every effort has to be made to protect these men and to bring them back if caught. Thus the flag is wrapped around the personnel, if not the funds, that go into covert operations.

So Super Secrecy is at the heart of Congress's problem in fulfilling its function of oversight of CIA operations. Even the authorization for CIA activities was promptly distorted in secrecy. The National Security Act authorized the CIA to: "perform *for the benefit of the existing intelligence agencies* such additional services of common concern as the National Security Council determines can be more effectively accomplished centrally; perform such other functions and duties *related to intelligence* affecting the national security as the National Security Council may from time to time direct" (italics added).

But secret directives promptly expanded these functions. Overthrowing governments, secret wars, assassinations, and fixing elections are not done "for the benefit of the existing intelligence agencies," nor are they duties "related to intelligence." It is entirely possible that a court might rule such actions unauthorized by statute. Yet within the executive branch, secret directives authorize special operations of all kinds provided they are small enough to be plausibly deniable. Unfortunately, these directives do not cover the impossible-to-deny operations: U-2 flights, Bay of Pigs, the Iranian coup, the Laotian war, etc.

A traditional method of Congressional control is through the power of the purse—the control of funding. The Constitution explicitly supports this power of Congress when it asserts in Article I, Section 9, Clause 7, that: "No Money shall be drawn from the Treasury, but in Consequence of Appropriations made by Law; *and a regular Statement and Account of the Receipts and Expenditures of all public Money shall be published from time to time*" (italics added). CIA expenditures are in violation of this constitutional clause, since no accounting whatsoever is made public. Indeed, the burial of CIA expenditures in the accounts of other departments puts the latter accounts in violation of law. They cease to be accurate.

Complete control of funding for covert operations is evidently delegated only to subcommittees of the Armed Services and Appropriations committtees. Thus, Senator Stuart Symington would not be permitted to discuss CIA appropriations, although he is on the Appropriations Commmittee and the CIA oversight subcommittee of Armed Services, because he is not one of the five senior members who make up the CIA oversight subcommittee of appropriations. The full committees do not vote on these matters, nor are they discussed on the floor of the Senate sessions on the CIA.

The failure of Congress to approve covert operations hampers its activities in other ways as well. Congressmen cannot properly assess the implications of many foreign events unless they understand the extent to which these events were shaped by covert American operations. The Gulf of Tonkin affair may have been encouraged by ongoing covert operations in the Gulf, but ignorant of these activities, Congressmen considered any attack on U.S. ships to be "unprovoked."

Similarly, interpretations of the true desires of Chileans may have been based on election results in Chile which in fact were manipulated by covert American campaign contributions. The Laotians may desire to avoid fighting, but a secret war financed by a covert operation may persuade Congressmen that Laotians want to continue the struggle.

Today covert operations are what most require the Super Secrecy of the CIA. Electronic intelligence-gathering does not require it, nor does intelligence assessment. It is the potentially explosive disclosure of interference in the internal affairs of other countries that does.

CIA employees must take a special oath to maintain CIA secrets. By restricting them from discussing these matters with their Congressman or Senators, the oaths interfere with our political system. Moreover, they constitute a special security system, unauthorized—on top of a variety of other unauthorized systems ("sensitive," etc.).

Super Secrecy has led to the widespread use, inside the CIA, of lie detectors. This may be a handy method for detecting double agents and for other use in covert operations. But their use spreads to all CIA employees, to other branches of government, and into the society at large. The funds available to the CIA make it possible for it to pioneer in a technology that undermines traditional judicial and ethical processes.

Super Secrecy as required by covert operations threatens the freedom of the press. For fifteen days, in the first prior restraint order in the history of the country against a daily newspaper, the *Washington Post* and the *New York Times* and other papers were restrained from publication of the Pentagon Papers. Part of the government's objection to publication was its fear of revealing covert operations and intelligence collection. And the only permanent injunction against free speech in the history of the United States has been issued against Victor Marchetti, a former CIA official—based partly upon his secrecy oath and partly on the need to keep secret the covert operations of which he might have knowledge.

Covert operations have led to Presidential requests to the press not to publish articles. In the case of the Bay of Pigs, President Kennedy urged the *New York Times* to do just that. When the covert operations are based in the United States, they can also interfere with individual rights. An effort to hide the fact that Tibetans were being trained in Colorado mountains led armed men to surround, and hold at gunpoint, a number of civilians who happened to witness their departure. And then the government apparently asked the *New York Times* not to publish the story.

Covert operations tend to distort the perceptions of foreign policy held not only by Congressmen but also by scholars and, in turn, the public. The entire image of U.S.-Soviet relations during the cold war would have been significantly different if U.S. penetrations of Soviet airspace had been made known. It would have shown that not all the Russians' fear of encirclement was "paranoia."

It is possible, with covert operations, to induce reactions from other nations which are self-fulfilling. Castro's anti-American attitude can be shaped by American sabotage of which he is cognizant but the American public is not. The Chinese knew that Downey and Fecteau were CIA agents; the American public did not. The North Vietnamese gauge our willingness to stay in Indochina by assessing, in part, the commitment shown through covert operations; the American public can not. In these matters, Super Secrecy is effectively directed only at the American public. The "enemy" may understand only too well what is happening, and sophisticated observers in third countries may also. But the American public is the last to know.

Government credibility suffers not only from acts of omission but also from the necessity to lie, to cover up. It was a sensation when President Eisenhower lied to cover up the U-2 incident. The extensive lies covering up the Bay of Pigs included Ambassador Adlai Stevenson's unwittingly untrue assertions in the U.N. Security Council. (Such acts are less sensational now because government credibility has sunk so much lower.) Even Presidential candidates are forced to lie. During the Kennedy-Nixon debates in 1960, both candidates were forced to wrestle with their secret knowledge of plans for the invasion of Cuba. What to say about Cuban policy in the face of this knowledge?

The Watergate affair amply documents the corruption of the political process by graduates of the CIA covert operations branch. Some of the CIA operatives hired at the lower level of the caper thought they were still working for the Agency. A more sophisticated operative is said to have gotten help in locating a suitable locksmith from a CIA roster. Throughout, the skills and techniques of CIA operators were ready and waiting. And those at higher levels directing the operatives had seen *Mission Impossible* and knew, or thought they knew, how the game was played.

The public's response to Watergate was to question why anyone should take such risks for so little. The answer probably lies in the fact that the administration had "institutionalized" dirty tricks. The same people had performed other "mission impossible" assignments, including breaking into a safe in Las Vegas, into Daniel Ellsberg's psychiatrist's office in Los Angeles. The resistance to covert operations was lowered; those who otherwise might have warned of the danger were, to that extent, silenced.

Watergate also reveals the dangers of permitting "hardened" operatives to work freely in American society. Ordinarily, only a criminal would be available to do these break-ins. The criminal element would have few contacts with a normal administration and would lack sophistication and reliability. But a gang of Cubans led by a covert master spy like Howard Hunt is another matter. They can inspire confidence and encourage assignments from an administration.

The use of private institutions for covert operations tends to bring them all under suspicion. This is what happened when it became known that the CIA had financed the National Student Association and about 250 front organizations and conduits. President Johnson appointed a panel headed by Under Secretary of State Nicholas Katzenbach to review the ground rules for such operations. It concluded:

1. It should be the policy of the United States Government that no Federal agency shall provide any covert financial assistance or support, direct or indirect, to any of the nation's educational or private voluntary organizations.
2. The Government should promptly develop and establish a public-private mechanism to provide public funds openly for overseas activities or organizations which are adjudged deserving, in the national interest, of public support.

The first resolution was adopted. But it left a number of loopholes. In the first place, organizations that seemed to be "private voluntary" might not be. They could be quietly organized as "for profit" and few would know. Alternatively, philanthropists might be enriched, perhaps through stockmarket operations, and they would then endow organizations with covert uses. Meanwhile, private businesses could continue to be funded by CIA.

The second recommendation does not seem to have been adopted. The infiltration of private organizations forces people to defend their "cover stories" and lose their integrity. Friends become unsure whether they can believe each other. Persons wonder whether they should accept funds from this foundation or that. To this day, legitimate "Stern Foundations" are confused with the conduit "Stern Foundation," which the CIA used in 1966. The Asia Society and the Asia Foundation have both suffered from the decision of the latter to accept CIA funds. Suspicion spreads.

V. Distortions of American Foreign Policy

When foreign countries are aware of U.S. covert operations and the American public is not, the possibility arises of having our government blackmailed by foreign governments. For example, they may insist on foreign aid they might not otherwise receive in return for participating in our covert activities. They may seek ransom for captured pilots—as Indonesia did in a case much like that of Gary Powers. They may hold prisoners until the United States admits they were CIA agents—apparently China's approach. And since covert operations, unlike electronic intelligence, require assets in place, the sensitive problems of purchasing and maintaining such assets can increase the risk of blackmail.

But even when pressure is not applied, CIA covert operations can lead to greater recognition of or commitment to a government. A U-2 base at Peshawar can buttress a particular regime in Pakistan. A country that gives us a base for invading Cuba, as Guatemala did, can discover that we are committed to maintaining stability there, if only to protect the base.

Because these commitments are undertaken indirectly and without full debate, it is difficult for anyone to be sure where they will lead. Laos is a good example. The commitment and involvement may outrun the conflict in Vietnam which reinforced them. Meanwhile, the secret war may decimate the population and otherwise dramatically change the original conditions of conflict.

For businesses abroad, the charge of their possible involvement with CIA cannot be answered. The Johnson administration took the view that one could not legislate "private morality" and that, in any case, it was not improper for businesses to cooperate with a government agency in securing information. But here, as elsewhere, the securing of information is something of a "cover concept" for covert operations. While it might not be immoral, it is poor policy to permit a government agency like the CIA to get involved with businesses around the world. In the long run, American business relations will suffer and the inevitable charges of government interference wherever American business rears its head do our foreign policy no good.

The ITT case shows how successive levels of degeneration in function are revealed when dirty tricks are institutionalized. First, the NSC is requested to order covert operations on an occasional basis. In time, the CIA is proposing these operations to a passive NSC. Then, in turn, the businesses through which the CIA operates, as in the ITT case, make proposals to the CIA and try to use the Agency for its own ends. Thus work expands to fill the covert possibilities available. Secrecy debases control.

The credibility, efficiency, and authority of State Department officials are undermined by the presence of covert CIA operatives. The CIA has better communications, better logistics, larger and more available sources of secret money, and greater security of communications. Under these circumstances, its authority in the field can hardly be matched. If there are CIA operatives around, why should sources of information talk to diplomats? The reported closeness of the late President Nasser to American CIA representatives rather than to Foreign Service representatives is a case in point. Nasser may have thought that the real power lay with the CIA.

CIA operatives undermine the effectiveness of the Foreign Service not only by competing with it but by implicitly smearing it. The legitimate diplomatic operations abroad cannot prove that they are legitimate. While some sources are attracted to the CIA, others are repelled. Members of diplomatic missions are suspected of being CIA agents much as American civilians might wonder if a Soviet diplomat is really a KGB agent.

The internal power balance in a foreign country can be distorted by the alliance of the CIA with certain elements in it rather than with others. Ramon

Magsaysay in the Philippines may have risen to power on the basis of help or information provided him by the CIA. Others who do not cooperate find themselves disadvantaged, relatively, even if no action is taken against them. From the CIA's point of view, small services can be of great significance—a few weapons, money, some investment advice, dirt on other members of the government, and so on.

Part of the purpose of CIA political operations is to gain just such influence as these operations make possible. But even when these "benefits" are not intended, CIA covert operations can still pervert a foreign government's structure. It is hard for a CIA operative to be passive. Some sources will be cooperating with him; others will not. Gradually, even without direct effort, the CIA—and the United States—may become aligned with and encouraging X rather than Y.

Covert operations seem to encourage rebellions or revolutions without hope. In Laos, teen-agers were encouraged to fight against the North Vietnamese troops until they were destroyed. In Tibet, guerrillas fought against the Chinese in hopeless uprisings. In the Bay of Pigs, miscalculations only somewhat less obvious were made. The dynamic of covert activities seems to have a logic that can produce violence which, on later reflection, is not worth it.

VI. Conclusions and Recommendations

The very existence, much less the mode of operation, of the CIA's Directorate of Plans is a legacy of the World War II Office of Strategic Services (OSS). In the hot war of the OSS, any and all tricks were considered consonant with the worldwide struggle against the Axis. Many imaginative and creative persons were drawn into its operations. After World War II, the OSS was institutionalized in the CIA. Many of the OSS operatives left, but some stayed. The pattern of imaginative involvement in covert operations remained. The cold war was seen, as late as the early 1960s, as a "long twilight struggle"; CIA covert operations fell neatly into that twilight—a gray area, whose propriety was buried in secrecy.

Today, with the cold war waning, the CIA is bidding for permanent institutionalization of its structure and role. Richard Helms argued that America's role as a "great power" demands a CIA even if the cold war does not. Thus what began in a hot war and grew in a cold war may come to base its right to exist simply on the permanent fact of American power.

Meanwhile, the effectiveness of the CIA's covert operations in the industrialized world has vastly diminished. In Europe, the instability of the post-World War II period is over. We no longer need to bribe Italian dockworkers to unload our goods. In the Communist industrialized world (and in China), CIA covert operations are of little effect, even if desirable. And electronic intelligence is providing more than we want to know about most subjects of interest.

As a result, the institutionalization of covert operations is certain to lead to its influence being applied to the Third World—an area with which we are not at war, and from which we are not in danger. The governments are penetrable. The agents have room for maneuver. But there is little work that needs to be done.

In the Third World, nationalism is a proven force against the rapid Communist expansion once feared. Soviet, Chinese, and American interference in Third World states tends only to produce resistance to a large power's further involvement. The problem ceases to be one of fighting fire with fire. It becomes one of giving competitors enough rope to hang themselves. No situation better illustrates these principles than Egypt. Unusual needs in Egypt, and unusual Soviet willingness to help, has nevertheless produced a history of strained relations between the Egyptians and the Soviets and a drain on Soviet resources.

The time has come for America to change its strategy from covert intervention to nonintervention. When there is no emergency, it should be an easy choice to stand for principle. In the long battle for respect and support in the Third World, principles and integrity will be the most important force. The short-run opportunist approach embodied in the CIA's Directorate of Plans sells the long run short.

Furthermore, it will be increasingly difficult to keep covert operations secret. As each operation is "blown," our reputation will suffer; we live in an era that is increasingly impatient with such manipulations. Each covert operation is a time bomb waiting to go off.

Covert operations diminish the flexibility of American foreign policy when it is most required, in a stage of disengagement. They tend to link us to established forces and to encourage the existing tendency of American policy to resist the popular aspirations in underdeveloped countries.

Especially important, covert operations pose a serious threat to democracy at home. James Madison wrote to Thomas Jefferson on May 13, 1798: "Perhaps it is a universal truth that the loss of liberty at home is to be charged to provisions against danger, real or pretended, from abroad." The effort to suppress information about covert operations abroad has already damaged freedom of the press and freedom of speech in America. The Pentagon Papers case and the Marchetti case may be precedents for still more ominous incursions on the First Amendment. Covert interference abroad is interference with freedom at home.

Finally, the greatest Presidential scandal of modern times has arisen from the injection of covert CIA methods, used by CIA graduates, into American society. No greater signal can be given of the danger of these methods to the highest interests of Americans.

We believe, therefore, that it is time for a drastic overhauling of the Super Secrecy system surrounding the planning and conduct of covert intelligence collection and covert operations. We recommend that certain operations and structures be abolished and that the secrecy surrounding others be eliminated.

The United States should continue to conduct operations involving the collection of intelligence materials by technical means, but not in any greater secrecy than other government activities. Implementation of this purpose would mean the elimination of the special classifications surrounding these programs and a public acknowledgment of their existence.

In this category we would put the various satellite collection programs for the gathering of data by photographic and other means, as well as ships and planes carrying electronic equipment. The government should carefully review all such programs to determine which ones in fact produce information of significant importance to the United States. An assessment should be also made of which programs are provocative—running high risks of penetrating the air spaces or territorial waters of other countries. The United States should make a public statement in general terms about the activities to be continued. The budgets for such programs should be publicly identified and be a regular part of the budget of the Defense Department. Officials of the Defense Department should be required to justify them as they justify all other programs. The organizations that operate and conduct them and the responsible officials for them should be publicly identified and be made a matter of public record.

There is, of course, a case for keeping some aspects of a program secret. For example, the technology of the most advanced cameras in satellites might justify continued secrecy. However, such secrecy should be within the context of an ongoing classification system and should be treated within the government like other classified material.

We do not believe that electronic intelligence-collection programs, if any, which penetrate the air spaces or territorial waters of other countries (or run a high risk of such penetration) should be continued.

Our proposals regarding covert operations are more drastic. We believe that the United States no longer needs a large establishment whose function is to conduct covert operations and gather intelligence covertly. Accordingly, the entire covert-operations section of the CIA should be dismantled. The CIA should become what it was originally meant to be—an intelligence evaluation and coordinating organization with no operational responsibilities. This would mean eliminating the entire Plans division of the CIA and the career service of covert operators. It would mean also that the CIA would no longer have clandestine agents in overseas embassies. Their clandestine contacts with government officials and opposition groups abroad should be taken over, to the extent necessary, by State Department officials and military attachés.

Adoption of this proposal would permit the CIA to emerge from the shadows. Its functions would be discussed publicly. Its budget could be publicly identified and its functions largely explained in a public defense of its budget and operations. The intelligence-analysis branch of the CIA would become the dominant career service, with intelligence analysts rising to top positions, including that of Director.

The gains from these proposals would include the elimination of the costs to executive-branch decision-making, American society, and to American foreign policy discussed above. The adverse consequences would be minimal. If the United States government decided to conduct a limited covert operation—for example, obtaining information from a spy within a potentially hostile government—it could be carried out either by the military attachés or by State Department officials. But there would no longer be a group whose *raison d'être* was such operations, a group constantly looking for ways to employ covert means as an instrument of American foreign policy.

Index

Index

ABM (anti-ballistic missiles), ix, 23,
111-138, 144, 156, 158; arguments
for and against, 125-127; and Congress, 120-121, 128; deployment
decision questions, 113, 127-134;
and Johnson, 121-123; and Mc-
Namara, 111-113, 119-120; organizational interests in, 114-123; and
politics, 122, 128-129, 130; and
"rules of the game" in Executive
branch, 123-124; and "shared
images" of U.S.-Communist enmity,
124-125
ACDA. *See* Arms Control and Disarmament Agency
AEC. *See* Atomic Energy Commission
AID (Agency for International Devel-
opment), 14
ARPA. *See* Advanced Research Proj-
ects Agency
AT&T (American Telephone and Tele-
graph), 139 n.8
Abrams, Creighton W., 152
Acheson, Dean, 148
Advanced Research Projects Agency
(ARPA), 117, 128, 137
Air Force, 9-14 *passim*, 19; and ABM,
116-117; and Gaither Report, 56,
62; and Skybolt, 3
Albania, 168
Algerian war, 18, 19, 22, 26
Allison, Graham, 12-13
Alsop, Stewart, 65 n.9, n.18
Anderson, George, 150
Anti-submarine warfare (ASW), 156
Armistice Agreement (1954), 34
Arms Control and Disarmament
Agency (ACDA), 124, 139 n.9, 146,
154
Army, 8-14 *passim*, 19; and ABM,
115, 123, 133, 134, 136, 137; and
Eisenhower, 150; and Gaither Re-
port, 55-56, 67, n.48
Asia, 39, 160, 161, 162
Asia Foundation, 177
Asia Society, 177
Atlas, 82, 101
Atomic Energy Commission (AEC),
55, 147, 150

Baldwin, Hanson, 68-69 n.73
Batista, Fulgencio, 168
Baxter, James, 48
Bay of Pigs, 11, 146, 147, 149, 152,
168, 169, 171, 174, 175, 176, 179
Bell Labs, 139 n.8
Bomb shelters, 48, 52, 55, 57, 83-84,
93-95, 126
Bombers, 102-103, 156, 159, 163
Bradley, Omar, 144
Bridges, Styles, 58
Brown, Harold, 140 n.20
Budget Bureau, 55, 57, 123, 136, 137,
139, 146, 149
Bulganin, Nikolai, 68-69 n.73
Bundy, McGeorge, 120, 147
Bureau of European Affairs (State
Dept.), 4
Bureau of Intelligence and Research
(State Dept.), 166
*Bureaucratic Politics and Foreign
Policy* (Halperin), ix, x
Burma, 39

CADOP (Continental Air Defense Objectives Plan), 99
CIA. *See* Central Intelligence Agency
COMOR (Committee on Overhead
Reconnaissance), 13
Calkins, Robert, 48
Cambodia, 39
Carney, Robert C., 65 n.14
Castro, Fidel, 171, 176
Central Intelligence Agency (CIA), x,
9, 10, 11, 165-182; career covert
operators (spies), 166, 168, 169,
176, 177, 181; and Congress, 165,
169, 172, 173-175; and constitutional system, 173-177; covert operations vs. intelligence evaluation,
172-173, 174, 181; and Cuba, 12-13,
169, 175, 176, 179; deceptions of,
166-180 *passim*; and decision-
making, 169-173; and JCS, Defense,
and State Dept., 166-167; Directors,
172, 173; domestic interference of,
168, 177, 178; electronic surveillance by, 168, 177, 179, 181; and
foreign policy, 169, 176, 177-179,

185

Central Intelligence Agency *(cont.)*
180; Forty Committee, 166-167,
170, 171; and freedom of speech
and the press, 175, 180; funding of,
174, 181; and Gaither Report, 50,
53; Intelligence Branch, 167, 172,
181; intervention abroad, 168, 169,
174, 175, 177, 178-179; monitoring
of, 171-172; Plans Directorate
(DDP), 165-166, 167, 172, 173,
179, 180, 181; and President, 146,
147, 154, 165, 171, 172, 173; range
of, 167-169; recommendations for,
179-182; and secrecy, 167, 169-173,
174, 175, 176, 180-181; structure
of, 165-167; and U-2, 11, 13, 168,
169, 176
Chiang Kai-shek, 33, 34, 38
Chile, x, 169, 175
Chinese Communists, 23, 37, 40, 160,
168, 179, 180; and ABM, 112, 113,
118, 121-138 *passim*; and CIA, 176,
177; and Gaither Report, 68-69
n.73; and Korean war, 20, 24, 25,
144; and Offshore Islands, viii, 7-8,
31-34
Chinese Nationalists, 31-44 *passim*
Civil defense, 66 n.29, 78, 81, 86,
93-97, 126. *See also* Bomb shelters
Clark, Joseph S., 58, 59-60, 65 n.18
Clifford, Clark, 147
Colby, William, 172
Cold war, 168, 176, 179
Common Market, 4
Congress, 58-60, 63, 144, 150, 157;
and ABM, 120-121, 122, 126, 128-
129, 131, 135, 137, 138; and CIA,
165, 169, 172, 173-175
Congressional Record, 58
Constitution, 174, 180
Corson, John J., 48, 50
Council of Economic Advisers, 154
Cuba, 168, 171, 178. *See also* Bay of
Pigs; Cuban missile crisis
Cuban missile crisis, 12-13, 150
Cutler, Robert, 48, 69 n.75

DDP. *See* Central Intelligence Agency,
Plans Directorate
DDR&E. *See* Defense Research and
Engineering, Director of
Dahl, Robert, 12-14, 16-17, 19

Defense budget, 13-14, 20, 155-164;
and ABM, 122, 123, 136; ceilings
on, 156-157; and CIA, 174, 181; and
Gaither Report, 48, 52-63 *passim*,
69-70 n.84, 103; for general purpose
forces, 159-162; and McNamara, 7,
16, 115; and President, 147, 148-
149, 150, 154; projections, 98-99,
100; size of, 155-157; shape of,
157-159; and Skybolt, 3-4; for strategic forces, 162-164; and war
termination, 22-24
Defense Department: and ABM, 136-
137; autonomy of, 7-8; and CIA,
166, 167, 181; and defense budget,
3-4, 13-14, 103; and Gaither Report,
49, 50, 52, 70 n.87, 84-85, 103; and
President, 147-154 *passim*; reorganization of, 84-85, 151-152; and Skybolt, 3-4
Defense Program Review Committee
(DPRC), 146, 148, 154
Defense Research and Engineering,
Director of (DDR&E), 117-118,
128, 130, 134, 148
Defense Unification Act, 147
de Gaulle, Charles, 3, 22, 26
Doolittle, James H., 65 n.14
Downey, John T., 176
Draft Presidential Memoranda (DPM),
118, 130
Dulles, Allen, 171, 172
Dulles, John Foster, 147, 148; and
Gaither Report, 53, 56-57; and Off-
shore Islands, 31-40 *passim*

Egypt, 180
Eisenhower, Dwight D., 3, 156, 159,
176; and Gaither Report, 14, 47-64
passim, 65 n.9, 67 n.51, n.55; and
the military, 144-150 *passim*; and
Offshore Islands, 31-39 *passim*, 44,
45 n.22
Electronic countermeasures (ECM), 83
Electronic surveillance, 177, 179, 181
Ellender, Allen, 173-174
Ellsberg, Daniel, 176
Ely, Paul-Henri, 26
Enthoven, Alain, 117, 118-119
Espionage. *See* Central Intelligence
Agency
Europe, 160, 161, 162

European Defense Community Treaty, 168
Executive Order 10501, 167

FCDA. *See* Federal Civilian Defense Administration
Far East Bureau (State Dept.), 44
Fast Deployment Logistic (FDL) ships, 10
Fecteau, George, 176
Federal Civilian Defense Administration (FCDA), 48, 52, 55, 85
Fisk, James B., 65 n.14
Fitzhugh Panel, 145, 149
Foreign Service (State Dept.), 9, 143, 145, U.S. embassies and CIA, 166, 172, 178
Formosa Resolution, 35, 36
Forty Committee (CIA), 166-167, 170, 171
Foster, John S., Jr., 117-118, 136, 140 n.20
Foster, William C., 48-57 *passim*, 60, 61, 66 n.30
Fox, William, viii
France, 25, 89, 168; and Algeria, 18, 19, 22, 26; and Indochina, 18, 20-21, 24, 26
Freedom of speech and the press, 175, 180

GNP (Gross National Product), 50, 78, 87, 100
Gaither, H. Rowan, Jr., 48, 49, 53, 58, 65 n.9, 66 n.36, 68 n.59
Gaither Committee Report, viii-ix, 14, 47-64, 65 n.18, 67 n.46; and active defense, 102-104; and defense costs and economic consequences, 87-88, 98-99, 100; and deterrent power, 81-82, 89; and early missile capability, 101; and foreign policy, 86; membership roster, 105-109; and passive defense, 93-97; and projected federal receipts and expenditures, 100; and "pro-spending cluster," 62, 63, 69 n.83; and public education, 88-89; and reorganization of Defense Dept., 84-85; text, 71-109; time table, 90-92
Gates, Thomas, 148
Germany, 26, 89, 149

Glassboro Conference, 131, 132, 138
Goodpaster, Andrew, 146, 147
Great Britain, 89; and Skybolt, 3-4; and Suez crisis, 24, 25
Green Berets, 9, 16, 19, 151
Guatemala, 178

Harriman, Averell, 147
Helms, Richard, 172, 179
Hill, Albert C., 65 n.8
Hilsman, Roger, 69 n.82
Hitch, Charles, 3, 4, 115
Hoopes, Townsend, 12
Hornig, Donald F., 140 n.20
Hull, John E., 65 n.14
Hunt, Howard, 177

ICBM (intercontinental ballistic missiles), ix, 51, 81, 82, 84, 89, 90-92, 101, 104; Communist, 133, 134, 163; costs, 98-99
IOC (initial operational capability), 81, 82
IRBM (intermediate range ballistic missiles), 51, 66 n.23, 82, 98-99, 101
ISA. *See* International Security Affairs
ITT (International Telephone and Telegraph), 178
Ichiangshan Island, 34-35
Indochina, 18, 20-21, 24, 26, 44, 176. *See also* Cambodia; Laos; Vietnam
Indonesia, 39, 168, 177
Initial operational capability (IOC), 81, 82
Institute for Defense Analysis (IDA), 65 n.7
Intelligence operations. *See* Central Intelligence Agency
International Security Affairs, Office of (ISA), 117, 119, 138 n.5, 167
Iran, 168, 174
Italy, 168

JCS. *See* Joint Chiefs of Staff
Jackson Committee, 57, 61, 65 n.18
Jackson, Henry, 121, 122, 128
Japan, 23, 24, 25-26, 39
Jayne, Edward Randolph, II. 138-139 n.5

Johnson, Lyndon, 22, 37, 44, 59, 60, 156; and ABM, 113, 120-137 *passim*; and CIA, 177, 178; and the military, 146, 147, 148, 149
Joint Chiefs of Staff (JCS), 20, 102; and ABM, 113-137 *passim*; Chairman of, and Service Chiefs, 151-153; and CIA, 166-167; and Gaither Report, 49, 50, 52, 56, 67 n.47; and Offshore Islands, 33, 43-44; and President, 143-154 *passim*
Jordan, 168
Jupiter, 82

Kahn, Herman, 66 n.29
Kanter, Arnold, x
Katanga, 168
Katzenbach, Nicholas, 177
Kelly, Mervin J., 65 n.14
Kennedy, John F., 3, 37, 38, 44, 45 n.22, 63, 119, 122, 156; and CIA, 171, 175, 176; and the military, 146-152 *passim*
Killian, James R., 65 n.14, 140 n.20
Kissinger, Henry, 120, 147
Kistiakowsky, George B., 140 n.20
Korean war, 18, 20, 21-22, 24, 25, 31, 32, 34, 38, 39, 69-70 n.84, 87, 136, 144, 147, 149
Kosygin, Aleksei, 132, 135, 138
Krock, Arthur, 65 n.18, 68-69 n.73
Kuzmack, Arnold, 159

Laird, Melvin, 7, 128, 148
Laos, 39, 152, 168, 172, 174, 175, 178, 179
Latin America, 169
Lawrence, Ernest O., 49
Leahy, William, 146
Limited-war capability, 51-52, 56, 62, 63, 67 n.48
Lincoln, George A., 49
Lovett, Robert A., 53
Lubell, Samuel, 67 n.55

MAAG (Military Assistance Advisory Group), 32-33
MIRV (multiple individually targetable reentry vehicle), 127, 158, 163
MRBM (medium-range ballistic missiles), 11, 14
MacArthur, Douglas, 18, 24, 25, 26,
144, 147, 149
McCloy, John J., 49, 53
McCormack, James, 65 n.8
McElroy, Neil, 56, 66 n.30
Macmillan, Harold, 3
McNamara, Robert, 7, 16, 148, 153; and ABM, 111-138 *passim*, 140 n.27; and Skybolt, 3, 4
McNaughton, John T., viii, 117, 119
Madison, James, 180
Magsaysay, Ramon, 178-179
Malaya, 39
Marchetti, Victor, 175, 180
Marine Corps, 10, 11, 19, 116
Marshall, George, 148
Matsu. *See* Offshore Islands
Military Assistance Advisory Group (MAAG), 32-33
Military attachés, 166, 181, 182
Military forces: confidence levels of, 161-162, 163; and defense budget, 155-164; and force structure, 157-159; and forward defense, 161; general purpose forces, 159-162; and length of war, 160-161; and mobilization lead time, 161; and simultaneity of requirements, 160; strategic forces, 162-164; and tactical nuclear weapons, 159-160
Military interests, 6-14; and ABM, 115-117, 124; autonomy of, 7-8, 20; and defense budget, 13-14, 20, 157-159; and Gaither Report, 55-56, 67 n.48; and intelligence operations, 166, 172, 181; and Presidency, 143-154; service vs. command, 151-153; in war termination, 17-21
Military strategy: one and a half/two and a half war, 155-156, 160; triad, 156, 163-164
Minuteman, 3, 10, 117, 118, 119, 124, 129, 133, 140 n.27, 163
Missile: capability, 101; interception, 103-104
Mutual Defense Alliance Agreement (1951), 32
Mutual Defense Treaty (1954), 34, 35

NASA (National Aeronautics and Space Administration), 11, 16
NATO (North Atlantic Treaty Organization), 3, 86, 140 n.27, 161, 162

NSC. *See* National Security Council
Nanchi Island, 36
Nasser, Gamal Abdel, 178
National Security Act (1947), 165, 166, 174
National Security Adviser to President, 120, 123, 146, 147, 154, 166, 167
National Security Agency, 166
National Security Council (NSC), 47-64 *passim*; and CIA, 165, 166, 174, 178; NSC-68, 69-70 n.84; and President, 143, 145, 146, 148
National Security Decision Memorandum Number 40, 166
National Student Association, 177
Navarre, Henri, 18, 26
Navy, 9, 10, 11, 12, 19, 116, 150, 156
Neustadt, Richard, 67 n.51
New York Herald Tribune, 58, 65 n.18
New York Times, 58, 65 n.18, 175
Newspapers, 58, 65 n.18, 171-172, 175, 180
Nike-Hercules/Talos, 82, 98-99, 104
Nike-Zeus, 126
Nitze, Paul H., 49, 56, 57, 133, 136
Nixon, Richard, 22, 23, 37, 57, 68 n.58, 122, 137-138, 163; and CIA, 169, 176; and defense budget, 155, 156, 158; and the military, 144-149 *passim*
Norstad, Lauris, 66-67 n.45
North Korea, 168
North Vietnam, 12, 129, 149, 176, 179
Nuclear Test Ban Treaty, 149
Nuclear weapons, tactical, 159-160

Office of Defense Administration, 85
Office of International Security Affairs (Defense Dept.), 6
Office of Management and Budget, 149, 154
Office of Strategic Services (OSS), 179
Office of the Secretary of Defense (OSD), 116, 117
Offshore Islands, viii, 7-8, 31-44
Oliver, Edward P., 65 n.8
Organizational interests, 6-14, 19-20; and ABM, 114-123; in war termination, 17-26

Pakistan, 178
Pearson, Drew, 65 n.18, 68-69 n.73

Penkovsky, Oleg, 168
Pentagon Papers, 173, 175, 180
Perkins, James A., 48
Perkins, James R., 65 n.15
Pescadores, 33, 34, 35, 36
Philby, Harold, 168
Philippines, 39, 179
Polaris, 3, 9, 10, 82, 98-99, 101, 116, 150, 163, 164
Politics, 58-59, 60, 171; and ABM, 122, 128-129, 130, 135, 137
Poseidon, 129
President: and CIA, 165, 169, 171, 172, 173, 175; and the military, 143-154
Prim, Robert C., 48
Pueblo, 168

Quemoy. *See* Offshore Islands

Rabi, I.I., 49
Radford, Arthur W., 36, 41, 43, 45 n.22, 150
RAND Corporation, 48, 49; 65 n.21, 66 n.29
Rankin, Karl Lott, 32, 33, 35, 39, 46 n.28
Readings in American Foreign Policy (Kanter and Halperin), x
Republican Congressional Policy Committee, 128
Research and development (R & D), 84, 98-99, 115, 118, 163, 164
Reston, James, 60, 65 n.18
Revolutions, 25-26, 168, 173, 174, 179
Rhee, Syngman, 34
Ridgway, Matthew, 24, 26, 150
Roberts, Chalmers, 58, 65 n.18
Robertson, Walter, 36, 41, 43, 45 n.22
Rockefeller, Laurance, 57
Rockefeller, Nelson, 122, 147
Rockefeller Brothers Fund, 70 n.85
Romney, George, 128
Roosevelt, Franklin, 146
Roper, Elmo, 57
Rostow, Walt W., 120, 129
Rusk, Dean, 4, 40, 123, 139, 148
Russell, Richard, 121, 122, 125, 128

SAC. *See* Strategic Air Command
SALT. *See* Strategic Arms Limitation Talks

SOSUS (sound system for underwater surveillance), 104
SUSAC (Soviet Union Strategic Air Command), 90
Satellites, 168, 181
Shilling, Warner, 140 n.21
Science Adviser to President, 123, 124, 130
Science Advisory Committee, 48, 58, 137
Scoville, Herbert, 139 n.9
Secrecy in government, 167, 169-173, 174, 175, 176, 180-181
Security Resources Panel. *See* Gaither Committee Report
Sharp, Ulysses S., 152
Skifter, Hector R., 48
Skybolt, 3-4
Southeast Asia Treaty Organization, 34
Soviet Union, ix, 31, 40, 180; and ABM, 111-138 *passim*; economic capability of, 78-79; and Gaither Report, 54, 57, 68-69 n.73, 78, 86; military capability of, 50-51, 79-81, 89, 90-92, 160, 162, 163-164; and SAC, 82, 89; and U-2, 168, 176; and U.S. defense budget, 156, 158
Special Assistant to Joint Chiefs of Staff for Counter Insurgency and Special Activities (SACSA), 166-167
Special Projects Office (Navy), 150
Spies, 168, 176, 177
Sprague, Robert C., 48, 49, 50, 53, 57-58, 61, 68 n.58, 69 n.83
Sputnik, 50, 60, 61, 62
Stanford Research Institute, 139 n.8
Stanton, Frank, 49, 57
State Department, 4, 6, 10, 11, 13, 85, 124, 137; and CIA, 166, 167, 172, 178, 181, 182; and Offshore Islands, 32, 44; and President, 146, 147, 148, 154. *See also* Foreign Service
Stennis, John, 121, 122, 173-174
"Stern Foundation," 177
Stevenson, Adlai, 176
Stone, Jeremy J., x
Strategic Air Command (SAC), 9, 51, 54, 59, 62, 81, 82, 89, 90-92, 101, 104, 116; costs, 98-99
Strategic Arms Limitation Talks

(SALT), 121, 127, 130-132, 135, 146, 163
Strategic forces, 162-164
Strategic systems. *See* Military strategy
Student Conference on United States Affairs (SCUSA), 66 n.30
Submarines, 104, 156, 163, 164. *See also* Polaris
Suez crisis (1956), 24, 25
Symington, Stuart, 174
Systems Analysis, Office of (SA), 117, 118-119, 153

Tachen Islands. *See* Offshore Islands
Tactical Air Command (TAC), 9
Taiwan (Formosa), 31-44 *passim*
Tallinn, 128
Taylor, Maxwell, 67 n.47, 146, 150
Thailand, 39
Third World, 180
Thompson, General (Brit.), 149
Thor, 82
Thurmond, Strom, 121, 128, 129
Tibet, 168, 179; Tibetans in U.S., 175
Titan, 82, 101
Tonkin Gulf, 175
Treasury Department, 57
Triad strategic system, 156, 163-164
Truman, Harry, 21, 26, 32, 37, 47, 64 n.1, 69-70 n.84, 156; and CIA, 172, 173; and the military, 144-150 *passim*
Tsou, Tang, viii

U-2, 11, 13, 168, 169, 174, 176, 178
ULMS (undersea-launched missile submarine), 156, 164 n.2
United Nations, 24, 42, 144, 176
United Press International, 111
United States: economic capability of, 78-79; military capability of, 50-51, 79-81, 89, 90-92; two-China policy of, 38-39, 42-43, 44

Vance, Cyrus, 129, 136
Vietnam, 8, 11, 12, 19, 21, 22, 24, 37, 39, 44, 120, 121, 123, 130, 133, 134, 136, 146, 148, 149, 152, 159, 162, 168, 169, 173, 178

War, length of, 160-161

War termination, 17-26; and civilian interests, 21-26; and military interests, 17-21
Warnke, Paul, 117, 119
Warsaw Pact, 162
Washington Post, 175; *Washington Post and Times Herald*, 58
Washington Special Action Group (WSAG), 154
Watergate, x, 176, 180
Weapons, "good" and "bad," 158, 162, 164

Webster, William, 48, 50
Westerfield, H. Bradford, 69 n.82
Western Electric, 139 n.8
Westmoreland, William, 152
Wheeler, Earle, 148
Wiesner, Jerome, 48, 50, 140 n.20, 149
Wohlstetter, Albert, 65 n.21, 66 n.26
World War II, 19, 23, 24 25-26, 87, 179

York, Herbert, 140 n.20

About the Author

Morton H. Halperin is currently directing a study for the Twentieth Century Fund on national security information and constitutional procedures. Mr. Halperin taught at Harvard University from 1960-1966. Subsequently, he served in the federal government as Deputy Assistant Secretary of Defense and later as Assistant for Planning on the staff of the National Security Council. After leaving the White House in 1969, Mr. Halperin was a Senior Fellow of the Brookings Institution. He is the author of numerous books and articles, including *Bureaucratic Politics and Foreign Policy*, and is a coeditor of *Readings in American Foreign Policy* and *United States-Japanese Relations*. Mr. Halperin has been involved in a number of recent court cases relating to national security and civil liberties, including his own wiretap suit occasioned by the electronic surveillance of his home telephone.